NLP in 21 Days

Harry Alder
and
Beryl Heather

D1329252

PIATKUS

✿ Visit the Piatkus website!

Piatkus publishes a wide range of bestselling fiction and non-fiction, including books on health, mind, body & spirit, sex, self-help, cookery, biography and the paranormal.

If you want to:
- read descriptions of our popular titles
- buy our books over the internet
- take advantage of our special offers
- enter our monthly competition
- learn more about your favourite Piatkus authors

VISIT OUR WEBSITE AT: **www.piatkus.co.uk**

Acknowledgements
We would like to thank John Seymour, a leading NLP trainer and writer, for his help in compiling the glossary. He is the author of *Introducing NLP* and *Training with NLP*

Other books by Harry Alder
NLP: The new art and science of getting what you want
NLP for Managers
Train Your Brain
Think Like A Leader
The Right Brain Manager
Corporate Charisma
(with Paul Temporal)

First published in 1999 by
Judy Piatkus (Publishers) Ltd
5 Windmill Street, London W1T 2JA
email: info@piatkus.co.uk

This paperback edition published in 1999

Reprinted 2000 (twice), 2001, 2002, 2003

**The moral rights of the authors
have been asserted**

A catalogue record for this book is available from the British Library

ISBN 0–7499–1829–2 (hbk)
ISBN 0–7499–2030–0 (pbk)

Data capture and manipulation by
Phoenix Photosetting, Chatham, Kent
Printed & bound in Great Britain by Biddles Ltd, *www.biddles.co.uk*

Contents

PRESUPPOSITION: People make the best choices available to them.

Foreword

Many years ago we took our NLP Trainer's Training to become Certified Trainers of Neuro-Linguistic Programming (NLP). The training itself was challenging, exciting and provocative. One of the most memorable points was when Richard Bandler asked us to define and explain NLP. Boy, did he know how to quiet a room of trainers!

NLP is such a broad subject that it defies easy description. Dr Harry Alder and Beryl Heather have synthesised the NLP practitioner information and brought a new clarity to the field. Each of us as individuals has unique talents. While Harry and Beryl are not the developers of NLP, they play a critical role in moving NLP to the next level. Their work makes the subject clear, lucid and available to a large audience. This is a major accomplishment. In the past, NLP was oriented to a niche market – largely that of therapists. With the publication of *NLP in 21 Days*, the curtain has now lifted and the general public is invited to share in this very exciting, cutting-edge technology.

As you read this, NLP is really only in its young adulthood. The term NLP was coined in the mid-seventies by Richard Bandler and John Grinder to codify their work. Richard and John met at the University of California at Santa Cruz, while Richard was a student and John was teaching there. To make some money (so the legend goes) Richard started editing Gestalt Therapy transcripts. Being the genius he is, he quickly recognised the *structure* of what the therapist was doing to create successful change. Up until that point, the therapist was not even consciously aware of this.

From this early experience, Richard and John developed the basic process upon which all NLP is founded: *modelling*. They realised they were onto something BIG, because they could go into any area (therapy, business, sports) and find the underlying structure that ensured success in that field. They worked with the US military, major sports teams, the US government and major corporations. And they were successful; the only problem was, they were ahead of their time.

Generally speaking, it takes approximately two generations for something new to become widely accepted. The first operational fax existed as early as 1947, and you know how long it took for personal computers to be accepted into the business and home. As you are reading this, you are fifteen to twenty years ahead of mainstream society! That is why this book is of vital importance. It picks up where John and Richard left off and moves NLP forward to ensure that one day it will be part of the mainstream.

You, too, have a role in helping NLP to grow. You can use it to model the excellence that you observe in the world around you. You can use it to communicate better with your spouse; to help your children get better grades; to create a life for yourself that you really want; and to serve others whose needs are greater than your own. You can participate at any level and transform your life to whatever degree you want. The choice is yours.

As you do, the field of NLP will continue to transform itself through the energies of creative, competent and ethical trainers who really care about the people they teach. The authors are two such people. Beryl Heather has been a highly regarded Corporate Trainer for twenty years. She is deeply committed to exploring the boundaries of NLP and pushing past them to create new patterns and new training programmes. She is respected in the United Kingdom and throughout the world for her contributions to business, NLP and training. Because of her accomplishments, she has been designated a Master Trainer of NLP which is the highest level of recognition in our field.

Dr Harry Alder is the epitome of an NLP modeller. He has written a dozen or so books ranging from the classic *NLP: The New Art and Science of Getting What You Want* to *Masterstroke: Use the Power of Your Mind to Improve Your Golf* and *Think Like a Leader*. Harry has the uncanny ability to go into any field and extrapolate the most valuable information, translating it in a way that we can all readily utilise. He is a master modeller who has thoroughly integrated the spirit of NLP. He is, at once, an Everyman and a Renaissance man! It is a pleasure to know him and count him as a colleague.

As we approach the millennium, this book includes vital keys to personal and global transformation for the next century. Who would have thought, sixty-five years ago, when Alfred Korzybski, the founder of general semantics, wrote in *Science and Sanity*, 'The map is not the territory', that these words would have rung so true? The map is *not* the territory and you will learn about this in the very first chapter. The map is only our interpretation of the territory – and in a world of six billion people it's important that we recognise this. This is the value of NLP – these six innocuous words comprise the entire philosophical foundation of our field. Without such a premise, NLP is meaningless – there is no hope for humanity because our maps account for what we think is real vs. not real; what is possible vs. what is not possible; and who we are vs. who we are not. We are each the drafters of our own maps that we call 'life'. Eventually all these maps lead back to the same territory: back to the source, back to you.

The 21-day format outlined here provides you with a time-tested map to make rapid and lasting change. It also offers extra little-known refinements for the NLP Practitioner (the trade secrets!). We whole-heartedly recommend this book, as a valuable contribution to advancing the field of NLP and the lives of those who explore it. As you read on, enjoy exploring the landscape of your mind. Discover its richness, its depth. Discover its dreams. Find out

who you really are and who you can really be ... and share
that, when the time's right!

John Overdurf, CAC, and Julie Silverthorn, MS.
Certified Master Trainers of Neuro-Linguistic Programming
Co-developers of Humanistic Neuro-Linguistic
Psychology™
Ocean City, MD, USA

Introduction

NLP stands for Neuro-Linguistic Programming, a revolutionary approach to human communication and personal development. Some people call it 'the art and science of personal excellence' or 'the study of subjective experience'. It offers state-of-the-art skills in interpersonal communication and practical ways to change the way you think and behave. Millions of people have used its simple principles and techniques to build better relationships, establish a new level of confidence, and achieve success in every aspect of their lives.

Anyone can learn NLP and benefit from its long-lasting results. You can apply what you learn at work, at home and in any part of your life. You don't need any prior knowledge of the subject. This book provides an easy-to-use introductory guide to NLP, as well as a complete training manual for anyone who wants to become a certified practitioner. You can start to apply the techniques and experience changes in your life immediately.

We have based the book on the successful practitioner training programmes run by *Realisation at Stenhouse*. We introduce each topic gradually, with full explanations and real-life examples. Simple daily exercises help you to remember what you learn as well as enjoy immediate benefits. Most of the exercises can be done in the course of your normal job or everyday life, so you don't need to set aside a lot of study time. Expect to see changes within days.

WHAT CAN NLP DO FOR YOU?

NLP enables you to achieve personal goals more quickly and effectively than ever before. In other words, you can do more of what you want, get more, know more, and, especially, *be* what you want. Applying its powerful communication techniques, for instance, you can build rapport with others. To do this you will draw on mental resources (the 'neuro' part) you never knew you possessed. And you will learn how to use language (the 'linguistic' part) in very specific ways to help achieve your goals. You will also learn how to control your state of mind, and how to align your beliefs and values to bring about the results you want – the 'programming' part of NLP.

This degree of personal control will give you confidence as well as boosting your self-esteem. It will also create spin-off benefits in personal achievement, relationships and longer-term self-development. What's more, NLP principles and techniques will enable you to deal with problematic situations in a creative, resourceful way.

NLP places more emphasis on *doing* than *knowing*. Most students of NLP find it starts to make sense when they apply it practically. Many experience major personal changes, from which changes in other people and circumstances follow. In summary, understanding and practising NLP will help you to:

- Build personal relationships
- Increase your persuasive skills
- Have a positive mental attitude
- Increase your self-esteem
- Overcome the effects of past negative experiences
- Focus on goals and channel your energy into achieving them
- Perform at your best
- Control the way you feel
- Align your values and beliefs with what you want to achieve
- Change unwanted habits
- Feel confident in whatever you attempt to do

- Achieve goals you previously considered impossible
- Establish rapport with clients, customers and work colleagues
- Find creative ways to solve problems
- Enjoy activities you used to fear
- Use your time more effectively
- Increase your sense of purpose in life
- Acquire the skills you admire in others
- Get more pleasure out of life

In this 21-day programme, the practical exercises allow you to test what you learn each day. Just have an open mind, and give things a try. By learning, then doing, one step at a time, you can expect more or less unlimited change for the better.

You may need to place a little trust – not in a guru or in some ancient wisdom, but in your own amazing neuro-physiological system. Once you trust the system – just like a computer or a cashpoint machine – you will start to get the best out of it. *You* will have control. NLP enables you to actually do what your awesome mind–body system gives you the potential to do. It provides a structure that allows you to train your unconscious mind in goal-achieving habits.

YOUR OWN DIY MANUAL

This book has two main purposes. First, it provides an introduction to NLP, for which you need no prior knowledge. While taking you from little or no knowledge of the subject, it treats many of the topics at a level of detail not found in other texts. Second, it provides a complete training manual for NLP practitioner certification, covering a programme which complies fully with the internationally generally accepted Certification Standards (Practitioner Level). We have included the syllabus as an Appendix.

NLP practitioner training requires a minimum number of hours, and you can choose between different versions of the programme. One may involve, say, two-day seminars, with the programme spanning several months. Another may require full-time, intensive study over two or three weeks but comprise the same number of hours and the same content. The international syllabus prescribes the topics, leaving the form and style of the training to individual Certified Trainers. So different training providers have their own characteristics and distinctive style. *NLP in 21 Days* follows the *Realisation at Stenhouse* intensive programme but at the same time provides a comprehensive manual to accompany any leading training programme.

We have tried to translate the live seminars into easily digestible book form, creating in effect a Do-It-Yourself manual. If you want to become a certified NLP practitioner, you can use the book as your training manual and reference guide. If you want to learn about NLP to enhance your work and personal life, simply work through the book and do the exercises.

E-PRIME

We have written this book in a language style known as E-Prime. This term simply refers to the English language without the verb 'to be'. Although the most-used verb in the language, it does produce a lot of imprecise, ambiguous language. The passive tense, for instance ('it was understood', 'it is believed'), beloved by bureaucrats but much frowned upon by modern writers, depends upon this little verb. We address the pitfalls of using the 'to be' verb, and the many benefits of using E-Prime, both in written and spoken English, in Day 8, 'The Power of Language'. Because of its extraordinary impact on communication, and even the way we think, E-Prime has gained popularity in NLP circles. Applying it to a full NLP text takes it a stage further, and you can judge the result for yourself. At the very least, it has encouraged us to express ideas in different, perhaps clearer ways, while drawing on the vast wealth of the English language. After Day 8 you can have some fun trying it for yourself.

PRESUPPOSITIONS

Over the years NLP has adopted certain ideas and concepts as general principles, sometimes referred to as presuppositions. These do not have the same validity as scientific or mathematical laws, and you need not treat them as hard and fast rules. However, they provide a philosophical basis for what you will learn, and you can consider them as 'useful' rather than absolute truth. They concern how people think and communicate and, once you understand their meaning, will probably seem no more than common sense. They provide an important foundation, however, for many of the NLP techniques you will learn.

No authorised canon exists of these presuppositions. They may number half a dozen to two or more dozen, and they comprise different versions and NLP schools of thought. We have selected 21 which cover the needs of introductory or practitioner-level training and conveniently span this 21-day course. To spread your learning and start with the right foundation, you will meet one presupposition each day (chapter), although they do not necessarily relate to that day's topics. In most cases they have a more universal meaning which you can apply in many contexts.

You will find some of these presuppositions quite self-explanatory, and others a little cryptic. Some date from the earliest NLP writings and underlie the basic thinking of NLP, whilst others have a lower status, and may seem to duplicate other presuppositions. We have treated them accordingly, explaining some at length, whilst addressing others briefly. It helps if you memorise them, although the real benefit comes from understanding the ideas behind the presuppositions and applying them in practical ways.

HOW TO GET THE BEST OUT OF THIS BOOK

You can take as long as you like to complete the book, working through each day's topics as time permits, at your own pace. Alternatively, if you wish, you can work through it in just 21 days, keeping more rigidly to the daily learning and practical exercises. We have written it as an easy-to-digest introduction. But at the same time it covers all the topics and skills that practitioner training demands, and to as much depth as you will require.

Day 1 introduces NLP as a whole, then on each following day you will learn new topics. Although some topics stand alone, we suggest you read the book sequentially. Each principle or technique you learn adds to your earlier learning – so they all stay valid. You always build on what has gone before, even if what you meet later puts things in a different light.

We explain any technical terms when we introduce them. Later on, if you wish, you can refer to the glossary of NLP terms at the back of the book. We have also suggested a short list of books you may want to refer to. These include a few seminal works by the founders of NLP and also the recommended reading list for the *Realisation at Stenhouse* practitioner programme. However, because this book fully covers the recognised syllabus you don't have to buy any other textbooks unless you wish to.

You will learn a highly practical subject such as NLP best from direct experience. The simple 'To Do' exercises each day provide practice in the essential skills you will need. Depending on the nature of the exercise, you may wish to have someone to work with you. Otherwise you may wish to use the book as a background manual while taking part in a live certification programme. But its DIY format allows you to go as far as you wish on your own.

Ideally, you should read one chapter, then start applying what you learn immediately, before carrying on with the next one. For instance, if you read the book in the evening, you could start to put the 'To Do' exercises into practice the following morning. You should not need to change your routine much, as we have designed the exercises to fit into your everyday life, whether at home with your family, at work, or socially. Alternatively, you may want to start by reading the book right through quickly to get the flavour of the subject. You can then go back and work through the programme in depth. This way, you can estimate the time required more accurately and schedule more methodically. But remember that the benefits of NLP come from *doing* and not just knowing, so you will need to commit yourself to working through the practical exercises.

For a sound introduction to NLP, simply read the book and apply the principles and techniques in your everyday life. This way, you will gain important skills and knowledge from the outset. For those who want to gain a recognised qualification, we have included details of *Realisation at Stenhouse* programmes at the back of the book, and look forward to meeting you in live seminars. If you have queries as you work through the book you can fax or e-mail us and we will do our best to help. Enjoy your journey of personal discovery and fulfilment.

DAY 1

How People Tick

This chapter covers:

- **Subjective experience**
- **Thinking and doing**
- **Personal excellence**
- **Modelling success**
- **The NLP model**

Choose any movable object and put it on a table. Now relax and focus on the object, allowing your mind to associate it with whatever meaning it has for you. Its colour, for instance, may take you back to some childhood memory. Or its shape may set your imagination going, just as you see things in clouds or when gazing at a fire. As soon as you stop seeing the object in an objective, conscious way, and start allowing your *unconscious* mind to interpret what you see, some meaning will emerge. Something will 'enter your mind', stimulated by your observation of the object.

Close your eyes if you wish, and see the object in your imagination. In some cases you will recognise the connection between the object and what it makes you think about. In such cases you will 'logically' account for the association, however obscure or indirect the link may seem. In other cases a thought may come into your mind that appears to defy logic, even when clearly stimulated by the object in some unknown way.

This sort of process often happens when we daydream or just allow our thoughts to wander. For instance, when driving a car, we often make such mental links with things we drive past. What happens if 100 people look at the same object? Based on our repeated experience in seminars, they will come up with 100 different 'meanings' – from the fascinating to the bizarre. This shows how very subjectively we experience what we see, hear and feel in the so-called objective, material world around us.

Our reaction to what we 'sense', or our perception, dictates our behaviour – what we do. Each individual's mysterious, unique, inner, wholly subjective interpretation of the external world shapes his or her individual behaviour. So while we may see and feel the same things, we act differently. For instance, the same object in the above exercise might make one person sad, and another very happy, because of its particular associations for them as individuals. All our behaviour, and consequently our achievements, depends upon our subjective experience. Today, on Day 1, we consider some of these important ideas.

First, a little background to NLP and some definitions: Neuro-Linguistic Programming builds on the ideas of the anthropologist Gregory Bateson, developed in the 1970s by John Grinder and Richard Bandler. Grinder specialised in linguistics and Bandler in mathematics and information technology, with an interest in psychology. The subject deals mainly with interpersonal communication, 'experience' and the pursuit of excellence. It offers a *structured* approach to how people think and behave. Some people call it the structure of human experience. So it takes much of the mystique out of the subject, and reduces the random, hit-and-miss aspects of understanding people. We defined NLP in the introduction as 'the art and science of personal excellence' or 'the study of subjective experience'. Colloquially, we might call it 'learning how people tick'.

NLP boasts an impressive academic pedigree. However, its increasing popularity probably has more to do with the rapid changes it can produce in behaviour and achievement – the fact that it *works*. Its applications turn up everywhere – for example, sport, therapy, training, education, personal development, and a range of business areas such as sales, negotiation, human resources management and customer relationships. In each case its highly practical, results-based approach sets NLP apart from other methodologies. In this book we show you how NLP can help you in practical ways – in your job and career, in the home, socially or in your personal development.

We described NLP at the outset as 'the art and science of personal excellence'. Why do we call it an art? Because subjective thinking and experience do not fit neatly into the objective scientific method as used in the physical sciences. And also because some of the subtle interpersonal communication skills used in NLP owe more to art than science. Why do we call it a science? Because, as far as possible, NLP tries to give structure to experience and has developed robust principles and models and a 'language'. So, within the limits of a highly subjective field of study, it applies every possible scientific rigour.

SUBJECTIVE EXPERIENCE

'Subjective experience' includes what goes on inside your mind, as well as in the outside world. Nobody really knows *how* anybody else thinks, let alone *what* they think. We each think we know 'reality'. So-called 'experience', therefore, differs enormously from person to person. We each perceive the world in which we live uniquely and subjectively. We see things differently. We have our own attitudes, beliefs and values, which together make up our 'mindset'. Our mindsets may not make sense to other people. And the way some people think and behave often doesn't make sense to us. None of us, however, has a monopoly on what scientists might call 'objective reality'.

Unfortunately, unlike external phenomena, we can't examine our unique, subjective experience in a laboratory. NLP accepts this, and simply sets out to understand subjective experience in order to help individuals do what they do better.

It explains experience using simple models about how we think, and how what we think affects what we do. Specifically, it shows how what we perceive through our five senses translates into understanding. In particular, NLP identifies how, through the five senses, we translate the world around us into meaning, understanding, and *experience*. This enables us to communicate more objectively about very subjective things. In this way we can understand other people better, communicate with them more effectively, and take more control of our lives.

THINKING AND DOING

> **By thinking differently, you will behave differently, and get different results.**

We tend to do what we think about most. NLP offers some simple techniques to help us change *how* we think – the 'neuro' part of neuro-linguistic programming. Our behaviour then inevitably changes. As Descartes once said, 'I think therefore I am', and the Bible tells us, 'Whatsoever a man thinketh, so he is'. What we think about most translates into the actions that cause change. Thoughts become outcomes, results, achievements, successes or failures.

Philosophers have for centuries probed the mysteries of the human mind. However, what we call subjective experience has all but baffled experimental scientists. They do not feel at home in the laboratory of the human mind. NLP, on the other hand, accepts this inherent subjectivity. Rather than ignore the invisible or mystical, NLP deliberately sets out to find a process or structure that makes sense of this very subjectivity.

It accepts what most of us accept intuitively – that we have a mind, a consciousness, a thinking 'black box' that sits somewhere between external causes and their effects.

TOWARDS PERSONAL EXCELLENCE

We can all achieve excellence. We may often complain that we lack talent or natural ability, pointing to someone better than ourselves. But, in terms of our potential for more or less unlimited learning and improvement, we all start from a level playing field. Each of us *owns* a customised, almost godlike goal-achieving resource, cleverly wrapped up in a three-pound lump of grey matter. And, according to the experts, we hardly use a fraction of our brains. Through NLP, anyone can tap into this *technology* of excellence, this limitless potential. To get the most out of NLP you need no greater starting qualification than an open, expectant mind. You can then draw on the fantastic neuro-physiological resources you already possess and start your journey towards personal excellence.

MODELLING SUCCESS

You can 'model' success. Using NLP, you can observe excellence in other people – the best you can find – and adopt *their* successful strategies and skills into your own life. By tapping their skills and so-called 'natural talents', you can speed up the process of learning, sometimes benefiting from their many years of trial and error. When you combine this know-how with the fantastic power of your own innate resources, you can accomplish just about *anything*.

'Natural Talent'

We sometimes envy other people's 'natural talents', whether social, professional, athletic or artistic. Yet we *all* have such skills and abilities. For example, you can do many things 'without thinking' (with what NLP calls *unconscious competence*) that others admire and perhaps envy. Perhaps you have a talent for swimming, riding a bike, doing mental arithmetic, making a soufflé, tying a reef knot, painting a water colour wash or making friends easily? These skills may seem very commonplace to you. But invariably *somebody* will ask 'How do they do that? They make it look so easy.'

We would all like to do things that friends and colleagues seem to take in their stride. But people don't often know just *how* they do what they do so well, or even admit to their own 'excellence'. Using NLP you can tap into these skills and – to an extraordinary extent – replicate them in your own life.

The Strategies of Excellence

NLP tries to remove the mystique from human excellence and make it more accessible. In any 'excellent' skill or behaviour we can discover a 'strategy'. Even when unknown to the person displaying the skill, this strategy comprises a sequence of thoughts and actions that consistently add up to success. You will learn about strategies and modelling in more depth on Days 16 to 18. Using these modelling techniques, you can draw on the thinking and behavioural strategies of the people up to whose level of excellence you want to perform.

Originally the NLP founders applied the idea of modelling to famous therapists renowned for their extraordinary communication skills. Today, people use it in every aspect of their personal and business lives. In particular it has raised interpersonal communication skills, whether verbal or non-verbal, to a new technological level.

THE NLP MODEL

As we have discovered, experience goes beyond externally observable behaviour and includes what goes on in the black box of the mind. So NLP has little truck with mechanistic, cause-and-effect approaches to personal experience, or the so-called 'behaviourist' approach (based on meticulous time and motion studies and methods that applied more readily to physical science). It addresses 'how people tick' – not just as a species but as unique individuals.

We all see, hear and feel things differently. Sensory inputs go through a myriad of mental 'filters' formed by our memories, memories of memories, feelings and past perceptions. Given these unique filters, we experience *only* our own, limited interpretation of the world – what we call our own *reality*.

The NLP model, shown in Figure 1.1, illustrates experience as a process, or system. It incorporates the familiar five senses, but adopts these as the way we think *inwardly* as well as outwardly. It illustrates the unity of mind and body. Using the analogy of an iceberg, the NLP model reflects not just 'above-the-surface' experience, but inner, subjective, 'below-the-surface' experience. It recognises that people behave according to unique values, feelings, beliefs, desires and motivation. Your 'experience' differs not just from mine, but from *everybody's*.

NLP helps us to understand and come to terms with this humbling reality. In particular, it helps us to understand how we *represent* or interpret things; and how, in the process, we generalise, distort and delete so much of the available information. Most importantly, we start to understand how these perceptions affect every aspect of our behaviour – and, in turn, what we achieve.

Creating Experience

The mind–body 'system' handles more than outside sensory stimuli. As you can see from the NLP model, we also see, hear or feel *internally* – recalling memories and having imaginary experiences.

Having formed experience from external stimuli, you can

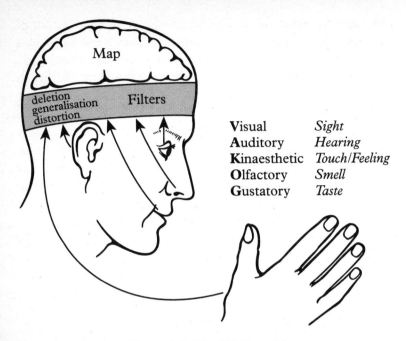

Figure 1.1 The NLP model

manipulate it to create new experience. For instance, you can recall a memory and change it, whether intentionally or unintentionally. The simple act of remembering a 'fact' may involve a distortion of an earlier distortion or 'filtered' experience. In due course you might end up with a *memory of a memory of a memory* which bears precious little relation to the original light waves that reached your optic nerves or sound waves that entered your ears.

This ability to manipulate experience offers a simple route to personal change. For example, you can change how you feel, or your state of mind, by 'representing' the offending thought and memories more positively. As well as just imagining different outcomes, you will learn, on Day 7, how to change the very structure of memories. You can even, if you wish, change long-standing attitudes, values and beliefs.

You can also *originate* your own experience – without your

physical eyes, ears or sense of touch – or *synthesise* experience by mixing memories and ideas in a novel way. In other words, you can *imagine*. Furthermore, you can imagine an experience in the future, or something happening across the world, just as easily as you can recall memories. In some circumstances, like vivid dreams and daydreams, internal experience seems just as real as real life. The ability to clearly visualise a desired outcome increases your chances of fulfilling it. The skill of creating and manipulating thoughts requires practice just like any physical skill. But it repays the effort many times over.

Through NLP you can start to understand subjective experience and, where necessary, change it for the better. In this way you can *create* experience, and a different future.

Knowing Yourself and Others

This means, for instance, that you can *create* experience rather than just *reacting* to outside circumstances or past conditioning. It means you can have more *choice* – controlling your life and creating your own future. You can, consciously and positively, *work the system* to achieve what you want.

With such self-knowledge, you can understand other people better. To start with, you will *accept* that their perceptions differ, by their very nature, from your own. But you can now *identify* their perceptive filters and appreciate how they have affected that person's interpretation of events. You can then *compare* these rich and varied perceptual filters or mental 'maps'. Better still, you can *use* them, trying things out for yourself in a different way and adding new perspectives. In this way you can enormously enhance your own, already awesome, mental resources.

We can all achieve personal excellence. It becomes a reality when we understand and direct our experience towards real outcomes.

PRESUPPOSITION FOR TODAY

> **The map is not the territory.**

We each have our own subjective 'map' of the world. It represents what goes on around us, what things mean to us, and what we believe and feel about them – our perceptions, or what we understand as experience or reality.

All this map-making goes on in our minds as we try to *understand* the world in which we live. And with such a 'tidy' mind, every bit of experience has to have a place – a pigeon-hole or classification. Things have to *make sense*.

Your personal map comprises the neural networks of your brain that have formed electro-chemically throughout your life. So every person's map differs. Your unique personal history acts as a filter on the thousands of sensory experiences you encounter moment by moment. And all this happens automatically, or unconsciously. Over a period, you can add to and amend your mental filters – you can literally *change your mind*. NLP gives you the choice to make these changes consciously and deliberately in order to achieve your desired outcomes.

What about the 'territory'? Because we each see the world through our own perceptual filters, none of us sees things as *reality*. We cannot. Thus 'The map [our subjective, limited perception] is not the territory [of reality]'. Some people find this idea quite disconcerting. But it can enrich your learning when you discover that other people experience and interpret the world differently. *Acting* on this awareness can enrich a person's whole life.

Now think about what this presupposition can mean for you. We saw earlier that by *modelling* another person's strategy of excellence you can do something better. Their strategy may relate to a skill or task, or a state of mind (like staying motivated, calm or confident). Or they may simply see things from a different perspective – have a different outlook on things. At the same time you can share with others your own strategies of excellence, as we all excel in one way or another. By discovering other people's *maps* of reality, you enlarge and enrich your own experience, gaining a better understanding of the *territory* of reality.

Start to think about this presupposition in whatever situation you find yourself.

- Notice how people will often argue that 'black is white' rather than change their views.

- Notice how an optimistic person sees a glass as half-full while a pessimistic person sees it as half-empty. This illustrates the universal tendency for people to see things from their own, unique perspective. 'Beauty [and half-emptiness or half-fullness] is in the eye [in fact the mind] of the beholder.'

- In insurance reports, witnesses to accidents often give hugely differing accounts of the events they have seen. These reflect, of course, the subjective point of view of the witnesses and confirm how widely 'real experiences' can differ. Watch for such differing interpretations in everyday life, and note that your own, if you witness a behaviour, experience or event, forms just another 'view'. Consider other 'maps of reality'.

- Notice how we arrive at strangely different conclusions, apparently based on the same data. You may see this in meetings at work, in conversations socially, or even in the way family members react to news and information. Note how we interpret even apparently objective 'facts' subjectively.

All these differences, of course, occur in our individual minds. Each person's lifetime of personal experience acts as an unconscious filter on everything they see, hear and feel. It forms an increasingly unbridgeable barrier between that person and the 'territory'. It sometimes distorts and demeans your experience, and limits you in what you want to achieve.

Once aware of this self-imposed limitation, you will realise that you have choices that never occurred to you. And having choice greatly improves your chances of success.

For the moment, watch out for examples of this presupposition in action. Listen to conversations at work. Note the vast differences of opinion in newspapers; on the television; between countries, races and political parties; and between parents and teenagers. Notice all the maps, their diversity, originality and uniqueness. Look for realities other than your own map. Enrich your own experience by looking from other perspectives.

TODAY'S TO DOs

- Memorise the presupposition for today (see p. 10) and notice three or more situations in which it seems to apply. Whenever remembering anything, use your imagination to the full. Consider using mnemonics, mind pictures or anything that helps make the thing memorable.

- Think of a person you often disagree with or cannot get on with. List some of the filters each of you usually applies to 'facts' – for instance, your values and beliefs, the influence of friends or relatives, your education and upbringing, how you feel at the time, and so on. Note how, logically, you will form different maps of reality. Then notice how you now feel about the person.

- In preparation for tomorrow, think of several personal goals you want to achieve. You can choose specific objectives or just desires, wishes or dreams. Write them down. Tomorrow you will learn how to increase your chances of fulfilling them.

DAY 2

Getting What You Want

This chapter covers:

- **The technology of goal achievement**
- **The four-stage success model**
- **The elements of a well-formed outcome**

Having given a brief overview of NLP, we now introduce the central NLP topic of goals. We all know people who never seem to accomplish anything because they do not have clear goals. Most of us also know people who set themselves daily, weekly or monthly personal targets and seem to achieve outstanding results. Their ability to focus on clear, measurable goals accounts for their success. As you think back over your life, you can probably relate your own successes and failures to whether or not you had clear and positive goals.

Setting and achieving goals (whether described as dreams, desires, outcomes or whatever) lies at the heart of human experience. As well as giving pleasure, positive goal-setting really can change your life.

Many business leaders and entrepreneurs seem driven by an ambition or dream. Motivating goals act as their yardsticks of success. Organisations may have their own versions of goals and outcomes, such as MBO (management by objectives), corporate planning and budgetary control systems. But company managers and leaders usually achieve what they do as *individuals*, sometimes despite the inertia of an organisation. Individuals translate well-formed goals into motivation, self-belief, persistence and all the human characteristics that bring about eventual success. So, not surprisingly, a few key individuals often account for the success of an organisation.

Think Like a Leader (Harry Alder, Piatkus) includes several examples, such as the young man hardly out of school and doing menial production work who 'saw himself' as a manufacturing manager by the age of 25. He described how he carefully honed and developed the image and feeling, and the elation of finally sitting in the manager's chair and experiencing what he had mentally experienced so realistically. He then went on to use the same 'system' of visualising and soon occupied the CEO's chair in a leading corporation.

In other cases ambition may relate to the company, and how it will look and feel. People like Archie Norman at Asda, Stanley Kalms at Dixons, Timothy Waterstone of bookselling fame, Ian Smith at Lunn Poly and Keith Oates at Marks and Spencer, Anita Roddick at The Body Shop have all realised major corporate as well as personal goals through visionary, imaginative thinking as well as hard work and commitment. Stretching your imagination clearly brings infinitely more dramatic results than stretching your work hours or developing your will power.

THE TECHNOLOGY OF GOAL ACHIEVEMENT

The idea of working towards goals seems a part of human nature. We possess a goal-achieving instinct, somehow linked to the universal tendency to seek pleasure and avoid pain. A person behaves in a certain way because they think that behaviour will benefit them. In other words, we tend to do things for a reason, or purpose. Whether we express it or not, we have an outcome in mind.

So behaviour has a *purpose*, to fulfil some outcome or other. And we *interpret* what we do as having a purpose. And we *give* it a meaning, even in hindsight. In a sense, we have an *excuse* for everything we do.

By setting your goals consciously and precisely, as 'well-formed outcomes', you have a better chance of translating them into behaviour and achievement.

NLP builds on this innate goal-achieving tendency and desire for purpose and meaning. Evidence abounds that human beings act as goal-achieving *systems*. Whether to get, do or know something, or just to survive and procreate, our goals seem to *systemically* underlie all our behaviour. This does not mean that we embark on every little activity with a conscious goal in mind. Indeed, we usually act without any conscious intention. We just do something without thinking about where our behaviour will take us. But, even when we don't realise it, we nevertheless pursue some underlying motive or goal.

Some highly successful sportspeople and businesspeople, for example, have relentlessly striven to overcome early educational or social disadvantages. Without consciously identifying their motivation and the source of their extraordinary energy and commitment, they have nevertheless pursued a personal vision more powerful than any corporate business plan or conscious career ambition. For instance, the outstanding generation of young Russian and East European gymnasts a couple of decades ago all shared a driving ambition to succeed, powered by their vivid dream of excellence and world recognition. A fertile, unconstrained imagination turns out, in such cases, to have more impact than all the will-power and dedication that most of us can ever muster. These individuals live out their dream, perhaps without even realising they have one.

Many such stories seem to date back to childhood, events and circumstances in early life, or the influence of a particular person. Sometimes it may seem like luck, chance or serendipity, and thus outside our control. However, the NLP approach to goal-setting differs from other popular business approaches in that it focuses on what happens unconsciously as well as consciously.

Anyone can call upon and trust this inbuilt goal-achieving mechanism. It will faithfully process whatever, consciously or unconsciously, we input into the system. We will give you the tools you need to harness your natural goal-achieving ability in this and tomorrow's module.

THE FOUR-STAGE SUCCESS MODEL

Before discussing goal-setting in more detail, we need to place it in the context of your overall progress towards excellence. Goal-setting forms part of a simple but vital process called the four-stage success model, which illustrates how we programme our personal goals.

The following four-stage model underpins all effective learning, especially for hands-on skills, and encapsulates much of NLP.

1. Decide what you want (set your goal).
2. Do something.
3. Notice what happens.
4. Change what you do until you get your desired outcome.

As you work through this 21-day programme, you will learn about each of these stages in more depth. This simple model applies to all our behaviour and achievements. Most of the time we don't think about the process, as we self-steer towards goals. It happens naturally. But sometimes we don't steer towards the *right* goals. If you start to consciously apply the four-part success model, you will soon see for yourself how it works in all sorts of situations.

A fine line usually separates success and failure. And it usually boils down to missing out or under-performing on one of these stages (such as not setting clear goals, or not learning from experience). Over the next few days you will develop knowledge and skills to equip you for each stage, and thus get more consistent results.

The rest of today's module addresses the first stage – deciding what you want, or setting your goals. In NLP terms this is learning how to have a 'well-formed outcome'.

THE ELEMENTS OF A WELL-FORMED OUTCOME

You may have already come across the widely used SMART goal characteristics:

Specific
Measurable
Achievable
Realistic
Timely

However , the SMART model only tells part of the story. For really effective goal-setting you need to follow NLP's goal-setting guidelines, known as 'the elements of a well-formed outcome'.

Today you will learn these elements or test criteria, and how to apply them to your own goals. We cannot overstate their importance as the foundation for effective behaviour and achievement. You should establish them as thinking habits and constantly apply them. Some overlap the SMART criteria, and you may find them expressed in different ways, as a longer or shorter list. We have summarised six elements to apply to your goals:

1. State your goal positively.
2. Put your goal in context.
3. Express your goal in specific, sensory terms.

4.   Choose a goal you can fulfil yourself.
5.   Evaluate honestly the effects of achieving your goal.
6.   Choose a worthwhile goal.

In this section we explain each one and then suggest a number of questions to help you apply it. These will help ensure that each goal you set has the best chance of success. In particular, they will uncover aspects of your goals that may not consciously occur to you, although relevant to your success or failure. Don't worry about your *answers* – just ask yourself the questions. Some questions may seem more relevant than others. If a question helps to confirm your goal, or makes you think you should change it in some way, it has done its job. As you learn these outcome tests, start to apply them to any goals and objectives you set, until it becomes a habit.

A word of advice: don't rush this exercise. Let's face it – we don't rethink our life's goals very often, and the potential benefits will well repay the time and effort spent. Many people have radically improved different aspects of their lives by using this approach to setting and achieving goals.

If you have not yet made your initial list of goals, desires, wants or wishes, do it before learning these rules. By applying them to real-life goals you will understand them better, and they will immediately benefit you by increasing your chances of success. Amend your written goal, if necessary, as you apply the rules and ask the questions. In a few cases you may have to abandon a goal completely. Doggedly sticking to a goal that has little chance of success makes little sense. Get ready to set new goals. You may well find you can achieve your *ultimate* desire in a different way.

1. State Your Goal Positively

When asked about their goals, many people respond by saying what they *don't* want rather than what they *do* want. So, first, state what you *want* – make it positive.

The brain actually works in such a way that stating a goal in negative terms can have completely the wrong effect. Parents sometimes tell their children what not to do ('Don't trip', 'Don't spill it', 'Don't do so-and-so'), only to find that they seem more inclined to do the very opposite. And this doesn't just apply to children. A cricketer enthusiastically encouraged 'not to miss this one' as the ball arcs through the sky will more than likely do just that. He will think about missing rather than catching it! The negative thought becomes self-fulfilling.

> **What most occupies your mind, whether intentionally or unintentionally, tends to turn into behaviour and reality.**

To 'understand' what you don't want, you have to make some sort of mental representation, including probably an image of the thing you don't want. Your mind uses that same mental imagery – especially if vivid – as its 'assumed outcome'. So your imagined 'don't want' almost inevitably turns into reality.

Although we do not understand all the brain neurology involved, this aspect of how we perceive things often fascinates people. For instance, if I tell you not to think about your left foot you *have* to think about it in order to know what not to think about! Or try *not* thinking about an aeroplane propeller or a fish finger. . . .

Unfortunately, when it comes to goal-achieving, the instinctive internal negative image can do its damage before you apply the negative injunction. So the golfer who thinks about the obstacles (the tree, the bunker) tends to produce what his or her mind imagines. He carries out the 'mind instruction' and the ball *succeeds* in landing in the bunker or hitting the tree. Inveterate worriers similarly tend to live out their fears, like a self-fulfilling prophecy. This confirms their worst imaginings ('I told you so') and they carry on achieving efficiently just what they didn't want.

Saying what you do want
Thinking positively does not come easily to everyone, of course. So how do you not think about what you don't want?

The answer: focus only on, or *represent* (in sights, sounds and feelings) what you *do* want.

Some recent research into the brain can help here. For instance, it seems we can only think *consciously* of a handful of things at once. So, once we use up our 'ration' by thinking about the sights, sounds and feelings of what we *want*, we simply cannot think about anything else. In fact when we think about something very vividly – in big, bright imagery, if you like – we can do little more than think about that single thing. As we say, it 'occupies our mind'. In this way we can overcome the tendency to imagine negative outcomes.

In positive goal-setting you exclude everything else – not just goals you don't want, but even thoughts about *how you will achieve* what you want. Just carry out one stage at a time. Focus first on the goal itself, rather than the means of achieving it.

You can easily learn to focus on what you want, although it may take some practice. Let's give some more examples. For instance, do you really want to *lose* 10 pounds in weight? Or do you want to reach a certain weight within a certain time? Do you want to stop arriving late or start arriving on time? *Rewording* your intentions to make them positive may require no more than a simple reversal. Language and syntax influence the mind, just like vivid mind pictures, so you can use this simple device to your advantage.

Try it out. Scribble down a number of wishes, goals, desires, whatever, without thinking too deeply about them. Then check whether you have expressed them positively. If not, rewrite them in positive terms. If you cannot do this by a simple reversal, then spend a while thinking about what you *really* want, and make *that* your positive outcome. You might think of several things you want that had not occurred to you, rather than the thing you started out not wanting.

Goal-testing questions

Asking yourself these questions will help you to clarify your goals and express them positively. If working with a partner, ask 'What do you want?' and so on. With practice you will acquire the habit of *literal* positive thinking, one of the rules of a well-formed outcome.

What do I want?
What do I hope to change now?
What outcome do I want to have?
What would I like to achieve?
What would I like to change?
What do I want to do differently?
Do I have an outcome in mind?
What outcome do I have in mind?
What would I like to do?
So, let's think, I want. . . .

2. Put Your Goal in Context

Next: when, where, and with whom do you want this outcome? Setting a goal entails more than just writing it down. Your goal forms the internal reality, or *multi-sensory blueprint*, of what you create.

> **What you see, hear and feel inside gives a foretaste of what will actually happen.**

Your outcome has to 'register' as realistic. You cannot kid your goal-achieving mind with vague abstractions or hazy images. Moreover, seeing, hearing and feeling does not happen in a vacuum, but in some context. Perhaps at work or in your hobby? Perhaps involving other people and what they say to you? Perhaps in a certain building or room?

If unsure about context, just apply the 'W' questions to your goal – what?, where?, when?, who? Imagine or 'mentally rehearse' each as you answer.

A tree has more meaning when surrounded by its natural landscape; in the same way your outcomes will have more meaning when imagined in a real-life context. You may even find you don't want a certain goal in a certain situation. So, sooner rather than later, you should identify the context of your outcome.

Goal-testing questions

Asking yourself these questions will further clarify your outcome by putting it in a real-life context. It will also add *feelings*. In this way you will get a foretaste of your outcome and increase your motivation and commitment. You will also firmly establish it *internally* as the target towards which your goal-achieving system will steer.

> Where will the change take me to?
> In what context would I use my new outcome?
> When do I want this?
> Where do I want this?
> In every relationship? In every situation? With whom?
> In what contexts might my chosen outcome not benefit me?
> In what other contexts might my outcome prove useful?
> In what contexts would I use my new skills?
> Do I want this all the time in all areas of my life?
> How long do I want to take to do or get this?
> When do I want to do or use this?
> Will it suit every situation?
> In which contexts will this outcome have importance for me?

3. Express Your Goal in Specific, Sensory Terms

What, specifically, will you see, hear and feel when you actually achieve this outcome? You can really go to town on this. What emotions will you enjoy? Put yourself into the future and enjoy your fulfilled outcome. What colour carpet will you have (if your outcome includes a carpet)? What will the person's voice sound like (if a voice forms part of the outcome)? And what will it feel like to sit in the chair (if any)?

This sort of visualisation practice will prepare you for some of the exercises you will do later. You can now start to familiarise yourself with your internal sensory world where you conceive goals and create experience.

Initially you may find it hard to visualise things, but easy to hear voices and sounds. Or vice versa: sounds may prove more difficult than visual images. But, with practice, we can all enjoy a rich inner sensory world. Start with easy things – like visualising a person you know very well, listening to their voice, recalling a time when you felt happy with him or her. Always start with what comes easily and go on from there. Close your eyes and imagine sitting in the next room and seeing as much as you can of yourself in the present room. Or think back to a holiday you enjoyed, an interesting person you met, or a job you did well. See how clearly you can recall these.

Soon, as well as memories, you will learn to clearly imagine whole new experiences that will form rich 'raw material' for your future outcomes. These comprise your personal, priceless inner resources and the very basis of your future.

> **Everything created in the world around us started as a thought in somebody's mind.**

Go for outcomes that easily translate into sensory experience. Develop your innate sensory ability and start to 'create' in a more literal sense. This process doesn't just help to clarify and build a goal. It actually 'tunes' your neurology, and in effect rehearses the links your brain needs to make in order to achieve success. Vivid sensory representations of your outcome set up a sequence of neural *associations*. These 'steer' you from inner experience to external reality.

As with the story of any success, one little idea or thought triggers another. Ideas may seem to come from nowhere. But in fact your clearly expressed goal forms a channel into which these associations mysteriously fall. They not only reinforce your goal or *destination*, but give insights as to how you will achieve them along the *journey*. And all this stems from having clear, sensory images of what you want.

On Day 7 you will develop more skills to create your outcomes, using the strongest sensory characteristics.

Goal-testing questions

You should now start to form your own questions to stimulate your own imagination – we have just given a few examples. Answer these questions in mental pictures, sounds and feelings as well as in words and you will help to create your eventual outcomes.

What will I see, hear and feel when I have achieved my goal?
How will I confirm I have reached my goal?
What evidence will I need to know I have achieved my goal?

4. Choose a Goal You Can Fulfil Yourself

You need to initiate and maintain your outcome *yourself*. Don't allow room for blaming people or circumstances for failure. People and circumstances often seem to dictate what actually happens, of course, and we may sometimes feel like pawns in a bigger game that we have little control over. A real achiever, nevertheless, takes responsibility for his or her goals and tries not to depend on other people.

Do not fulfil other people's goals. Make every goal you want to achieve *your own*, whoever may benefit in the end. You may well have worthwhile goals for other people (say your children), or goals that depend on other people. But you need to have reasonable *personal control*, however good your motives on behalf of others. Whilst you may not personally fulfil your child's goal, you can set goals for yourself that might *help* your child to fulfil *their* goal. For example, you can help with their education, you can spend more time with them, you can make some provision for them to start a business, or whatever. You can measure yourself fairly against those goals, in so far as *you* can bring them about.

This does not mean that you have to abandon your goal if it concerns somebody else. But you may have to rethink it and restate it in such a way that you play the prime role.

> **Achieving goals means achieving *your* goals.**

You can certainly take on board the goals of others (like those of your employer, boss or partner). In other words you can *adopt* a goal. But for a well-formed outcome you must then have the power to bring it about.

Sometimes you will meet borderline situations. A manager, for instance, depends on other people to fulfil many, perhaps most, of his or her goals. As we know, managers have to delegate, especially in large organisations. Does that mean that such work goals fail the test? Not necessarily. As long as you can *influence* the outcome, even indirectly, by virtue of your position, knowledge or resources, you can assume it as your own goal. It will depend on the circumstances.

For example, as a junior member of a project team, you will not have the authority to set firm completion dates and performance criteria, nor responsibility for the final out-come. But, as project *leader*, you should have the position, power and (hopefully) the necessary skills to bring about your outcome, albeit through others.

Similarly, you can produce a draft report *recommending* a certain change in your organisation without taking responsibility for the implementation. Your goal stops where your responsibility and power stop – where you can no longer ful-fil it personally. You can write a book, for example, but you cannot determine how it will sell. This need not present a problem, however. Sometimes you can amend a goal, or restrict it to the part that you can play personally. Ask the question: to what degree can I *own* this outcome, both in set-ting it and in bringing it about? When applying any of these criteria you may need to lower your horizons a little. But you will achieve more in the end by confining yourself to goals over which you have reasonable control.

A similar situation applies in teams, and only *you* can judge whether you can reasonably control the team outcome. You don't necessarily have to do everything yourself, but you have to *make it happen*. Ask yourself: could I reasonably excuse myself in the event of failure, by blaming other people? If so, rethink your outcome before you embark on it.

Sometimes circumstances, rather than people, will affect your goal. For example, a goal that depends on interest rates or exchange rates, commodity price levels, the performance of stocks or the weather, hardly rests within your own power.

Control the controllable and let the rest take care of itself.

This means only setting goals within your 'reasonable' control (*intuitively*, perhaps, rather than logically reasonable).

Goal-testing questions

Asking these questions will make you the central player in any goal you set, eliminate possible excuses for failure, and make you feel positively motivated.

What will I do to achieve this goal?
What have I already achieved for myself similar to this?
What form does the similarity take?
Might anything get in the way of me achieving my goal?
Can I take charge of the changes required?
What will this outcome mean to me?
What will the change allow me to do?
What difference will that make to me?
How can I achieve my goal?
How do I see myself doing it?
What possibilities could I conceive to achieve this goal?
Do I need any help to achieve this outcome?
Does it depend on me alone or on someone else?
What will it enable me to do?

How will I personally affect this outcome?
What can I achieve with this outcome?
How much of the outcome can I control?
What can I do immediately?

5. Evaluate Honestly the Effects of Achieving Your Goal

Will you lose anything that you now have, *and want to keep*, by achieving this goal? This means thinking about your goal in a wider sense, including its effects on your other goals and how it might affect other people you care for. Fulfilling a career goal, for example, may well mean losing out on your family life or spending less time on a hobby or leisure pursuit. Conversely, achieving a leisure goal may mean sacrificing career advancement if that requires working long hours and at weekends. If you want to stop smoking, for example, don't kid yourself about the pleasure and perhaps the indirect social benefits you now get from it. Think honestly about what you may lose in the process of getting something else.

Achieving an outcome means moving from one state to another. These states include how you *feel* and the invisible pros and cons, spin-offs and downsides, as well as the visible, external aspects – the 'ecology' of the change (see Day 3).

Consider any positive (to you) aspects of your present state *before* you embark on your new outcome. Otherwise you may end up feeling cheated, or still unhappy and unfulfilled, even though on the face of it you have 'succeeded'. Alternatively, you may *not* achieve what you consciously set out to achieve but still finish up losing some of what you had when you started out.

Even if you apply all your will-power to a badly thought-out goal, the positive benefits you now enjoy (and unconsciously hold on to) will tend to thwart it somewhere along the way. On a hiding to nothing, you may not realise why you keep failing to achieve your conscious goal.

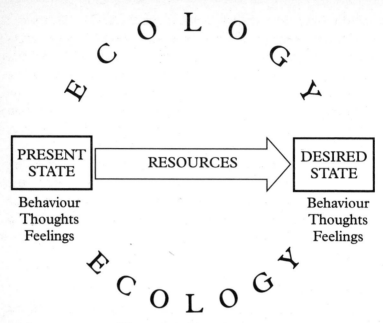

Figure 2.1 Changing state

Always look for another, better, cheaper, quicker, way to attain your desired outcome. If no other route exists, whereby you can maintain the benefits of what you now have, re-evaluate the cost of your goal.

> **Evaluate the total change involved in achieving your outcome.**

Even if your other goals and intentions remain unaffected, the goals of other people you care for may suffer. If you consider this important, you will lose out. In the end it will mean giving up something, such as a relationship. So you need to evaluate this as a possible trade-off.

It doesn't take a superman to climb up an organisation leaving a trail of hurt, misused people behind him. But what will he forfeit in the process, especially in the longer term? Sooner or later, events catch up with us. No outcome stands alone. We cannot act independently of those around us. To what extent will you either ignore or adversely affect other people's outcomes for the sake of your own? You decide. If the new outcome replaces or exceeds all the positive aspects of your present state, fine. If not, do some rethinking *before* you embark on your outcome, rather than after your world (and perhaps the world of others) has fallen apart.

Ideally, you will come up with a win-win situation in which you keep what you have got (not so much the behaviour, but the benefits it brings) while achieving some new outcome which offers its own benefits. Such win-win outcomes usually depend on following well-formed outcome principles.

Goal-testing questions

Answering these questions will help you reflect how well, on balance, your goal-achieving mechanisms have served you – at least in terms of self-preservation and survival. Don't give up too quickly what you have for the glittering prize of some new goal. Aim to recognise and maintain the best from the past, while creating an exciting new future.

Am I sure I really want this?
What will I get once I have reached my outcome?
What do I really want?
How will my life differ, having achieved this outcome?
How will I integrate this outcome into my present life?
What will it mean to me to have this outcome?
Would this outcome seem appropriate in every situation?
What effect will it have on my life?
What will happen after I achieve my goal?
What advantages will result from my achieving it?
What impact will achieving this have on the rest of my life?
What would *not* happen if I achieved this?
What would happen if I *didn't* achieve it?
What would *not* happen if I didn't achieve it?

Are there other areas of my life where achieving this outcome could have benefits or disadvantages?

How do I see this outcome as important?

6. Choose a Worthwhile Goal

Finally, your goal should feel worthwhile to *you*, not necessarily to others or the world. To apply this rule, you need to identify the positive *consequences* of your outcome.

This doesn't just mean testing your outcome against another benefit you will lose, but against your identity and long-term purpose in life. Does it fit with your personality and values?

Rather than making a snap judgement, take some time to reflect and imagine possible scenarios. Mentally rehearse both the benefits and the downsides of your outcome and its consequences. Some aspects of your goal will not appear when you first embark on it. You may well have to rely on your intuition to apply this.

You may not usually think in this depth when setting and implementing day-to-day goals. Yet this forms a vital aspect of your motivation. Your unconscious mind helps you to achieve goals *cybernetically* (meaning that it literally *steers* you towards your outcomes). When you aim at positive, worthwhile targets, your 'system' naturally motivates you to achieve your goal and overcome the obstacles on the way.

Goal-testing questions

Asking these questions will help you discover any disharmony between your goal and you as a person, your values and beliefs. The answers may not come immediately. They may come when you least expect them.

Is the outcome worth what it will take to achieve it?

What consequences will follow my achieving this goal?

How will my life differ?
Does this goal reflect my identity and aspirations?
What will I get by achieving it?
And what then?
What further goal does it take me towards?
And for what purpose?

Achieving well-formed outcomes

You now have a checklist of guidelines for setting goals. You may have to amend or eliminate poorly formed goals, but those that remain will have a greater chance of becoming reality. The goal-testing questions will keep you focused and motivated throughout the process. If you follow these guidelines conscientiously and imaginatively they will *multiply* your chances of success in anything you set out to accomplish. And don't forget the rest of the four-stage success model (see p. 16).

Using these 'elements of a well-formed outcome' you can change vague or negative goals into positive, motivating, pleasurable outcomes. For instance, you can readily translate a vague, negative desire, such as 'I want to stop feeling a failure at work', into a well-formed outcome that you will actually realise. How might the test apply in this case?

1. **Positive:** I want to feel more confident in my work and use my abilities to the full.

2. **In context:** Especially in the Monday staff meetings and when I have to deal with Colin and the accounts people.

3. **Sensory terms:** I will feel confident and walk tall. My voice will sound firm and authoritative.

4. **Fulfil it yourself:** I will make sure I do my own work as well as I can.

5. **Evaluate honestly the effects of achieving your goal:** Do I gain something from feeling a failure? For instance, do I really feel ready for the new responsibilities of a promotion that better performance may result in? Will I lose the sympathy of my colleague who also lacks confidence? Perhaps my friend could join me in some useful, out-of-work training in the weak areas.

6. **Make it worthwhile:** How does this goal relate to my other long-term goals? For instance, what if my partner's relocation promotion, which we've both looked forward to, comes about? Or would I really prefer to make the break and start my own business? Then again, does work really matter that much to me? Perhaps I just need to counter-balance this work-related issue by developing and enjoying my family life, social life and leisure pursuits.

PRESUPPOSITION FOR TODAY

People create their own experience.

Compare this with the first presupposition: 'The map is not the territory'. Think about 'experience'. When daydreaming, for instance, does your experience constitute the reality in your mind or the external reality outside your present awareness? Or when reading an exciting novel, does your experience amount to sitting there reading or does your experience lie somewhere in the world of the story?

Experience seems to depend on what goes on in our heads rather than what goes on in the material environment around us. As we have seen, at best our experience can only amount to a filtered version of that material world, over which we have little control. But we can think what we want to think.

And we can thus create our own experience, including what we do and achieve.

Ask yourself: What triggers a real-life experience? What makes things happen? Could *anything* happen (like picking up a cup, throwing a ball, or building a cathedral) without someone first internalising it as an intention, an idea, a thought?

According to the evidence, what we think about most happens in reality. We sow the seeds, if you like, of our own destiny. Today you have seen the importance of fixing outcomes internally in specific sensory terms (in other words, making them as close to real experience as possible). Keep in mind today's presupposition as you subjectively (inwardly) create your own objective (outward) experience.

TODAY'S TO DOs

- Memorise today's presupposition and think about it in terms of your life and what you want to accomplish. Can you decide upon things now that will influence what you achieve in the future? If you can 'see yourself' doing something and feel strongly motivated, will this produce a real outcome? Do you have choices for the next minute of your life? How can these choices change you for the better? If you think about the presupposition in this way it will open up new ideas, solutions and possibilities. It will give you a more positive outlook on your future.

- List *all* your goals. Initially do not differentiate between definite objectives and things you want but have not thought through. Include some really big things, as well as some short-term desires of no great consequence. You can add wishes and dreams. Then go through them, one at a time, applying all the elements of a well-formed outcome (see pp. 17–31). If possible, bounce them off a friend or colleague who might have a more objective view than you. Some people seem to know us better than we know ourselves. Change or eliminate any goals that do not satisfy all the criteria. New goals might come to mind as you do the exercise. Make a note of them and put them through the same process. Then put your list to one side and come back to it after a while, perhaps tomorrow. You may find this outcome exercise gives you a new sense of direction and meaning.

- Try vividly imagining one of your goals as if already fulfilled. Notice how your expectation, feelings about it, and behaviour change. Note how you experience a foretaste of the final pleasure you will experience in achieving your goal. The *process* of goal achievement offers its own pleasure.

- Watch out for evidence of different 'maps' of reality. Everything you have learnt so far remains valid and today's new knowledge and experience builds on it. Always remember and apply *yesterday's* learning. You can always find new significance in the oldest wisdom. Start to look for the *personal benefits* of getting to know how other people think.

- Memorise the four-stage success model (see p. 16). And think of three or more skills or behaviours you possess, or have observed in others, that incorporate this process. Think about what might happen if you missed out any one stage.

- Think of a goal you would like to fulfil. At this stage don't choose something earth-shattering, but a specific task or achievement you have repeatedly put off or failed to achieve. Choose something that, if successful, will happen very quickly and bring immediate benefits. Then, without any further learning, apply the four-stage success model. Commit yourself to your goal and conscientiously apply each stage. Enjoy the sense of fulfilment as you turn something in your mind into reality.

DAY 3

Knowing What You *Really* Want

This chapter covers:

- **Outcome ecology**
- **The role of your unconscious mind**
- **Representing your outcomes**
- **Cartesian questions**
- **Values and outcomes**

You should now have some well-formed outcomes. The tests we applied on Day 2 had a common-sense, 'left brain' kind of logic. Today we shall consider some subjective, *right brain* ways to maximise your outcomes. (We associate the right brain with intuition, imagery and the unconscious mind.)

Using this 'dual brain' approach, you can access your full, extraordinary goal-achieving powers. You will learn, for instance, how to align the goals you set with your values – one of the secrets of goal-achievement. And you will learn how even unconscious goals can affect your success in achieving conscious goals. By addressing these and similar aspects, you can make your goals even more robust. This means that you will see a lot more of your goals to successful completion, and you can venture on to more ambitious ones.

Your progress towards excellence begins when you decide clearly what you want. Even a first, limited attempt at goal definition will multiply your chances of success *many times* as you align your thought processes and goals. People not naturally goal-oriented say that they focus better on what they want by applying the well-formed outcome criteria (see Day 2). Understanding these principles gives you confidence and a sense of control.

Today you will apply some important new tests to the goals you have already set. When these wider aspects of goals come into the equation, remarkable results follow. This applies particularly when goals align with a person's values and identity – suddenly they 'fit' the person. One or two of these factors could give you the key to success. You can then aim to make goal-achieving an everyday habit.

OUTCOME ECOLOGY

The traditional approach to goal achievement largely consists of the SMART process described on Day 2. But the NLP approach goes beyond SMART, by placing a unique emphasis on *ecology*. In this context 'ecology' refers to the wider and more indirect effects of your goals or outcomes. This includes the effect any outcome may have on your *other* outcomes. A further conflict, or a mismatch, may exist between your goals and values, or even your identity. The goal may simply not reflect *you*.

Yet another aspect of outcome ecology involves the effect of your outcomes on the welfare of other people who you care for. Their outcomes affect your own, and your outcomes affect theirs. We don't achieve things in isolation – at least not in isolation from those whose interests we have at heart. You will only succeed if you take account of other people's interests, in so far as they could indirectly affect you. You will have addressed this when you considered well-formed outcome element number 5: 'Evaluate honestly the effects of achieving your goal' (see p. 27).

As in natural ecology, all our desires, outcomes and values interconnect and interdepend. Some people never seem to get round to doing what they consciously want to do. In fact, other, unconscious outcome 'forces' may affect their behaviour.

How does this work? As we have seen, your goal-achieving system happily pursues the target that sits uppermost in your mind. Because you consciously do not want the *achieved* goal, you clock up another failure. What you *don't* want takes precedence. At the same time some 'secondary gain' (or *unconscious* intention) has its way in your unconscious. We call this a positive intention – positive, in the sense of fulfilling some inner rational (though unconscious) intention. And it often 'succeeds'. You get what you don't (consciously) want.

Take, for example, a person who displays psychosomatic symptoms. They may well crave the 'secondary gain' that sickness brings, like attention or sympathy, though not by design or conscious intent. *Consciously*, they may insist they only want good health. But other non-conscious goal-achieving forces may play a part. In such cases, as we know, the secondary, unconscious goals tend to win out when it comes to actual behaviour.

Other people, having achieved a *conscious* goal, find that some bigger *unconscious* outcome remains unfulfilled. Hence the feeling of anticlimax or something still missing when he or she should feel overjoyed with success. In fact, this means the person did not identify and pursue the *right* goal. More accurately, perhaps, he or she did not pursue the *ultimate* goal but just reached a stepping stone on the way. The real goal may lie further on.

One top manager, for example, explained how he did not have the same sense of pride and elation as his colleagues at the final commissioning of a major plant which he had masterminded. Why? Because he had already 'seen' it all. It had vividly occupied his imagination for a long time. His dream now centred on another, bigger, outcome already incubating in his mind. His fulfilment required not just present success, but an even greater future success.

So, to get the ecology right, you first need to check your whole *hierarchy* of goals, and what other goals they may affect. Then you need to think about the effect of your goals on other people. Directly or indirectly, such considerations will affect your own motivation and behaviour, and ultimate success.

The NLP approach suggests you can carry out this ecology check *before* you embark on your goals, rather than as a painful post mortem. Besides saving time, effort and sometimes pain, better definition of your goals increases the likelihood of success.

Identifying Ecological Outcome Factors

How can you identify these ecological factors? First you need to understand the way you *think*. You learnt, on Day 1, about subjective experience and the NLP model. These showed how we all think and act uniquely. You will already have started to understand yourself better as you worked through well-formed outcome tests and answered the goal-testing questions on Day 2.

Some of these ecological aspects may initially lie outside your consciousness. But in other cases you simply need to *think* honestly about the issues. As we have seen, simple but provocative questions can make us much more aware of our real desires and values. In some cases the effects of your goals will suddenly occur to you as you apply the six rules. Or perhaps an insight will come later when not thinking about them.

As we have also seen, some ecological issues affect other people. So they may have an important impact on your relationships with others as well as on your narrower, personal goals. You will start to notice some of these aspects of your outcomes as you ask yourself the different questions and ponder on your goals.

Outcome ecology builds on the first presupposition: 'The map is not the territory' (see p. 10). Our personal mind programmes constitute the 'map'. They include so-called 'meta programmes', our higher-level thinking patterns such as our values, beliefs and other personality traits. All this affects how you set and achieve goals, the key to personal excellence.

Each specific outcome you pursue needs to harmonise with these unique, personal thinking characteristics. As a multi-faceted personality, your 'parts' need to act in concert. Otherwise you reduce your chances of success. Start to *think about how you think* as well as the outcomes you want. The 'To Do' exercises (on p. 50) will help you further identify the issues surrounding your goals. The extra self-knowledge you gain will prove very valuable.

THE ROLE OF YOUR UNCONSCIOUS MIND

Your unconscious mind plays a part in everything you do. Business or organisational goal-setting methods usually omit this factor, as do personal goals set using a logical, systematic or 'left brain' approach. In fact we all pursue goals, all the time, whether consciously or not.

We differ fundamentally, however, in the way we think about our goals. For example, some people tend to go *away from* certain outcomes rather than *towards* others. Put another way, some people tend to focus on avoiding what they *don't want*, rather than going for what they actually *want*. We might describe these fairly fixed characteristics of their way of thinking and behaving as a 'negative' or 'positive' disposition.

We have other differences in our thinking styles. For instance, some people create vivid visual *images* of what they want, while others seem to experience the *feelings* of success. And the way we motivate ourselves also differs from person to person. For each of us, these unique characteristics form part of the goal-achieving process. Success depends on maximising these processes, and in particular on having clearly defined goals to aim for.

How can unconscious goals affect our behaviour? To go back to an earlier example, an *away from* person concentrates *mentally* (but unintentionally) on the very symptoms they want to avoid. The secondary, unconscious goal therefore takes precedence and 'succeeds'. So, just like the golfer who sees only the bunker and water hazards, they finish up experiencing the very scenarios they want to avoid. Hence well-formed outcome element number 1: 'State your goal positively' (see p. 18).

We seem to get what we think about most, even if we think about what we *don't* want. You can call this 'avoidance' system prudence, realism, caution, worry, or whatever. In fulfilling your internal goal, it works most efficiently. In achieving your conscious purposes, however, it often leads to seemingly unaccountable failure.

Creating Reality by Thinking

We often recognise these self-fulfilling mindsets in other people. Less readily do we admit to pursuing unconscious goals ourselves. Take giving up smoking. A person trying to give up smoking pursues a worthwhile *conscious* goal, despite its negative phrasing. But he or she may have to battle against the pull of other *unconscious* secondary goals, or 'secondary gains' (perhaps social), that come from smoking. In such a case, the *stronger* inner goals form the target to which the person 'self-steers'. And sometimes the unconscious secondary benefits – perhaps several – outweigh the declared goal. You may find it easy to spot negative goals in your own list by the words you use to express them. But you might find it harder to spot unconscious positive intentions, which can account for many years of apparent failure.

In any event, to achieve anything, you need to have a goal. And what takes precedence in your thoughts determines that goal. All your behaviour then tends to robotically follow that inner goal, whatever course you have consciously set. So, in setting conscious goals, you need to identify the different secondary outcomes and forces working in you that might affect them.

Once aware of these unconscious forces, and having honestly evaluated any 'hidden' or secondary outcomes, you may decide to stick with your present situation. You have the choice. But at least you will not then face repeated failure because you did not understand how the 'system' worked. With choice and control, you can start to put your effort into success rather than failure.

How to Identify Your Unconscious Goals

How can we take account of these unconscious goal-achieving forces? It sounds like a 'Catch 22' situation. You can't identify secondary goals because you have no consciousness of them, and you have no conscious awareness of them because you can't identify them. Fortunately you can overcome this dilemma. First, just accepting that secondary goals *may exist* will tend to bring these ecological factors to light. Only a very thin boundary exists between consciousness and unconsciousness, and with practice you can set up a dialogue with your unconscious mind. This way, you may suddenly become aware of things you would never have thought about, or conversely you may forget the strongest resolutions.

So first open your mind to the possibility of this dialogue. The six well-formed outcome tests you learnt on Day 2 will gradually reveal the less obvious aspects of your goals. And the goal-testing questions we have suggested, some of which may not appear to make logical sense, should help reveal these unconscious factors.

You may want to go through the six outcome tests in a more relaxed 'listening mode'. In this way you may identify less conscious desires and align them with your conscious ones, making necessary changes along the way. In such a mode, allow time for your mind to incubate the thoughts. Sleep on them. Rushed, half-baked goals make little sense in the context of a lifetime of personal achievement. As well as identifying unconscious goals you may conceive new ones, as you (literally) exercise your mind towards future outcomes.

REPRESENTING YOUR OUTCOMES

You have met the NLP model, which describes how we 'represent' the world around us, and illustrates how each sensory stimulus transforms into understanding. How do these unique mental representations affect our goals?

They actually *create* internal goals. Your values and beliefs in effect *suggest* to your unconscious mind what you want to accomplish. Put another way, your dominant thoughts form the target for your inbuilt goal-achieving mechanism. A strong value, for example, although not reflecting an identifiable goal, will tend to *pursue* certain types of goal. Honesty, for instance, pursues goals reflecting honest behaviour. Independence favours goals that might bring about independence, and so on. Values and beliefs *guide* us, and the direction they take us in clearly indicates our ultimate destination.

They dictate, for example, whether or not you achieve your conscious goals. A belief such as 'I can't organise other people', for instance, would militate against you fulfilling any goal concerned with managing people. Beliefs and values can thus generate a spiral of success or failure. So you can gain a lot by identifying and restating the values and beliefs that might underpin any outcome.

More generally, you need to know how you uniquely perceive the world (through your values, beliefs, *filters*, *map*) and how that affects both what you want and how you achieve it. By reflecting on your own style of thinking and values, you get to know yourself better and, in doing so, get better at achieving your outcomes. And by better understanding your personal mental 'map', you see more clearly goals important to you as an individual. You identify bigger life purposes to which you want to give your time and energy. You *align* what you wish to achieve with your identity as a person.

CARTESIAN QUESTIONS

Different techniques can help you to tease out these less conscious aspects of your goals. Cartesian questions, for instance, can help.

Converse	Theorem
~A B	A B
What wouldn't happen if you did?	What would happen if you did?
Non-Mirror Image Reverse	Inverse
~A ~B	A ~B
What wouldn't happen if you didn't?	What would happen if you didn't?

Figure 3.1 Cartesian questions

Using one of your specific goals, ask the four questions in the matrix:

- **'What would happen if I did** (fully achieve my outcome)?'** You will have already gone through this process on Day 2, when you applied element number 5 (see p. 27), and in particular when you visualised the fulfilment of your goal.

- **'What wouldn't happen if I did?'** This question allows 'secondary gain' to surface. It will help you identify the benefits from a present behaviour which you might forfeit if you achieved a new outcome. You may have to *forego* little pleasures, even though you would not normally have identified them. (And even if you did, you might not readily admit to valuing them.) You decide. The process creates choice. This sort of ecological outcome-testing demands honesty, of course, as well as time for relaxed, unhurried introspection.

- **'What would happen if I didn't** (achieve my outcome)?' This will emphasise the cost or pain of carrying on in the same way. Your deliberate choice to go ahead may provide the motivation you need to make the change.

- **'What wouldn't happen if I didn't?'** This question has the effect of confusing your left brain. It gets beyond your conscious mind and gets your brain working along different neural channels, making you think about things in a new way. It can make you aware of values and inner forces you had not thought about at all. So experiment with answering this question in an intuitive rather than a logical way.

Problem-Solving and Other Applications

Let's apply this method of questioning to a simple example: 'I really want that promotion.'

Using the Cartesian form of questions, ask:

- What would happen if you did get that promotion?
- What would not happen if you got that promotion?
- What would happen if you didn't get that promotion?
- What would not happen if you didn't get that promotion?

All sorts of secondary issues can arise from this sort of questioning. As we have seen, the last, sometimes confusing question, often brings to the surface previously unidentified aspects of a goal. Use these questions to open a dialogue between your conscious and unconscious minds. In this way you have more chance of exposing what an outcome really means for you.

You can also apply Cartesian questions to business and organisational goals. At the very least, they will help you clarify woolly, imprecise goals. And, more than likely, they will open up insights about the goals that will take you a long way towards actually achieving them.

VALUES AND OUTCOMES

We have met values a number of times in the context of setting goals. Now you need to consider how you can define and identify your values, and how they affect your goals or outcomes. You will then start to see your outcomes in the light of your values, beliefs and other thinking patterns. This can give you extra insight and act as an important ecology check. You may also find that understanding yourself better has spin-off benefits. As well as understanding where they come from and how they affect you, in this section you will learn how to identify specific values, put them into an order of importance, and, if you want to, *change* them.

Understanding Values

A value has *importance*. Ask yourself the question: 'What do I consider important?' Your answer will contain values or beliefs about what you consider (or know) as *true* – you believe it. We often tend to use the terms 'values' and 'beliefs' interchangeably. For example, 'I consider honesty important' (a value); 'I believe in honesty' (a belief). Sometimes we make less direct links: 'Bosses just look out for themselves' (a belief); 'You should put your own interests first' (an implied value); 'We should eradicate racial discrimination in this company'(a belief based on a value of equality).

We create such beliefs and values over a lifetime. They

affect, as mental filters, every representation we make of the world, moment by moment. Consequently, they affect all the outcomes we set for ourselves and the decisions we make. In short, they steer our lives completely, motivating our actions, determining what we achieve, how we perceive ourselves (our identity) and how we develop as individuals. They help to form our personal map of the world and reality.

Identifying Values

You can relate your values to the specific goals you set on Day 2. Just ask: 'What importance does this outcome have for me? In what contexts or situations?' It may help to apply the questions to different areas of your life so that you don't miss less obvious goals. This process may well reveal conflicting values, such as between work and home life. It will often bring to the surface what you have *felt* all along. For example, think about your:

- Work and career
- Family
- Social life
- Hobbies
- Interests
- Personal development
- Spiritual matters and purpose

And any other life categories you can identify.

Work questions, for example, might include: 'What's important about my career as a nurse (accountant, plumber or whatever)?' Or, 'What's important about working at ABC Ltd?' Answers may include: 'Security', 'Respect', 'Meeting people', 'Helping others', 'Making money', and so on. Your answers will reflect your values. Try to keep your responses to single words or very short phrases. Just having to think of an appropriate word may mean you have to reconsider the value deeply. Some words will recur, and you will soon settle on a list of values.

Your Values Pecking Order

Then ask, of each value that comes up, 'Why do I consider that important?' Your answers will form sentences that may well include further values you had not thought of. At the same time, values you have identified will keep cropping up and you will soon get a feel for your values pecking order – from the most important down to the least important.

You can rank your values by simply asking: 'Of these values, which do I consider the most important?' Then, for those remaining, ask the same question, and so on, fully ranking your list. You can further test your pecking order of importance by asking: 'How does so-and-so compare in importance with so-and-so?' For example, how does 'honesty' rank with 'loyalty'? A final order will soon emerge.

You may not find it easy to deal with so-called nominalisations, like 'independence' or 'security'. Try to put questions into a real-life context to elicit their relative importance. For example: 'If I had to choose between a job giving me independence, and one offering security, which would I choose?' *Imagine* both, then your intuitive answer will confirm your values. This concentrates the mind.

The same sort of questions can apply to a hobby, or to any other area of your life. A pattern will emerge, as values usually apply across the board in a person's life. However long your list, your top few values will affect whether and in what way you achieve your goals. You can now apply your values list to the well-formed outcomes you set on Day 2, by asking the question: 'Does this goal conform to my values?'

Where Do Your Values Come From?

Having identified your values, you will gain further insight by identifying their source. For example, have you gained them from your family or friends, your church or religion, school, your geographical position, your economic position, the media, or a mentor or person you respect?

You may think of other sources of your values. In some cases you may tie it down to a specific person ('I'll never forget what she said . . .'), or a time and place ('The moment it happened I decided . . .'). Although not vital for change, identifying the source of values tends to confirm their random origins and sometimes their irrelevance to your present goals. Conversely, the 'pedigree' of a value may confirm its relevance to your present situation. In short, values present you with fully negotiable choices. You can change them as you wish. And the more you can align your goals or outcomes with the ecology of your values, the more chance you have of achieving them.

Changing Your Values

You can 'negotiate' your own values just as you can your outcomes. NLP stresses the importance of choice. Values and beliefs that you have accumulated historically may (or may not) have served you well for past outcomes. But, by reappraising your values, you create choices, based on your *present* goals and values. Things and people change. Exercising your moment-by-moment choice means that you have control, over whether and how you change. In respecting other people's mental maps, you respect their choice also.

You can change your values just as you can change your goals: 'This no longer seems important, but that does (now)'. Or change their ranking: 'This (now) seems less important than that'. We can and do change our values and beliefs. Their resilience over time, however, means we usually have to have strong reasons for changing them. Sometimes this results from a major change in circumstances or lifestyle, such as a new partner, job, house move, accident or illness. But you can change values *by conscious reappraisal* as part of an outcome-setting process. Once you have identified and pondered a value of little use, you will probably soon amend or replace it. A more useful, empowering value can then take its place.

PRESUPPOSITION FOR TODAY

> **A person is not his or her behaviour.**

By identifying with our behaviour in an absolute way we can soon become stuck with it ('That's just me'). This can apply, even if what we do does not reflect our true identity and values. However, we sometimes have to differentiate between our behaviour and our identity. 'I lost' may well constitute a fact. 'I am a loser' (note the *am* of identity) no doubt untruthfully caricatures the person.

We can relate today's presupposition to the dictum 'Love the person, change the behaviour'. Our naturally diverse and variable behaviour reflects all sorts of circumstances as well as how we feel and perceive things at any given moment. We can all sometimes act *out of character*.

Your identity, although complex and multi-faceted, does not have the transitory characteristics of moment-by-moment behaviour. So you can separate yourself from your behaviour. Although *responsible* for your behaviour, you do not need to make it *equate* to your identity. And you can change *both* – how you see yourself as a person, and what you do.

TODAY'S TO DOs

- Memorise today's presupposition. Think of examples of things you have said and done which seem out of character. Recall times when you have 'labelled' someone because of a single behaviour.

- Choose three of your well-formed outcomes from Day 2 and apply the Cartesian questions. In the process, notice whether you feel differently about the outcome, and whether you want to change it. Expect also to gain insights and new perspectives about your outcomes.

- Choose one area of your life and, using the process we have outlined, list your main values in order.

- Choose a goal from the same area of your life and note how each value affects it, how you feel about it, and how you intend to make it happen.

- Go through your goals again, to see whether you feel differently about any of them and want to make changes. Then experiment with putting them into some order of priority. Revisit your list as often as you like, concentrating especially on the important ones. Enjoy an added sense of control and purpose in your life.

- Spend some time imagining these goals or outcomes – seeing, hearing and feeling them as if already achieved. Enjoy all the benefits and pleasure they bring. You have begun to create your own future.

DAY 4

How To Win Friends And Influence People

This chapter covers:
- **Matching**
- **Building rapport through matching**

The ability to get on with others helps ensure success in almost every walk of life. If your job depends on interacting with people, managing them or otherwise depending on them, you will need this communication skill. And we all need it in any family or social context. We sometimes call this interpersonal skill 'rapport'. Having a good rapport with another person creates the right conditions for an effective exchange of thoughts and ideas, whether in selling, negotiation, interviewing, counselling or any ongoing relationship.

Good communication does not just comprise what we say or even the external gestures we use. It involves far more complex and not always observable interactions. Sometimes rapport comes easily and we might describe the successful ingredient as positive 'chemistry'. You just 'hit it off' with a person immediately. Or you may find the reverse, and experience negative chemistry. In such a case you might want to keep clear of the person, but you may find that hard to do in a work or family situation. And, in any event, you might miss out on what could have proved a worthwhile relationship.

Using NLP, you can take a more mature, professional approach. As a more effective communicator, you can have far more control over your relationships and outcomes. Sometimes you might enjoy a natural rapport, as with a very close, lifelong friend. You do well to maintain and value that kind of rapport, and 'leave well alone'. But you can also use NLP techniques to create or build rapport in all sorts of situations when it might not otherwise have happened.

The skill of building rapport may well support the goals you have addressed over the last two days. These often involve getting your point of view across: influencing, persuading, or having an effect on somebody to bring about change. Any *communication* goals should, of course, fulfil the six well-formed outcome criteria discussed on Day 2. But other goals may also need communication skills, perhaps as a stepping stone to bigger goals. Having applied the different outcome criteria on Days 2 and 3, using effective rapport skills will help you communicate even better and achieve more.

MATCHING

We tend to like people *like* ourselves. We get on better with them, and so communicate with them more effectively. And they, in turn, get to like us. Effective rapport therefore involves matching. People who have a rapport tend to *act like each other* in a number of ways.

Today you will learn how to build this rapport with people. You can start to use some simple matching skills in minutes. Others involve quite advanced skills and require practice, but will reward your effort many times over. Thousands of NLP students have enjoyed developing these matching skills, and have found them highly effective in creating rapport.

To learn and improve, you first need to recognise what creates or breaks rapport. This involves cultivating a sensitive awareness, or 'acuity', both about yourself and about the other person. The skill usually exemplifies what NLP terms *unconscious competence*, something we observe in people who act with ease and excellence. The field of communication relies particularly on apparently innate skills. You can observe this in selling, negotiation, counselling or other interpersonal skills. Initially, learning this skill can seem like very conscious, hard work. As with any skill, however (like driving a car), unconscious competence comes with practice. Achieving consistent rapport means *doing* it, according to the four-stage success model you learnt on Day 2.

Conscious awareness, given the rapport skills you will learn, enables you to *choose* more empathetic, sensitive behaviour. You can choose to *intervene* in a communication, for instance, rather than simply trusting your unconscious skills. Just as when driving a car, you can thus develop the right habits, to replace the wrong ones. For a while you may seem to go backwards in skill and competence, but in the long run you will learn more effectively.

Rapport skills offer benefits far beyond your professional or work life. They may well affect the goals you set, especially those involving other people. The secret lies in matching. You can build rapport by matching in the following areas:

1. Physiology – body posture and movement

2. Voice – tone, speed of speech and other voice characteristics

3. Language and thinking style – choice of words and 'representation system' (seeing, hearing, or feeling)

4. Beliefs and values – what people hold as true and important

5. Experience – finding common ground in your activities and interests

6. Breathing – a more subtle but powerful way to match someone

BUILDING RAPPORT THROUGH MATCHING

We will address each of these areas separately, in sufficient depth for you to start applying the skills in your everyday life. Before we do, you need to understand a few vital points about matching.

Firstly, always remember the importance of subtlety and respect. Don't abruptly change your posture or voice, or mechanically copy gestures. Make any change gradually and as far as possible imperceptibly. Avoid attracting the other person's attention by your body language, but rather help them to achieve rapport unconsciously. Otherwise you may annoy or insult them, rather than create rapport. Although highly conscious at first, your actions should gradually become natural and spontaneous. Have respect for the other person as a unique individual, especially when it becomes apparent that their behaviour and mannerisms differ from yours.

Secondly, you also need to respect your own body. We all have different ways to stand, sit and carry out basic behaviours and these may differ from those of the other person. This means that in some situations you will feel decidedly uncomfortable when matching, and this will come across to the other person. You may find it physically difficult to act 'out of step' with your normal posture and mannerisms.

You may get away with uncharacteristic behaviour when relating to a stranger, such as a new sales prospect. But anyone who knows you well will spot you acting 'out of character', and this will break any rapport you would have built by acting naturally. So stay within your comfort zone and the natural boundaries of your personality. That does not mean that you cannot match; simply that you need to choose behaviours that you can match comfortably, or partly match.

1. Matching Physiology

People who get on well together tend to adopt the same body posture when communicating. Look at people locked in conversation and you will often see their silhouettes mirroring each other. An old couple, after many years of marriage, frequently almost seem to look alike.

As well as overall posture, people tend to use similar gestures and mannerisms. For example, they may both lean back with arms clasped behind their heads, or face each other with hands open on the table, or with arms or legs crossed or uncrossed. This happens completely naturally and we hardly ever notice it. Once in rapport, our interest centres on the other person and the content of the discussion rather than any external physiology. All this physiological matching provides *evidence* of rapport, which we can therefore *calibrate* or measure.

As well as using physiological matching to measure rapport, you can use it to establish and build rapport. For instance, you can:

- Sit or stand in the same overall way, aligning your back similarly, or positioning your head to one side to match the other person.

- Cross or uncross your arms and legs, and match the other person's general body movements.

- Make the same sorts of gestures with your hands, face and body.

Part matching

Matching happens progressively. You don't have to immediately match every aspect of the person's body language. Start with just one aspect – say the overall posture or stance. Then gradually match the angle of the head, crossing limbs and limb movements, size of gestures, voice volume and pitch (see p. 60), and so on. Matching forms a continuum rather than an either/or approach. So you can experiment with any level of part matching while you gain experience and develop your skill.

If someone sits or stands in a particularly marked or idiosyncratic way, consider just moving *part* way to matching their posture. You need not *mimic* the person exactly in order to establish and maintain rapport. For example, you may prefer to use part matching in the following situations:

- Early in the communication, to establish and measure rapport

- When you would otherwise have to move out of your comfort zone, as we saw above

- When confronting a particularly emotional person whose body language reflects that

- When, in the case of very unusual physiology, the person might notice you matching

- When you have established reasonable rapport and just wish to maintain it

- When you first attempt matching

What about facial expressions? A person with pronounced expressions who raises their eyebrows, pops or rolls their eyes, purses their lips, grimaces and so on, will not feel at home with a passive, poker-faced person who does not betray their feelings. They expect a like response. To such a person facial movements seem normal. You will find these expressions hard to fake so stay within your comfort zone, going part way rather than not matching at all.

With very overt physical positions, such as crossed and uncrossed arms or legs, it helps to allow some delay before matching so that the movement appears quite natural.

You can use variations on the theme of part matching, sometimes called 'crossover matching'. For instance, if the person folds their arms you could cross your legs, or vice versa. If the other person clasps their hands you might just place one hand on the other. If they rub their hands together you can shuffle your feet. If they fiddle with a plastic cup you can click your pen, and so on. As with 'going part way', you need not match exact item for exact item.

These categories mostly require both large- and small-scale (macro and micro) physiological matching. And some may require more acuity than others to spot.

Macro matching

As well as specific matching, think about your overall position, say within the room, or *vis-à-vis* furnishings, in relation to the other person. You can, for example, match a person sitting across a desk, or with chairs facing, just like a mirror image. Alternatively, you can sit together, facing the same direction (as when on a couch), and still match gestures and body position. The latter behaviour will more likely create a sense of unity of purpose and rapport – you have literally got the person 'on your side'.

On the other hand, you may have little opportunity for eye contact, or even to observe their overall body language. In this case, you may choose to have your chairs at right angles

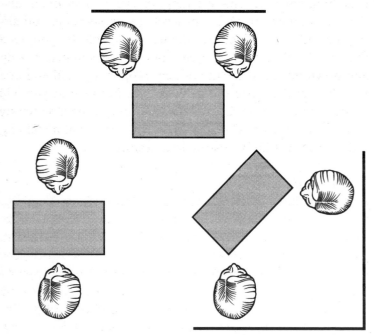

Figure 4.1 Positioning yourself for rapport

to each other so that you both effectively 'face the same direction' but with better eye contact, and, if you wish, still look at the same document.

A flip chart, white board or common document to refer to can often help to focus attention and establish rapport. The object forms a neutral reference point and brings you together. It can also help rapport if you both contribute ideas and explanations in words or drawings on a single notepad. In this way you not only match physiology but can also match the person's preference to draw doodles or diagrams to communicate. Similarly, swapping the same marker pen and jointly contributing to a diagram, flow chart or list of ideas on a flip chart can also help create rapport. Simple things like this can all help to establish a genuine meeting of minds. Communicating means getting closer to a person in more than just a physical sense.

The respective heights of chairs can also have an effect. Matching aims for win–win rapport, rather than manipulation or domination. Different levels (as in standing and sitting respectively) might give the wrong signals. So you need to match levels as well as orientation. If a person marches up and down talking you will not help rapport by reclining in a low chair at the other end of the room. In this case you will either have to join in the mobile discourse, or part match by at least standing up. Consider all macro aspects of matching, rather than just body posture and gestures.

Micro matching

As well as the degree of matching, the type of matching also forms a continuum. Finer *micro* matching, for instance, might include the subtlest physiological changes. Although requiring keen observation skills, in this case you can achieve strong rapport inconspicuously. By observing someone carefully you will soon start to notice numerous little mannerisms, all of which offer matching potential. The communicatee remains unconscious both of their own behaviour, especially at this micro level, and also your matching behaviour. But rapport none the less follows, almost magically.

Some of these techniques might seem contrived and even a bit far-fetched but matching *does work* in creating rapport. What happens when the other party notices the matching process? This hardly ever happens. If it does, it probably means you have broken some of the rules we have explained, gone beyond your comfort zone or forgotten the importance of subtlety and respect (see p. 55).

What about communicating with someone already familiar with the techniques of matching? This sometimes applies with skilled salespeople and negotiators. Interestingly, we have found that they will usually respect you for your professional communication skills. After all, as we have seen, matching does not involve manipulation, but understanding the other person better, and achieving a win–win outcome for both parties.

2. Voice Matching

Sometimes you will find physiological matching inappropriate or impossible, such as on the telephone when you cannot see the other person. But the pitch and tone of your voice also represent a major part of any communication. And, according to research, this may have more impact than the actual words we say. The more aspects of a person you can match, the more effectively you can create rapport. So aim to understand and match every area.

The qualities you can listen for in voice patterns include:

- *Volume* – do they speak quietly or loudly?
- *Tempo* – how fast or slowly do they speak?
- *Rhythm* – can you detect a flowing melody in their sentences or do they pronounce their words in a more separate, staccato way?
- *Pitch* – high or low?
- *Timbre* – what qualities do you hear in their voice? Clear or husky, for instance?

- *Tone* – what emotions do they convey in their tone of voice?
- *Phrases* – do they use characteristic sayings or regional colloquialisms?

Once again, begin by matching one characteristic, then add others as you become more competent. Above all, stay with the *flow* of the conversation. Rapport has some of the characteristics of dance. Make any changes slowly and naturally as far as you can, and remember not to stray too much from your personal comfort zone.

Avoid matching a pronounced regional accent or idiosyncrasy as the other person may perceive this as a 'take off'! But certainly match in terms of the general level of the communication (as you would in speaking to a child or a much older person), and the style in terms of formality or informality.

3. Matching Language and Thinking Style

Once you notice how differently people behave in everyday communication, you will start to recognise their thinking style and preferences. Matching a person's thinking style produces powerful rapport. As we saw in the NLP model (on Day 1), the way we think in the three primary senses mirrors the way we use our senses externally.

Visual
People who think primarily in a visual way tend to use language that contains visual words and phrases, such as, 'I get the picture' or 'Let's try to put this into perspective'. You can create rapport by thinking in this way yourself, picturing internally the person's description and using the same sort of 'sensory words' (known in NLP as predicates).

Auditory
In the same way, auditory predicates, such as 'I hear what you say' or 'It sounds good to me', may indicate auditory

thinking. By matching these words and recreating the sounds in your head, you will start to think the way the other person thinks, identify with their thinking style, and create rapport as you begin to 'speak their language'.

Kinaesthetic

People who have a primarily kinaesthetic thinking style will tend to use words related to feeling or touch, such as, 'We are getting to grips with the problem' or 'Things are going smoothly'. Start to *get a feel* for how these people express themselves, and use similar words and figures of speech. You will see how (notice I use a visual predicate), sometimes almost miraculously, rapport increases as you share their experience.

For more on sensory preference in thinking style, see Day 6.

4. Matching Beliefs and Values

Matching can also include beliefs and values, which we discussed on Day 3. This can sometimes succeed where other sorts of matching fail, as when a person in a group situation (such as a meeting or training course) will not co-operate. Deep-rooted values have special importance to people, and by matching them you can sometimes touch a person's 'hot button'.

For example, you can appeal to the value a person places on time (a chunk of which they have already committed by attending a meeting or training session). By agreeing 'You should not waste time', you have matched a value, and brought a common purpose into the communication. Other values might concern not wasting money, fairness to fellow participants, 'doing unto others', or whatever. The higher the level of common values or beliefs (like 'everybody has rights'), the more easily you will find common ground and create rapport.

Universal, or macro, values and beliefs, like 'fairness',

'honesty' and 'courtesy' help to establish early rapport which you can build on, using physiological and other types of matching. As well as the training example above, this works especially well in difficult communication situations as may occur in mediation, counselling and negotiation. Once you find a common basis of understanding, other matching techniques will usually work well.

5. Matching Experience

Put one or two accountants together, or nurses, or aeroplane enthusiasts, and before long you will have plenty of conversation and rapport. The same thing happens when you meet a stranger from your home town or someone who attended the same school or university. Your experiences or 'maps' overlap, so you share common ground or 'likeness'.

You can use the experience-matching principle even more widely. When communicating with a random group of people, for instance, you can usually identify a common experience to which they can relate. Using the training analogy, for instance, all the participants have probably had to:

- Drive through traffic to the event
- Brave the weather
- Give up other important things, or
- Get work duties sorted out before leaving the office

Even a common experience like 'We have all given up a day of our life to attend today's seminar, so let's make the most of it' can create an initial rapport on which to build a successful training or similar group event. Keep in mind *perceived likeness*. Give a nod of assent at every stage in the communication, especially when establishing rapport. For a short meeting between two people you might establish common experience with comments such as:

- 'We both have plenty of other things to do so let's get this sorted out quickly.'

- 'We both stand to gain from this so I'm sure we can reach agreement quickly.'

- 'It feels very warm in here – shall I open a window? Do you mind the traffic noise?' (Either way, you match experience as a win–win step to rapport.)

Once again, the 'likeness' of common experience or a single purpose helps build rapport.

Salespeople use common experience a lot, readily noticing signs that let them know of a potential customer's lifestyle and interests. A photograph, picture or model in the person's office may offer a clue, for instance. Or, if the salesperson has done his or her homework, prior knowledge of a sport, hobby or pastime will pay dividends. You do not need to fake this. Usually some genuine common ground of experience will exist to start with, however tenuous. An indirect link to an interest may exist, for instance, through a friend or colleague, or even something you recall seeing on television. Listening and watching carefully will soon indicate the person's interests. People will always talk about what interests them if you give them half a chance.

6. Matching Breathing

As you learn to observe the 'micro' physiological movements and gestures covered earlier, you may also notice differences in breathing patterns. Breathing offers another opportunity for matching. Calibrating (or measuring) breathing takes practice and you may need to start using your movement-sensitive peripheral vision. While making eye contact you may notice peripherally the rise and fall of the person's shoulder which gives the rhythm of the breathing. You can then change your own breathing to match, which has the added benefit of allowing you to maintain control of your emotional state. Alternatively, you can crossover match by nodding your head in time with their breathing – again, usually undetectable but powerful in building rapport.

You now have a wide repertoire of ways to generate rapport by creating 'likeness' in any communication. You can use all the techniques together, but we suggest you experiment with one at a time at first until they feel familiar. Soon you will act in a natural, unaffected way. And remember that you don't need to rush things. The skill of rapport comes only with repetition. Concentrate not so much on what you *know*, but on what you can *do*. Aim to do things 'without thinking'. You have this power in your natural observation skills, which you can improve, and the simple techniques of matching which you can learn and perfect.

PRESUPPOSITION FOR TODAY

> **The meaning of a communication is the response it gets.**

Traditional communication training often concentrates on the message, the medium, and all the technicalities of correct presentation, but ignores the outcome – what you actually want to achieve. The study of body language, for example, involves giving precise meaning to each type of physical gesture and posture. But, whatever techniques you use, if your communication does not bring about your desired response or outcome, you can waste a lot of time and effort. A silent glance, if it conveys meaning and understanding between the parties, may constitute a highly effective communication. For this reason, NLP places much importance on observation or sensory acuity. Only by knowing the *effect* of what you do can you hone your skills to a level of excellence.

Matching has become important because of the evidence that it helps to establish rapport. And all the research points to the fact that rapport creates better communication. In other words, matching gets a response – it produces an outcome. According to this presupposition, an effective communication has to focus on the response it produces.

We suggested earlier that you focus on doing rather than knowing. But don't get so wrapped up in what you *do* that you forget what you *want*. Start with your outcome. What do I want to achieve from this communication? To inform, impress, entertain, shock, or whatever? To do this well, you have to put yourself in the other person's shoes and imagine what effect different words, media or behaviour might have on them. This means crossing from your 'map' to theirs. Such an approach, even when using an unorthodox communication process, will certainly produce rapport. And rapport will take you a long way towards a successful communication outcome.

TODAY'S TO DOs

- Start matching and notice how it affects rapport. Try out one skill at a time, gradually working your way through all of them. You might concentrate first on voice matching, for instance, then gestures, then sensory 'predicates', then experience. Make a start today. Your skill will develop quickly and you will soon wonder how you could ever have failed to notice these characteristics in people you know well.

- Memorise today's presupposition and think of three examples of it in your own experience. You may think of cases where a first-class communication did not bring the required response. Alternatively, you may remember an occasion where you felt you did not communicate well – say in a presentation or interview – yet you got what you wanted. What did you do that got the right response? What need you not have done?

- Go back to the goals you set on Day 2 and notice whether any of them involve relationships and rapport skills. How will what you have learnt today help you to achieve them?

DAY 5

Power Communication Techniques

This chapter covers:

- **Calibrating rapport**
- **Pacing and leading**
- **Mismatching**
- **Establishing relationships**
- **Matching with congruence**

Today you will learn more about rapport, how you can 'calibrate' it, and how you can change other people's behaviour by 'pacing and leading'. You will also learn more about how to create rapport in group situations, and how and when to 'mismatch'.

CALIBRATING RAPPORT

Once you have practised the different matching techniques you learnt on Day 4, you can carry on to perfect your rapport skills to any level you wish. As well as establishing rapport, you also need to recognise whether rapport exists, and to what degree. We have already stressed the need for careful observation (sensory acuity) so that you can detect or measure (calibrate) rapport.

Calibration, a term borrowed from engineering, refers in NLP to the way you can notice small reactions and 'measure' moment-to-moment changes in other people. You can then, if necessary, adjust your own behaviour. This resembles the 'noticing' stage in the four-stage success model (see Day 2). Calibration takes a lot of practice, and at first it may seem impossible to watch for so many things at the same time. On Day 4, we learnt about the different areas in which we can create and recognise rapport (matching physiology, voice, language and thinking style, beliefs and values, experience and interests, and breathing patterns). Now we introduce four more ways in which we can create and recognise rapport.

1. An internal feeling

You may get a sense of 'connectedness' with the person. This calls upon natural, 'right-brain' intuitive skills that may have atrophied if you have not used them much. However, with practice, you can *learn* to sense these internal feelings. You may have to take a few risks in trusting your intuition, as it may not seem to square with logic. Right-brain feelings or 'chemistry' may not spell out any 'message' clearly. So choose simple, low-risk situations in which to try this out.

2. Colour change

Watch for a change of colour in the other person's skin. This illustrates the micro changes in physiology you met on Day 4. You may not match such involuntary changes directly. But, having calibrated them, you may then match the *state* they indicate – in your own way. For example, you will build rapport if you match the other person's mood – excited, animated, serious, amused or whatever characteristic their changes in skin colour might indicate. Along with skin colour, other minute changes have individual significance, such as breathing (see p. 64), lip size, pupil size, facial muscle tone, and small movements in the hands and feet.

3. Spontaneous comment

People will sometimes literally *tell you* how they feel about a communication, and you may miss this if you only watch for hidden indicators. Listen for the other person making some positive statement, such as 'I agree', 'that's right' or 'absolutely'. 'We're on the same wavelength' or 'You must have read my mind' may indicate stronger rapport. In more formal situations, or with less explicit comments, you may have to detect and interpret such spontaneous indicators of rapport.

4. Ability to lead
Sometimes the other person begins to follow some of your movements, voice qualities or language. They 'keep pace' with you, and you 'lead' them. The next section discusses this in more detail.

PACING AND LEADING

Through pacing and leading you can establish and maintain rapport, and also bring about changes in the other person.

NLP uses the term *pacing* to refer to matching as an on-going process. The person with whom you wish to gain rapport sets the 'pace', including the speed and tone of voice and physical gesturing. Rather than instantaneous, reflex-like matching, you pace as if in a long race. In other words, you *stay with* the person. So you can use pacing as a strategic rather than a tactical skill, for instance in an important nego-tiating situation where you need to establish a meeting of minds. Although usually applied to physiological matching, you can also pace, for instance, experience, beliefs and values, and language, as we explained on Day 4.

When *leading*, you gradually change your own behaviour (whilst maintaining rapport), in such a way that the other person intuitively matches, or 'follows' you. Put another way, when matching or pacing, you *follow* behaviour to achieve rapport. Once in rapport, you *lead* behaviour to persuade, humour, influence or whatever – to bring about your communication goals or outcomes.

Through pacing and leading you can thus calibrate or

measure the rapport you have created. Your success in leading a person depends on the quality or level of rapport you have built up. At the same time, your *degree of success* in leading calibrates the *depth* of the rapport.

You can test your pacing and leading skill. Change your actions slightly and notice if the other person follows – allow for a delay. Do they adopt a similar behaviour, voice tone or whatever? If not, you need to return to simple pacing (matching) to achieve rapport, then try again. When the person does instinctively follow, you have evidence both of rapport and your ability to lead.

As well as affecting the other person's physiology, you can use leading to influence someone's feelings, approach, point of view or decisions. For example, if the other person's body language reflects a low emotional state, yours will too if you simply match them. But physiology and feelings closely relate. Thus, by changing your physiology, you can usually lead the other person to change their state. If you gradually pace and lead more positive physiology, voice patterns or language, you will help them regain a positive state of mind.

Pacing and Leading Difficult People

The principles of matching and rapport always apply, even when the situation does not seem conducive to successful communication. The principle remains the same: matching helps rapport, and you need rapport before you can bring about change.

Matching can apply particularly, for instance, when dealing with an angry or distressed person. When a person feels highly agitated their expressive, rapid movements usually reflect this. Common sense tells us that to take an opposite 'calm and collected' approach will more likely aggravate them further (although some psychologists advocate this very approach). So first *pace* their behaviour and state (within reason, in extreme cases) to establish rapport. Then *lead* them to your (and probably their) outcome.

This means that, to start with, you need to *join* the person, at least to some degree, in his or her behaviour. If they speak quickly, you do the same. If they use their hands a lot, do the same. Let them know, by your words and total body language, that you empathise with them – you *care*. Continuously pace, without judging the appropriateness of their actions.

In the case of extreme behaviour, you will find that partial or crossover matching, which we covered on Day 4, establishes the basic rapport. You can go part way, and still get results. In any event, to whatever degree, *pace* first, or you will probably not lead them successfully. Then gradually change one characteristic of your communication at a time and wait for them to follow. Lead them to a level of body movement, voice pitch and tone or overall position (say to get them seated, or at least standing still) more amenable to successful communication. Keep your outcome in mind (which, if win–win, will also benefit them). As a rule, for extreme behaviour, match *to the extent you need to*, to lead.

Putting Pacing and Leading into Practice

You can use pacing and leading to great effect in many situations, including:

- Putting interviewees at ease
- Getting sales prospects into a positive, buying frame of mind
- Pacifying an irate customer or staff member
- Humouring an angry boss
- Handling a difficult seminar delegate
- Taking the heat out of a situation
- Setting the tone of a meeting as chairperson
- Handling a bereavement
- Communicating bad news
- Handling unruly children
- Fostering a team spirit

- Taking control in a sensitive negotiation
- Getting a reserved, uncommunicative person to 'open up'
- Making a convincing case
- Changing a person's mood to one more conducive to communication – serious, light-hearted, etc.

In each case you need to ask yourself: 'What physical posture, movement, tone of voice, values and other characteristics in the other person will best support my communication goal?' For instance, standing up or sitting down, low-key or psyched up, intense or laid back, close or distant, still or moving? And which of these characteristics should I pace and lead to help bring about my desired outcome?

Clearly, with so many applications, you may need to adapt the process from person to person. This will depend upon the state of mind of the person you communicate with, and the state of mind you want to induce. For instance, you may need to bring a 'hyper' person down to a calmer level that allows better dialogue and two-way communication. Alternatively, you may have to motivate a more passive person.

Let's say you have to deal with a very irate hotel guest. The specific circumstances don't matter – anything can trigger emotion in some people at some times in some hotels. Some classic communication training insists you speak slowly and quietly, staying cool and calm. But in reality, the cooler you appear the more anger you may provoke. What husband or wife doesn't know the effect of responding with cool objectivity when a partner's emotions run high?

The likeness principle means that you start by joining – sharing, if you like – the world of the other person. Thus, you need to match (at least partially) their general body posture, body movement, and voice level and speed. Don't stay reclining in a chair or keep your arms tightly folded, for example, when trying to gain rapport with a human catherine wheel. When they perceive you as empathising with their plight the most unusual alliances can result. Use phrases like, 'I know just how you feel. I would feel the same way myself.'

Paradoxically, you can create rapport, even in a very animated communication, by using the matching principles you have learnt. Attempts at leading will then have more success. Gradually lower your voice and wait until the person starts to lower theirs (reflecting the universal human tendency to naturally and unconsciously match the other person). Then reduce the speed and perhaps pitch of your voice as a separate lead. (Build on even a minimal lead.) Gradually slow down and contract your hand and body movements to create a further lead. Aim to achieve, not just rapport, but a more conducive mode of communication to achieve your outcome. A further lead in this case, for instance, might involve leading the person (literally, at this stage) to a private room or office where you can do more justice to their needs and your own responsibilities and constraints. By leading incrementally in this way you can maintain rapport – the basis for successfully changing behaviour.

If you observe excellent communicators who have a natural ability to pacify, charm or win over, you will probably notice NLP matching skills in practice (more than likely, an example of unconscious competence). By adopting and practising successful communication strategies, you can go a long way towards emulating what, up to now, may have seemed like a personality or a natural, genetic talent.

Always stay within the context of your overall outcomes (what you want), and your communication outcome (what you want out of that particular interview, meeting, presentation or other interaction). And stay within your own capabilities in pacing and leading. Your goals should also conform to the six elements of the well-formed outcome you learnt on Day 2. These include seeking to bring about benefits for others as well as yourself (a win–win result) and respecting their map of the world. Few interpersonal skills, including pacing and leading, work in a vacuum. Base what you do on the principles you have already learnt.

Effective communication can make a massive contribution to your overall success in a job, career, or as a person. By choosing and using the skills you learn, you will refine even further your well-formed outcomes, and increase your success hit rate.

Pacing and Leading Groups

When communicating with more than one person you may not find it as easy to match different body language and voice patterns. You can, however, match beliefs, values and experience, as we saw on Day 4, by starting with 'common denominator' shared experience or values. And you can also, to some extent, apply the pacing and leading process to a group.

Large groups

Let's take a meeting as an example (though you can easily adapt the following to a workshop, seminar or other group situation). In the case of a meeting, the chairperson will typically need to use pacing and leading skills, but in fact any member can influence the way a meeting goes. Start by pacing experience. Express views in common with those present, or establish some group 'likeness'. Aim at the most basic level – a common purpose in coming together, a shared experience like lunch, a common source of pleasure or annoyance (the comfortable or uncomfortable surroundings, for example). This establishes an experience match or 'reality frame' (discussed further on Day 15).

At the same time, pace the general physiology of the group. For instance, don't come across as perky and 'raring to go' if they appear all 'down in the mouth'. Start at their level. Remember, you have a whole matching continuum along which to operate. Then lead them from a common experience, belief or value to where you want them to go.

If you want to motivate them to greater attentiveness or involvement, for instance, let them know the *benefits* of the change. Then gradually change your own demeanour as you lead them that way. Do this in small, subtle increments. For instance, you might first arouse their curiosity, then get their attention, then gain their commitment to getting involved and taking part, then go for agreement on a specific outcome.

At each level your total physiology will lead them, as well as the suggestions you make verbally. Pacing and leading in a group situation may require more emphasis on common experience, beliefs and values, rather than physiology, voice or sensory predicates.

Avoid appearing as 'all things to all people' when it comes to personal temperament, mannerisms and sensory pre-ference. By simply matching 'common' experience, acting sincerely, believing what you say, holding to your values and expressing this in every part of you, you can influence even a very large group.

Small groups

In a small group you can interrelate with individuals and, through them, have an effect on the whole group. This har-nesses the tendency for people in a group to act as one. Follow the same rules as for one-to-one pacing and leading. Watch out for those who indicate, by their mismatched pos-ture or movement, their lack of rapport with you or the main group. Work on them individually by first matching their body language to gain rapport.

Once you have achieved rapport, you can lead them to postures, voice characteristics and general demeanour more in tune with the state or point of view you want to get across. Influencing even one mismatched person in that way can mean success for you and the whole group. This applies especially in cases where a person has influence within the group. This may arise through their position in the company, their role or importance in the group (say technically), or their strength of personality. Spot the 'ring leader'. Aim to gain a 'critical mass' of rapport within the group, after which the group members will themselves reinforce rapport.

You can also build on rapport by pacing *positive* behaviour rather than trying to change negative behaviour. In this case, you need to move your attention and matching between those who show rapport. Elicit supportive contributions from them which will influence their colleagues. Again, aim for a critical mass of group rapport. This means leaving more of the matching to delegates, rather than doing it yourself. As rapport grows, this happens automatically. Your job then becomes one of *maintaining* rapport, or leading to outcomes as required.

MISMATCHING

You will soon start to recognise mismatches in your early attempts at rapport. As you observe people around you, you will see this happening unintentionally all the time. But you can use mismatching *positively* – to *break* rapport. Why should you want to break rapport? Perhaps to:

- End a communication you feel has no further purpose
- Redirect the flow of conversation
- Gain attention
- Positively interrupt a communication for whatever purpose
- End a relationship

You may have excellent rapport but the other person may not pay attention to the level you wish. For example, just enjoying the other person's presence, exchanging small talk, or communicating at an abstract level all provide a good *basis* for communicating, but do not necessarily constitute *effective* communication, through which you can fulfil an *outcome*. In such a situation, a slight mismatch can have the effect of giving the person a slight shock, thus regaining their attention. This prepares them for some important message you want to get across.

How do you mismatch? Essentially, you reverse the matching process. Go for *difference* rather than likeness. For example, you could adopt a different posture, voice tone or mannerisms to indicate that a meeting has come to an end. This could involve, for example, placing the palms of your hands on the table and leaning forward in an attitude that shows you intend to get up. Or you might look away in another direction, to indicate that something else now occupies your mind and the conversation has ended. Or, in the extreme, you might stand up and walk towards the office door. Many successful bosses can match and mismatch effectively without understanding the process. Watch people who do it well, and model their behaviour.

More subtle changes can work just as well. Try mismatching any body language or voice pattern, slight redirection of the eyes, any action indicating preoccupation or distraction, or just leave a long, 'pregnant' pause in conversation. If you have ever experienced someone glancing over your shoulder when chatting at a party or social event you will know how powerfully this subtle mismatch can say: 'I do not want to engage in this communication'. You can use this social device in all sorts of business situations as well.

Notice the effect of the *degree* of mismatch. A sudden, 'gentle' mismatch can regain lost attention and improve the effectiveness of the communication. Conversely, a very powerful mismatch can bring a communication to a sudden end, if you want that. In doing so you may jeopardise the relationship, but that may well fit your ultimate goal anyway. Once again, you need to apply your technical interpersonal skills to well-formed goals.

ESTABLISHING RELATIONSHIPS

Creating rapport does not mean you have created a relationship, other than a very transient or ad hoc one. Relationships tend to require longer-term thinking and behaviour. Even couples in love or close work colleagues experience the occasional lack of rapport, yet continue in a sound relationship. To establish a worthwhile relationship, you need to make rapport part of a bigger relationship outcome. Selling, for instance, involves creating rapport in order to get the person to like you, not just long enough to get their initial order, but with a view to referrals, repeat business, loyalty and a mutually beneficial relationship – 'relationship marketing'. It goes back to the 'respect' rule you met on Day 4.

Relationship Outcomes

A relationship involves more than just a longer timescale. You need to show competence and reliability in what you do. A person will not keep liking you, however positive the chemistry, if you keep letting them down. Act in a consistent and dependable way. Even people of very different temperaments establish lifelong relationships based on competence, mutual dependability and consistency.

However specifically you direct your rapport skills, they require the context of an *outcome* – what do you expect from this relationship? This outcome will appear higher up your 'goal hierarchy' than your specific communication outcome (which you might well adjust or even forego in order to achieve your longer-term relationship goal). At the same time your relationship outcomes should align with your other main outcomes. Remember your well-formed outcomes from Day 2. Each day's learning builds on what has gone before.

Power and Manipulation

Pacing and leading can have powerful effects and it pays to use these techniques wisely. Have clear intentions. Why do you want to lead? How will your leading affect the other person and their interests (ecology)? You might succeed in manipulating the other person on one occasion; but in the longer term the relationship will probably suffer, and you will lose out.

Sometimes in NLP we have to defend ourselves against accusations of manipulation. A tool or process cannot, in itself, manipulate – only the person who uses it. People manipulate with *intention*. Human beings have influenced each other for millennia, using all sorts of persuasive devices. If the intention brings mutual benefit, pacing and leading will help in just about any sales, negotiation, business meeting or learning situation. Used in a skilful, professional, morally sound way, it provides a powerful tool of communication.

MATCHING WITH CONGRUENCE

As well as matching with others, you need to match between the parts of yourself. This requires what we term *congruence,* simply meaning that what you say and how you express it (in your total physiology, tone of voice, etc) must harmonise. Research has shown that, although people may not always notice the actual body language a person adopts, they instinctively seem to spot disharmony between words and total physiology. Somehow we unconsciously pick up the communication signals. We also know from research that, when mismatched, people tend to take body language rather than the words we say as 'truth'. In fact, according to one major study, words alone account for a mere 7 per cent of the effectiveness of face-to-face communication.

You will find it hard to fake congruence. So follow the rules of respect and staying within your natural comfort zone (see p. 55) in all your communications. You can test this by applying the outcome criteria (goal-setting rules) in Days 2 and 3 to any communication or relationship outcomes. Problems of 'ecology', covered in Day 3, will usually lead to incongruence when expressing your outcomes and values. A fully congruent communication has enormous effect, whether a public presentation or a one-to-one conversation.

PRESUPPOSITION FOR TODAY

> **Experience has a structure.**

The linguistic aspects of thinking have had a structure for many years, but the mystical, subjective, 'neuro' part – the mind – has so far defied scientific method. Now the NLP model (see Day 1) allows us to think and talk about subjective experience, but based on a structure. The NLP 'five senses' model usually makes sense to ordinary people who easily identify with this simple approach to thinking. We can also now apply specific terms and annotation to describe thinking processes hitherto 'out of bounds' to lay people.

This has significance for the whole field of NLP, as it forms the basis for future enquiry. But it also affects individuals who can now start to understand and deliberately change their thoughts and feelings. All this has an effect, in turn, on our behaviour and the outcomes we achieve. We have begun to *harness* subjective experience. This gives us some personal control in a world of unpredictability, irrationality and countless individual perceptual maps.

TODAY'S TO DOs

- Try out your calibration skills – pace, pace, pace. At first it may seem like hard work, but you will soon start to notice things without trying.

- Having practised some more matching, experiment with simple leading skills. Wait until you have rapport before you lead, and don't rush it.

- Think of situations where you might want to bring a meeting or interview to an end and try the mismatching techniques you have learnt.

- Think about a relationship you value but which you want to improve. Use your rapport skills to establish or regain rapport. Think about the relationship also in terms of Day 1's presupposition: 'The map is not the territory'.

DAY 6

Making Sense of Your Own World

This chapter covers:

- **Seeing with your brain**
- **Trusting your 'autopilot'**
- **Representational systems**
- **Identifying sensory preference**
- **Eye movements**
- **Synaesthesia**

On Day 1 we introduced the concept of 'subjective experience', as illustrated by the NLP model. Today we specifically address the main senses, or representational systems, through which we each perceive our own world – seeing, hearing and feeling. You will also learn how to identify your own sensory preference, and the preference of other people you communicate with. This constitutes another important aspect of rapport (which we covered on Days 4 and 5).

SEEING WITH YOUR BRAIN

Let's start by discussing the way we sense or 'represent' things in our brains, and the importance of unconscious thought and 'automatic' behaviour. The NLP model you met on Day 1 gives some structure to 'subjective experience'. It also shows our thinking as a dynamic system, or continuous process.

According to the NLP model,

> **We don't 'see' with our eyes at all, but we see with our brain.**

Only when those light waves 'register' in the visual cortex do we really 'see', or rather *interpret,* what our eye has seen. And similar processes apply to the other senses. However sophisticated our sensory 'receptor' organs, the real sensing happens in the brain, where we store all our past experiences and the attitudes and beliefs these have formed.

Yet even this description paints a very incomplete picture of this amazingly complex sensory process. In practice, *physical limits* constrain our sensory receptors before we even start filtering the external data.

In the case of sight, for instance, we can only handle a tiny fraction of the light waves that reach us. This limited human sample excludes, for instance, the whole ultraviolet and infra-red worlds which, by design, we cannot perceive. The same perceptual 'filters' that distort and generalise also classify and simplify the constant bombardment of data. So, even perceiving a tiny sample of the external world, we can operate at high speed and with remarkable efficiency. We have at our disposal a staggeringly clever system. Next time you climb into your car, remember that the really awesome 'system' sits behind the wheel.

Nevertheless, even this fantastic survival system can let you down in the complex modern world of human relationships. 'Jumping to conclusions', for instance, saves a lot of valuable survival time, but does not make for very successful relationships. At best, we represent or interpret people and the world according to our own, personal criteria – the perceptual filters in the NLP model. NLP enables you to take more control of how you 'see' with your brain, giving you more choices as to how you respond to your environment and those around you.

TRUSTING YOUR 'AUTOPILOT'

This process happens automatically, of course. Although perhaps aware of our intentions (or some of them), we remain largely unconscious of the moment-to-moment *process* at work. In fact we can only think consciously of a handful of things at any one time. So we depend on our unconscious mind for the great majority of our actions. Even ignoring basic physical functions (like breathing or digestion), the simplest of actions – like reaching for a glass of water or catching a ball – involve hundreds of muscles in superb co-ordination.

Usually we simply don't know how, physiologically, we actually do what we do. And even if we did, we could not consciously think about all the parts of the operation at once. In fact, when we *do* try to think about an existing skill we usually mess it up (try, for example, demonstrating how to tie a necktie to a group!). Most of the time we just trust our 'autopilot' – we don't consciously think about it.

Only when faced with a new event or situation do we have to switch to conscious mode. We rely on familiar patterns of thought and habits of behaviour. We allocate every bit of sensory data we receive to a 'pigeon hole', however irrational our interpretation and classification. And we leave this to the same automatic control system that handles any other habitual behaviour. Different points of view or ways of doing things mean change, and tend to unsettle our comfortable version of 'reality'. So everything (as far as possible) has to have a blueprint or programme and become a habit. This way, we can use our precious ration of *conscious* thinking power (no more than about half a dozen bits of information at any one time) to think about *what we want*, rather than the hopelessly complex process of *how we get it*.

Unfortunately, when we think and act in this habitual way, we sometimes feel like the servant rather than the master of our thoughts and goals. Our minds seem to have minds of their own. We do what we don't really want to, and don't do what we really should or could do. By accessing these systems consciously and deliberately, we can become *effective* as well as efficient. We can harness and direct this 'neuro power' towards specific, worthwhile outcomes. NLP will help you to understand these processes, giving you more control over your life.

REPRESENTATIONAL SYSTEMS

You have already met the main visual, auditory and kinaesthetic thinking styles. We refer to these as modalities or representational systems – how we *represent* the world. Each of the five senses – seeing, hearing, feeling, tasting, smelling – has its inner equivalent or 'mirror' system. We remember, imagine and 'think' in these familiar modalities.

Everything that reaches your brain through your sensory organs translates into meaning and forms your subjective 'experience' – your *representation* of the world you perceive. The idea of consciousness draws on the same *sensory* mental model. We will now focus on 'rep' systems, and you will learn how to recognise sensory preference (a person's favoured representational system).

Although we all have more or less the same physical sense organs, we represent things in our own unique way. Our rep systems act as our special language of experience. This 'language' embraces all our mental processes (thinking, remembering, imagination, perception and consciousness). Even a basic understanding of these representation systems and their characteristics will allow you to take more control of your mind. Once you control the way you interpret things, you start to control your feelings, and in turn your behaviour. And, as we saw on Day 2, when considering outcomes, you can 'create' your own experience.

We take in, code and store information using the following four main representational systems:

1. Visual (V) – seeing
2. Auditory (A) – hearing
3. Kinaesthetic (K) – feeling/touching/moving
4. Auditory digital (Ad) – inner dialogue

We have not met the last one, Auditory digital (sometimes referred to as self-talk) before. The other two systems, Gustatory (tasting) and Olfactory (smelling), have far less significance in terms of everyday human communication. When you meet them in NLP they usually share the kinaesthetic category. Interestingly, however, sometimes a smell or taste can trigger a distant memory and in this special way they can sometimes have a greater effect than the three main senses.

Lead and Primary Systems

We use all these rep systems all the time. However, most of us tend to have a preference. You met this briefly on Day 4 when we discussed sensory language or 'predicates'. This bias or preference applies in two ways.

First we have a 'lead system', the representation system we normally use to *access* stored information. For example, if you recall an event that happened last week, will you first represent in your mind something you saw, something you heard or something you felt? The answer will depend on your lead system, the sense that normally leads you to a memory.

Second, we have a preference in the way we *process*

information, our 'primary system'. A person who tends to think in images and can easily 'picture' things will have a primary visual preference. This doesn't mean they only think in pictures, but that they prefer visual representation which to them seems the most familiar and readily available. So labels like 'a visual person', can sometimes mislead. Moreover, some people have the same modality for their lead and primary systems, while others may have one modality for their lead system and another for their primary system.

In establishing rapport, a person's representation system provides an important area of 'likeness'. The way that person creates and runs their 'mental map' reflects their true identity. If you can identify and use a person's primary representation system you will, in effect, 'speak their language' and will communicate better. Mutual understanding will increase because of the common system you both use. Using a different representation, however, means the listener has to 'translate' what you say. For instance, they have to translate a visual image into something that 'sounds' or 'feels' right. This may seem like hard work. And it can lead to misunderstanding. Hence the benefits of matching thinking style to achieve better communication.

As we saw on Day 5, when pacing and leading a group you need to use the whole range of representation systems to bring everyone 'on board'. However, at a one-to-one level you can match a person's rep system to create rapport, just as you can match their posture or movement. Most people don't like to stray from their preferred way of thinking. But, once you have established rapport, they will more readily *follow* you to another, less favoured thinking mode. So you can pace and lead in thinking style. For example, you may get a highly visual person to 'just listen' to you for a while, 'paint mental pictures' in the case of a non-visual thinker, or communicate your feelings to a non-kinaesthetic thinker. Extending our experience of rep systems means mutually enriching each other's 'maps'.

IDENTIFYING SENSORY PREFERENCE

If you can identify a person's sensory preference, you can match it, create rapport and communicate better. But how do you recognise a person's sensory preference? You can watch out for certain characteristics that indicate their favoured or primary representational system.

Visual (V)

People who favour a visual approach often stand or sit with their head and body erect and with their eyes pointing slightly upwards. They tend to take shallow breaths from the top of their lungs. They often speak quickly, in a higher-than-average pitched voice, and process their thoughts quickly when in conversation. They will characteristically sit forward in their chair and appear organised, neat and well-groomed. Visualisers memorise by seeing pictures, and sounds do not easily distract or interest them. They often have trouble remembering verbal instructions because their minds tend to wander. They tend to use visual words (or 'predicates') like 'I get the picture'. A visual person will take an interest in appearance – how things look.

Auditory (A)

People who favour an auditory approach tend to move their eyes sideways when accessing thoughts. They breathe from the middle of their chest. Easily distracted by noise, they typically talk to themselves silently, sometimes moving their lips as they do so. They speak in more resonant tones, not as high-pitched as the visual person, and their voice may sound rhythmic or even musical. They can repeat things back to you easily, they learn by listening, and they usually like music and talking on the telephone. Auditory thinkers often tilt their head to one side in conversation, as if 'lending an ear' or as if on the telephone. They memorise sequentially, by steps and sequences. The auditory person likes to *hear* feedback in conversation, and responds to a certain tone of voice or set of words. They tend to use auditory predicates, like 'That sounds OK', and take an interest generally in how things sound. As good listeners, they enjoy the spoken voice.

Kinaesthetic (K)

People who favour a kinaesthetic approach typically breathe from the bottom of their lungs so you can see their stomach go in and out as they breathe. They tend to look down and to the right when accessing memories. They often have quite a deep voice and talk slowly, with deliberate phrasing and perhaps silent gaps between phrases. They seem to process thoughts and speech more slowly than a visual person. They respond to physical rewards and touching. Kinaesthetic people also tend to stand closer to people in conversation than the visual person. They memorise by doing or 'walking through' something. They tend to use kinaesthetic 'feeling' predicates. They take an interest in how things *feel*.

Auditory digital (Ad)

These people will spend a fair amount of time talking things through to themselves. They tend to use complicated sentences and like a lot of detail. They often use abstract words without a direct sensory link and place importance on logic and what 'makes sense'. The auditory digital thinker will often exhibit characteristics of other major representational systems. Their eyes, during self-talk, will tend to point down and to the left.

These profiles just illustrate stereotypes, of course. Even a person with a strong preference may not match every trait. But, as your observational skills improve, they can help you identify thinking types (especially if you can spot more than one characteristic supporting a particular preference). They also give you a sound basis on which you can develop your matching skills.

Representational Systems and Predicates

We referred earlier to sensory words or predicates. We all use many such phrases and figures of speech – you will hear them every day once you start to notice them. You may want to add a few of your own to the following examples:

'He always looked on the bright side.'
'Everything went blank.'
'I can't seem to focus on the problem.'
'Everything moved along nicely.'
'She has had a very colourful life.'
'I need a bit of sparkle in my life.'
'Everything just flooded in on me.'
'I've put the past behind me.'
'I've got a lot to look forward to.'
'He really caught me off balance.'
'I don't like looking back.'
'Go on, I'm listening.'
'I need to slow down.'
'I can't seem to get moving.'
'She sounded quite upset.'
'I can't hear myself think.'
'The situation looks very bleak.'
'He's got the problem right out of perspective.'
'She's too high-powered for me.'

The following longer list of sensory predicates, classified by each representation system, should provide a helpful checklist for reference.

Visual	Auditory	Kinaesthetic	Auditory digital
see	hear	feel	sense
look	listen	touch	experience
appear	sound	grasp	understand
view	make music	get hold of	think
show	harmonise	slip through	learn
illuminate	tune in/out	catch on	process
clear	be all ears	tap into	decide
focus	rings a bell	make contact	motivate
imagine	silence	throw out	consider
picture	resonate	turn around	change
catch a glimpse of	deaf	hard	perceive
dim view	overtones	concrete	theory
get a perspective on	attune	get a handle on	insensitive
eye to eye	outspoken	touch base	distinct
in light of	tell	boils down to	conceive
make a scene	clear as a bell	come to grips with	know
mind's eye	call on	connect with	questions
pretty as a picture	clearly expressed	cool/calm/collected	be conscious
showing off	describe in detail	firm foundations	clever concept
take a peek	earful	get a load of this	process of
well defined	give me your ear	get in touch with	elimination
vivid	hold your tongue	hand in hand	
	voice an opinion	pain in the neck	
	word for word	slipped my mind	
		start from scratch	
		stiff upper lip	
		under pressure	

Other modalities

Occasionally you may also hear words or phrases that indicate olfactory or gustatory processing, such as 'something smells fishy' or 'a taste of her own medicine'. You can easily match these also when they occur. As mentioned before, when identifying sensory preferences, NLP usually includes these two senses with kinaesthetic.

EYE MOVEMENTS

You will recall from the profiles on pp. 89–90 that eye movements can help you identify sensory preference. Although quite reliable, 'body language' and verbal indicators have tended to attract a lot less attention in NLP than eye movements. If you notice the direction in which a person's eyes look when you ask them a question, or suggest that they recall an experience, you will notice distinctive directional movements that seem to relate to their thought processes. This applies whether imagining, remembering, or perhaps speaking to themselves. These eye movements probably reflect the processing of sensory information in different parts of the brain (which we know about from PET scans and post mortems on brain-injured patients). We sometimes describe the eyes as 'windows of the soul'. When we start to understand what these movements mean, we realise that the eyes can indeed convey more 'truth' than what a person says.

Eye movements, along with the many other characteristics we have already covered, indicate a person's preferred representational system. With this information you can more easily match the person and gain rapport, for example by using appropriate sensory language predicates. In some cases eye movements communicate things to you beyond the subject's consciousness, especially regarding the way they process thoughts.

The Meaning of Eye Movements

If you ask someone to imagine how velvet feels against their skin they will usually look down and to their right, the eye pattern for accessing kinaesthetic experiences. If they happen to have a visual lead system they will probably look up momentarily to their left first, the way we usually access visual memories. These cues form a pattern for visual (up) and auditory (sideways) representations. This in turn differs, depending on whether they remember (to their left) or construct (to their right) the visual image. A constructed representation *synthesises* (or recreates) images or sounds, rather than recalling an actual memory – for example, if you imagined your room with different decor and furniture.

K and Ad depart slightly from this pattern. Kinaesthetic eye access, as we saw in the example, looks down and to the subject's right. Auditory digital looks down and to the person's left. When looking at the person, you should reverse these directions, of course (see Figure 6.1). In practice, eye movements, invisible and largely unconscious for the subject, only have relevance when used with someone else.

These 'eye access cues' remain valid for the great majority of right-handed people, and for most left-handers. In the remainder of cases, a small minority, the reverse applies: left for V and A construct, and right for V and A remembered.

Fortunately, you need not, however, rely on eye movements as the only indicator of a representational system. Usually the words the person uses (predicates) will provide the same information, as well as the physiological and voice characteristics we described in the stereotypes earlier. In conjunction with other indicators, however, they provide a reliable, consistent test, almost impossible to 'fake'. You cannot stay aware of your own eye direction for more than a very short time. It happens involuntarily – hence the special reliability of eye movements in determining favoured representational system.

Eye movements can tell us a lot about how a person thinks and thus allow us to relate better to what they say and do. They can reveal disarmingly how we process thoughts in terms of the main representational systems. For this reason, once you have established a person's pattern – 'normal' (as per Figure 6.1) or otherwise – their eye movements will help you identify untruth or 'constructed' information.

However, such a fast, instinctive process – without any explanation of the internal process – can sometimes seem very confusing. The eye pattern alone may not seem to make sense. For instance, in order to internally 'see' something, a person may first mentally locate the object and feel it, or even hear it, before they have a good visual image. Hence apparently 'roundabout' eye movements, even when you request the person to 'see' something. If you ask a person to describe exactly how they do something *inside*, however, whether a memory recall or an imagined future event, it usually becomes clear. Typically, they will need to do it again and think about it, possibly for the first time. Such 'elicitation' may require different forms of questioning, and you may need to use more than one indicator as confirmation.

Eye Accessing Cues

Figure 6.1 illustrates these 'eye access cues'. The eye directions appear as when looking at the other person – their right

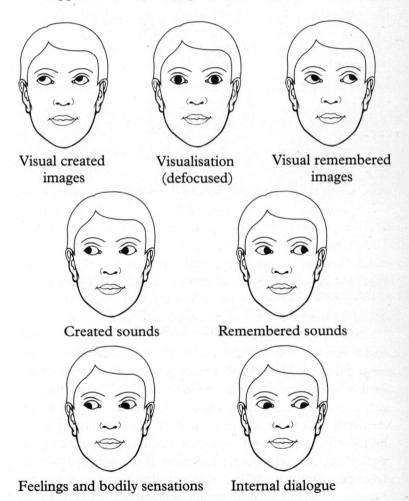

Visual created images

Visualisation (defocused)

Visual remembered images

Created sounds

Remembered sounds

Feelings and bodily sensations

Internal dialogue

Figure 6.1 Eye access cues

to your left and vice versa. More detailed descriptions of eye accessing cues follow, including examples of questions that will help elicit them.

Visual constructed

The person constructs an internal image of something they have not seen before, or synthesises in a novel way 'stored' images they have seen before. They literally 'make it up in their head'. To observe this cue, you might ask the question: 'What would your room look like if it had walls painted bright blue with yellow stripes?'

Visual remembered

The person uses a mental image to recall an actual visual memory. Note that some people access visual memories by defocusing their eyes, looking straight forward rather than up, and seeming to look through or beyond the other person. This seems to relate to readily available, or 'on tap' information, rather than less accessible memories. To elicit a visual remembered eye movement, you could ask: 'Can you remember what your best friend at secondary school looked like?'

Auditory constructed

Here the person constructs a sound they have never heard before, or synthesises 'known' sounds to make a novel, unfamiliar sound. They have to construct a representation, rather than just recall it from memory. You might ask: 'What would your boss sound like if she had Donald Duck's voice?'

Auditory remembered

In this case the person remembers a sound from the past, perhaps a voice. To get this cue, ask something like: 'What have I just said?' or 'Can you remember the sound of your mother's voice?' Or simply ask the person to think of a favourite tune.

Kinaesthetic

As we saw, people generally use this eye pattern when accessing their feelings. Ask, for example, 'What would it feel like to touch a wet flannel?' Or, 'Imagine sliding down a polished banister.' In these last cases the representation involves bodily movement as well as tactile sensations, another feature of the K modality. It also includes feelings in the sense of emotion, such as a 'tingling sensation' or a 'gut feeling'.

Auditory digital

This happens when people speak to themselves in the form of inner dialogue or 'self-talk'. To get this cue, ask the person, for example, to 'recite the national anthem to yourself'.

You can think of your own examples, and have fun trying them out on friends and colleagues. If you want to elicit specific eye movements (for instance, to test that they work), simply use examples that clearly require the representation system in question, and the constructed or remembered characteristic. Use specific sensory ('see', 'hear', 'feel') rather than 'neutral' predicates (like 'consider', 'think', 'recall' or 'imagine'). 'Imagine an oak tree', for example, might require any or all rep systems. Directing the person towards colour, on the other hand, will definitely require the visual sense, while the sound of leaves rustling in the wind will trigger the auditory system.

If you want to establish sensory preference, a series of more neutral questions will soon confirm the lead and preferred primary rep systems. Simply watch and listen for the modality the person uses most.

You will gain confidence in identifying eye movements by carefully watching over a period of days, in all sorts of face-to-face situations. This will hone your skill in observing fast and obscure eye movements. Practice also validates the general pattern of movements, which you will come to trust. These eye movements will give you another indicator of a person's sensory preference which you can then match to gain rapport.

SYNAESTHESIA

Sometimes you may notice that a person seems to use two rep systems at the same time. For example, he or she may indicate visual eye movements but use kinaesthetic predicates and body language. Termed 'synaesthesia', in this case two or more rep systems work in unison. For instance, a certain sound may have a feel or texture or colour. In other cases a strong memory may produce a negative kinaesthetic feeling linked with a positive visual memory. In such a case the person probably doesn't understand why they feel the way they do.

To speak the 'language' of such a person you may need to use *mixed* predicates. In the above case, for instance, you may say 'I can *see* how you *feel*'. Although grammatically strange, both predicates will have meaning to a person with VK synaesthesia, even when used in conjunction. So you will gain rapport.

People with synaesthesia often have good memories, because the more sensory 'recordings' we can call upon the better we recall memories. And, in any event, people with extraordinary memories tend to use more than one rep system – whether or not naturally synaesthetic. Memories, of course, mirror real, *multi-sensory* life. Similarly, a vivid imagination operates in multi-sensory mode.

We came across an interesting example of this when we did some work for UK television, following a 1996 interview with the late Princess Diana. The sensitive nature of the topics covered, including Prince Charles and the royal family, could have created all sorts of constitutional problems for the British monarchy, and the interview became a main news event. As 'neuro-linguistic experts', we monitored Princess Diana's eye movements from the video recording of the interview, in an attempt to determine her thought processes. As it happens, we found the movements easy to follow and consistent, and a textbook illustration of the eye accessing cues you have learnt about today.

It turned out that Princess Diana exhibited so-called Ad–K synaesthesia. This meant that when she talked to herself she triggered K emotions, and when she triggered a kinaesthetic representation she tended to use inner dialogue. One did not happen without the other. Thus she exhibited a distinctive down and to the left eye movement, signifying that Ad accompanied K language and physiology. Interestingly, and perhaps to the regret of the news-hungry broadcasters, no evidence at all emerged of *constructed* representations – typically associated with lying.

Synaesthesia may occur more widely than we think, and it seems normal, of course, to the person who has it (like colour blindness), until they learn that not everybody processes thoughts in the same way. One synaesthetic seminar delegate suddenly realised why he could do mental arithmetic more easily than other people. He could 'see' every calculation in vivid colour; he 'rated' bright or dim colours respectively 'easy' or 'difficult' to manipulate, and followed different mental processes.

PRESUPPOSITION FOR TODAY

> **Every behaviour has a positive intention.**

Although we do not always articulate it, nor even have awareness of it, we invariably have a purpose for what we do. Any action – at least to the person doing it – has a positive intention. We pursue some outcome, whether stated or unstated, conscious or unconscious. An action you or I might think of as anti-social or repugnant will no doubt 'make sense' to the person performing it. More than likely, he or she will have a *reason* for doing it, a cause or ideal that we (or society generally) may not espouse. According to that person's 'map of the world' their behaviour will bring about an outcome. Thus they act positively, and with intent.

For example, the immediate social benefits and short-term feelings of well-being induced by smoking or drug-taking may act as 'positive intentions', even though – rationally and consciously – a person may try hard to give up the behaviour. In identifying the underlying positive intention, you may well find an alternative behaviour which achieves the same intention but with fewer disadvantages. By acting *as if* every behaviour has some underlying positive intention we will become less likely to react to behaviour in a disapproving, unhelpful way. Rather, we can begin to explore and understand our respective maps of reality.

TODAY'S TO DOs

- Start to notice indicators of people's primary rep system. It may help to spread this exercise over several days, as it takes practice to notice more than one or two features at once. For instance, you can start with listening for sensory predicates – the seeing, hearing and feeling words listed on p. 92. You may then find yourself fascinated by eye movements. You can, if you wish, split your day into parts, concentrating on different indicators during each period, assuming you meet different people in your work or socially. Initially, don't match them (by changing your own words and behaviour) – that will come later, when you can confidently identify primary systems.

- Find a magazine article or a couple of pages of a novel and note all the sensory words or predicates you can find. Notice which kinds of prose – from business and legal documents to fast-paced novels and journalistic writing – have most sensory predicates.

DAY 7

Changing Your World

This chapter covers:
- **Submodalities and the meaning of experience**
- **Changing experience and behaviour**

On Day 6 we learnt about the main representational systems or modalities. But each representational system, or modality, contains certain characteristics, qualities or details. We refer to these characteristics as submodalities. They contain the secrets of human thought and experience.

SUBMODALITIES AND THE MEANING OF EXPERIENCE

Take as an example the first sensory system, seeing. Within this single modality you might describe an inner picture or image as: near or far, large or small, bright or dull, in black and white or colour, focused or blurred, appearing straight ahead or to the side, panoramic or framed, three-dimensional or two-dimensional (lifelike or a bit unreal), and so on. Submodalities give subjective meaning. They literally *make sense*.

Below, you will find lists of qualities or submodalities for each of the three main sensory systems:

Visual	*Auditory*	*Kinaesthetic (feeling)*
Associated or dissociated	Loud or soft	Temperature
Colour or black and white	Distance from sound	Texture (rough or smooth)
Location (e.g., to the left	source	Intensity
or right, up or down)	Words or sounds	Pressure (hard or soft)
Distance	Location of sound source	Duration (how long it lasts)
Brightness	Stereo or mono	Weight (light or heavy)
Framed or panoramic	Continuous or	Shape
Blurred or focused	discontinuous	
Contrast	Speed (faster or slower	
Moving or still	than usual)	
Speed (faster or slower	Clear or muffled	
than real life)	Soft or harsh	
Size		

Submodalities apply to any representation. Acting as a sort of code, they give the mind-picture *meaning*. They make the representation clear or confusing, pleasant or unpleasant. In other words submodalities determine not only what you see but how you interpret what you see and how you feel about it.

Submodalities give unique meaning to every sensory experience. For example, a visual image comprises more than light waves measured through a clever optical tool called the eye. It consists of your personal interpretation of the experience based on millions of neural firings that take place in your brain (which in turn interact with an existing network of billions of synaptic recordings). This enormously complex process makes the colourless energy waves of the universe into a beautiful red rose, a dramatic sunset or the face of a little child. It works a bit like tuning your television, but with infinitely greater richness and variety.

Giving Meaning to Time

These submodal characteristics also place the image in time. A visual image may recall something from your past or preview something in the future, whether yesterday or five years ago, tomorrow or in five years' time. We seem to locate time, at the submodal level, using such language as 'The past is behind me' or 'I'm looking ahead to a bright future'. For more on the way we represent time, see Day 13.

Creating Unique Experience

Submodalities give the fine distinctions to any modality and transform the objective, physiological processes of seeing, hearing and feeling into subjective experience. We all know that the same external sensory inputs can have very different effects on different people. What makes one person happy will make another person sad, for example, because we code these inputs in the brain, and filter them according to our past experience, beliefs and values. This produces the varied thinking characteristics that NLP terms submodalities.

Modalities and their submodalities, together, make up your experience – your reality. They represent your 'map' of the world. But, as you have learnt, this does not constitute the 'territory' of reality. Submodalities give meaning to experience.

> **As you consciously change submodalities, you change experience.**

The presupposition 'People create their own experience' thus has practical use in our everyday lives.

Content and Characteristics

Submodalities comprise far more than the *content* of a thought (such as the fact that you played tennis or went to the theatre). They determine the way you *feel* about an experience. They produce, from the representations we see, hear and feel, what we call our 'state of mind'.

You can put this to the test. Think of a pleasant memory and note as many of its submodalities as you can. Use the checklists on p. 102 if you need to. Then think of a very unpleasant memory, and similarly make a note of its submodalities. Now compare each set of submodalities and you will probably find that they differ. Those differences account for the different way you *feel* about each experience.

The circumstances or content of each memory differed, of course. But you can probably think of memories with very similar content which nevertheless evoke different feelings. For example, you may have won an event on two occasions but now feel differently as you recall each one. And sure enough, the memory submodalities will also probably differ.

To take another example, you may meet two different people for the first time, and each first meeting might evoke very different feelings or 'chemistry'. The content did not differ greatly – you had no earlier knowledge of either person and no logical reason to form particular impressions. But you unconsciously *coded* the two memories very differently. Each had different *qualities*. And your coding probably took the form of the various submodalities of the sort listed on p. 102.

Thought Qualities

All this helps to explain apparently random, illogical feelings and reactions. The secrets of our hang-ups, prejudices, irrational feelings and perceptions boil down to the way we code, in submodalities, our representation of the world around us. In other words, our personal map-making system depends on the qualities, or submodalities, of our thoughts.

For instance, an early attempt at a skill or activity, such as public speaking, might arouse painful feelings of embarrassment. The same activity, once you have overcome your initial fears, may well produce pleasure. If you remember or imagine such occasions you can identify the sort of visual submodalities listed on p. 102. As you test out examples from your own experience you should find that:

- All thoughts consist of visual, auditory and kinaesthetic representations.

- Each representation has degree and quality in its sub-modalities.

- Similar feelings or 'meaning' involve similar sub-modalities.

- Such submodalities, and the feelings they evoke, do not seem to depend on content.

- Certain combinations of submodalities tend to relate to happiness and pleasure, and others to pain and bad feelings.

In due course you will associate submodalities with more specific states of mind, but for the moment you need to get used to accessing thoughts in this structured way.

You can't do much about content when it comes to memories, of course. You can't turn the clock back and change what happened. But you can do something about the way you *represent* those experience recordings *now*. You can change the *qualities* or characteristics of the mind-pictures, sounds and feelings that constitute your experience. These, we have already learnt, do not equate to reality. They have already gone through the personal mental filters that result in the memories we record and the feelings they evoke.

So it makes sense, if you can change these representations, to do it in a way that supports your present outcomes and enhances your state of mind. Once you can identify sub-modalities, you can then start to manipulate them to create experience and change behaviour.

CHANGING EXPERIENCE AND BEHAVIOUR

Submodalities can seriously affect your state of mind! For instance, as stated earlier, because you can change them, you can change your *experience* of something. This means you can change how you feel, and any behaviour that follows from this. And we know, from the four-stage success model in Day 2, that what we do brings about results or outcomes.

Switching Submodalities

Try this out. Go back to the unpleasant memory you recalled, but this time *switch* the characteristics of the picture to match the submodalities you identified in the happy memory. *Replace* the 'unhappy' submodalities. For example, if in your happy recollection you saw big, bright images, then make them that way as you recall the negative memory. If your unhappy memory appeared blurred, out of focus and not in 'real life' colour, *replace* it to match your happy memory. You will probably meet many of the visual qualities we listed on p. 102.

Take another example. Perhaps in your unhappy memory you could *see yourself* there in the picture, whereas in the happy recollection you occupied your own body looking through your own eyes and experiencing it yourself. NLP uses the terms associated (seeing things through your own eyes) and dissociated (looking as if from the outside). This one important submodality can have a dramatic effect on how you feel about an experience. Switching to the associated state may, along with the other submodalities, apply the 'happiness' code to an unhappy memory content. These submodalities do not apply universally. But they usually remain valid *for you* as representing particular states.

Association tends to intensify a feeling. Conversely, recalling a traumatic experience in a dissociated way will typically cause less pain – you distance yourself or 'step outside' the experience. Thus, changing the main submodalities of thought means changing how you feel. And it makes sense to create more pleasurable, empowering feelings.

We often describe submodality processes in visual terms – in any event we use the visual modality most. The term 'visualisation' or '*imag*ining' for instance, often applies to imagining something in more than just visual images. But you can switch submodalities in any of the representational systems. Change the sounds or feelings. Change that nasty voice for the voice of a little child, or a cartoon character, and see whether it creates the same fear in you. Change that cold sensation for warmth and comfort. External experience involves all the senses, and changing internal experience requires the same multi-sensory realism. Switching sub-modalities gives you a powerful technique for change.

Kick-Starting Your Subjective Mind

You may already have experience of manipulating your thoughts in this way and noticed the change in how you feel. On the other hand you might think it impossible, incredible or just strange. This basic skill, which we all had as children, just needs *imagination*. It means doing what you want in your own mind, having your own identity, and changing what you want. If your powers of imagination have atrophied over the years, start with something simple, then practise, practise, practise. You can hone your mental skills, like any skill, through repetition and practice.

To get started, try the following:

- Imagine your boss with a silly hat on.
- See your desk sawn in two.
- Visualise your TV swinging from the ceiling.
- Imagine a blue dandelion.
- Change some colours, sounds, and feelings.
- Start saying different, more empowering things to yourself.
- Imagine a blue triangle/a short piece of string/a tree a mile high.

- Pretend that when you lost you actually won.
- Pretend that when you failed you actually succeeded.

Enjoy yourself. Treat your mind as a priceless, personal treasure.

Most educated Western people tend to think more objectively, having a preference for rational 'left-brain' processing. But you can now enter your precious, subjective world and relearn childhood imaginative skills more associated with your right brain. In this way you can start to access your creative, unconscious mind.

Once you become proficient in changing submodalities using non-threatening situations from your own experience, you can start to use your new skill more positively to create the internal experience and feelings you want. This, in turn, produces more positive, useful behaviour, enabling you to make important life changes.

Learning to Relax

It helps to relax when using any of these mental techniques. Most of us unwind at some time and have our own methods that work, such as listening to music, soaking in a hot bath, or getting away to a quiet place in our minds. It usually helps to think of each limb relaxing, one by one, then your neck, head, face and jaw. It also helps to breathe deeply and slowly. Some people, however, seem to like imagining their body as very light, and floating up rather than sinking down. And particular kinds of music can have a very different effect. Some people, for instance, find Baroque stringed instruments really relax them.

Once physically relaxed, you can get any busy thoughts out of your mind by visualising a pleasant, calming scene – say from a holiday or a place you once associated with peace and serenity. As you let your imagination wander, concentrating on all the sights, sounds and feelings that emerge, you will overcome the interference of your critical left brain. Although most people know how to relax, our crowded lifestyles often do not allow space for real mental exercise. Look on this as an investment in all the advantages that come from a fit mind as well as body – it will reduce your stress levels, help you to think more clearly and creatively, and give you greater control over how you feel.

Make sure you have a reasonable amount of time, without a telephone or interruptions, and can sit or lie in comfort. However, once you have developed the skill of relaxation, you can change your state of mind quickly to help you in whatever situation you find yourself. Start by consciously applying yourself and making time, then the unconscious habits of mind and body control will soon come.

Changing Your Neural Landscape

Every time you use your mind in such a way, real electro-chemical events occur in your brain. Different scanning techniques have shown this clearly, some in real time. While you think, your actual physical neural networks *change*. The very landscape of your brain (not just your intangible 'mind', however defined, but your 'grey matter') alters permanently, in form and chemical composition. Once you have mentally *created* a mile-high tree or a blue dandelion, you can't rub it out. It may *change* each time you recall it (unknowingly perhaps) but there it will stay, in some form, ingrained on your mental topography.

Now you can use this same phenomenon, consciously and positively, to change how you feel and so transform parts of your life. Test this for yourself with today's first 'To Do' exercise below.

You can only do so much to change the world. But you can do a lot to change how you *represent* or interpret the world, by identifying and changing your thought submodalities. You can change for the better how you think, what you do, and what you achieve.

PRESUPPOSITION FOR TODAY

> **The mind and body are part of the same system, and affect each other.**

We associate feeling with our bodies. But you can change your very physiology by the way you think. If you think 'confident' you look and act confident. If you think 'anxious' or 'afraid' your heart rate, voice tone and body language will match. If you think 'embarrassed' or 'self-conscious' your behaviour and physical mannerisms may well betray the fact. Conversely, by changing your physiology you can change your attitude, or 'state of mind'. It works both ways, as a single system over which you have control. Walk, talk and act confidently and you will start to feel confident. Here's what you can do:

1. You can *access* all your existing mental resources.

2. You can *change* any submodality as you wish.

3. By changing these submodalities, you can change the *meaning* of any experience, or how you feel about it.

4. You can begin to create and control your own experience, to conform to your goals (you no longer have to rely on chance or circumstance).

5. You can change what you do (physically) to affect your mind; and you can change how you think to affect your body.

6. You can change your basic body functions (like breathing, pulse rate and even brainwaves) by relaxing and becoming aware of subtle body changes.

TODAY'S TO DOs

- If you have not yet done the submodality switching exercise (see p. 106), have a go at it seriously today. In this case you may have to set aside time on your own when no one will disturb you, and first get into a relaxed state (see p. 108). Sometimes this works well in bed before you go to sleep. Apply the technique to any disempowering memories or 'hang-ups' and note the changes you can instantly make.

- Keep practising your pacing and leading skills (see Day 5). Start with non-sensitive situations until you have gained confidence and skill. Don't jeopardise a major contract or close relationship or try things out first on the managing director. Check back on the many ways you can create rapport by matching (see Days 4 and 5).

DAY 8

The Power Of Language

This chapter covers:
- **Using language to get what you want**
- **E-Prime**
- **The hierarchy of ideas**
- **Turning words into outcomes**

The word 'linguistic' fits in the centre of NLP so today we will think about language. We have already said a lot about 'body language' and non-verbal communication. But words also have a vital place in excellent communication – not just the words we use (which, you may recall, only account for some 7 per cent of a communication) but also the way we process language in the brain. All this has an impact on a communication, and even individual words can enormously affect meaning. How many times have you used a word, and heard another person use it, only to realise that you each meant something quite different? On other occasions we come up against the limitations of language, and readily admit 'I can't put this into words'.

USING LANGUAGE TO GET WHAT YOU WANT

Through NLP we can use language for better communication, but at a deeper level or in a different way from usual.

This comes from understanding the limitations of language just as much as its strengths. It also involves understanding the relationship between language and the way we represent and 'filter' things – the NLP model you met on Day 1. In effect language provides us with a multi-purpose tool, like a drill that can convert to lots of other uses. But we need to use it appropriately and effectively. Without wise application we just have a super-gadget, and a potentially dangerous one at that. Similarly, we can use language better by understanding what it can and cannot do, and by always matching the right tool to the job in hand.

Remember what you learnt on Days 2 and 3: keep your outcome or goal in mind – and don't get too wrapped up in the process of achieving it. Staying with the drill analogy, do you want quarter-inch drills or quarter-inch holes? Think about the *outcome* holes rather than the drill-bit *process*. You will then self-steer towards the right tool for the job – in today's case, the tool of language.

You will recall Day 4's presupposition: 'The meaning of a communication is the response it gets.' We consciously use language to get a desired response – to achieve an outcome. We need to choose words that will have the appropriate meaning for the other person, and fit their map of reality. Similarly, when receiving a communication, we need to determine precisely what people mean by the words they use, sometimes by asking appropriate questions. These skills will help any professional communicator and can also benefit anyone who wants to get more out of their life through better communication.

Over the next three days you will learn how to use language to achieve all sorts of outcomes. Have an open mind and you will soon start enjoying the benefits.

E-PRIME

We have written this book in a language style known as E-Prime. Developed by David Bourland, a linguist and

Harvard business graduate, the term simply refers to the English language excluding the verb 'to be'. Although the most-used verb in our language, it often leads to unclear meaning and sloppy grammar. For instance, for many years writers have frowned upon the passive tense ('It was understood', 'It is estimated', etc) which depends on the verb 'to be'. NLP typically responds, 'By whom?', or 'Who says so?'

The little word 'is' can make sweeping assertions, like 'This is true', 'He is a bad man' and so on. It assumes everything *is* black or white when real life proves otherwise. It 'labels' people and things so conveniently that we no longer need to make our language precise. The trouble starts when other people place a different meaning on our words, or we on theirs, causing a mismatch of meaning. Communication breaks down and relationships suffer.

Such linguistic distortion forms one of the many filters in the NLP model you met on Day 1. Even very common words, such as 'is', affect our perceptions and the meaning we place on things. For better or worse, language fundamentally affects the way we think, and E-Prime demonstrates this starkly. As well as illustrating how language affects meaning, it allows you to make changes using one simple language technique.

We take all sorts of short cuts in everyday spoken language or in tabloid writing. Having to replace 'is' and other 'to be' words forces us to think about the actual meaning we want to communicate. You can usually think of a better, clearer way to express something, often by using active 'doing' verbs and specifying who does the action. Fortunately, however popular the verb 'to be', the English language provides plenty of alternative words.

Two Dangers

The founder of general semantics, Alfred Korzybski, identified two particularly dangerous uses of the verb 'to be'. The first he called the 'is' of identity ('Joan is a nurse'), and the second the 'is' of predication ('Joe is stupid' or 'That leaf is green'). The verb 'to be' offers no compromise – something either *is* or it *isn't*. So we tend to make generalised or absolute statements that would not bear logical scrutiny. Joan, for instance, *is* also a mother, wife, student, swimmer, and keep-fit enthusiast. And she happens to work part-time as a nurse except in the school holidays. So what *is* Joan? Without doubt, what Joan *is* doesn't end there. So we lose out in really understanding about Joan.

In a similar way, 'Joe is stupid' might translate in E-Prime to 'Joe acted stupidly on that occasion'; or better still, perhaps, 'He *appeared to me* to act stupidly'. And 'The leaf *appeared* yellow – or rather, in the evening light, a yellowy, greeny brown, to John.' So we can make our meaning clearer and truer by simply replacing the offending little words. Just ask: 'What do I really mean to say?'

E-Prime forces more direct meaning into language, identifying who does or says what, and who has responsibility. It helps eliminate woolly, ambiguous generalisations and obliges us to replace 'to be' words with action verbs. Much of the passive voice, and broad generalisations or 'nominalisations' (beloved by bureaucrats and ivory-tower academics), simply disappear. Abstract words become concrete, sensory things we can imagine and understand.

Saying What You Mean

But E-Prime goes a lot further than mechanically replacing words. You may have to rethink precisely *what you mean*, rather than just changing *how you say* something. So it forces you to think clearly as well as communicate clearly.

In principle, E-Prime works quite simply. You just eliminate the verb 'to be'. But in practice it has an extraordinarily radical impact. As well as transforming the way you think, it can also affect your behaviour, achievements and relationships. We have already met the important link between thinking and behaviour, 'Whatsoever a man thinketh, so he is'. So, rather than a mere language device with proven communication benefits, E-Prime acts as a powerful agent of *personal change* – the very essence of NLP. Its applications continue to grow in areas such as problem-solving and personal achievement.

Even a limited use of E-Prime can bring about a radical rethink of what we and others mean by the words we use. You will get a chance to try it out yourself in some of the exercises later.

Writing and Speaking in E-Prime

Although simple in principle, most people find it frustrat-ingly complex to put E-Prime into practice. We have already referred to the treatment of 'is'. In fact the process involves eliminating the *various* forms of the verb 'to be', such as *be, been, were, was, will be, am, are, is, being*, including those concealed by apostrophes (e.g. 'it's ridiculous').

In translating this book into E-Prime we have made excep-tions, however, such as when we quote from other sources. Whether in contemporary, everyday spoken language or old, familiar sayings ('To *be* or not to *be*, that *is* . . .'), we depend his-torically on the verb. In fact some of the NLP presuppositions you will meet, long predating E-Prime, use the verb 'to be'. So, in these limited cases, you will meet a few 'to be' words.

We hope you will appreciate the benefits of this enormous grammatical omission, and the clarity of meaning it has enforced. See whether you 'notice the join', and miss the 'to be' verb as you read on. If not, we have achieved our main pur-pose in removing the various pitfalls of the verb, whilst keep-ing the text readable. Better still, if you meet an unfamiliar way of expressing something that causes you to think more deeply about its meaning, it will have an even greater benefit. You may have fun spotting how we have managed to do away with the most-used verb in the English language. And you will proba-bly appreciate its significance more as you relate it to what you learn throughout the 21-day programme, especially the language chapters. In due course, you can have a go at speaking and writing in E-Prime yourself.

THE HIERARCHY OF IDEAS

We use words to express ideas or concepts, and we can make them specific or general, with a continuum in between. At one extreme we use very specific and detailed language, and at the other extreme we communicate in a vaguer, more general way. In NLP we use the Meta Model when wanting to elicit detailed, precise information. The Milton Model, by contrast, uses what in NLP we term 'artfully vague' language. Both models can achieve extraordinary communication results, but in very different ways. We will cover these in detail on Days 9 and 10.

Although you will learn about these two models, in practice the way we use language represents more of a continuum. In speaking and writing we keep moving along it, adopting different degrees of preciseness or vagueness. To change the analogy, we adopt a *hierarchy* of preciseness or vagueness, and operate within that hierarchy, depending on the purpose and circumstances of our communication.

Figure. 8.1 The language continuum

A high-level concept word or nominalisation, like 'honesty' (as in 'Jean values honesty'), has only a general meaning. But, depending on the context, you can usually break it down into more concrete ideas (like 'She tells the truth to her boss' or 'She speaks her mind'), and eventually to specific actions as examples of honesty. Thus we form a hierarchy under 'honest', which will extend to almost any level of detail, until we reach the 'deep structure' of meaning.

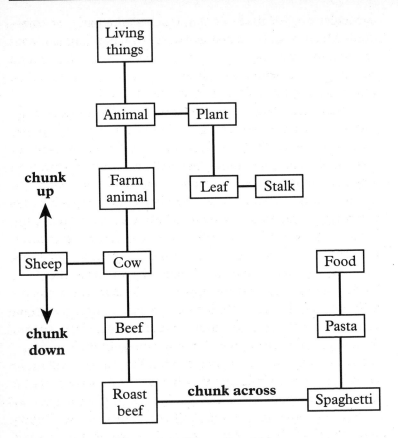

Figure 8.2 Hierarchy of ideas

Chunking

The hierarchy of ideas concerns the way we think and communicate in 'chunks' – big chunks (at a general or abstract level), or smaller chunks (to whatever level of detail we need). 'Chunking up' therefore involves lifting an idea to a higher, more general level. For example, instead of thinking of 'sheep' and 'cows', you can chunk up conceptually to 'farm animals', then further up to 'animals'. Chunking up further, you arrive at 'living things', and so on.

In the same way you can chunk a concept down. For instance, instead of talking of a dog, you might consider a particular dog, or part of a dog (such as the paw), or something which dogs do (such as barking). Chunking sideways or laterally, you stay on the same level. Thus dogs chunk laterally to cats, cows, kangaroos or any other mammals, of which they all form a lower chunk level.

Sometimes, when communicating, it helps to chunk up, and at other times you can get a better outcome by chunking down or laterally. Depending on your desired outcome or response, vague generalities may suffice. At other times you may need to deal in more detailed, specific information. On the one hand you want to 'see the big picture', or get a better perspective, and on the other hand you wish to 'focus on the detail'. Just as words can reflect our sensory preference, in the same way the words we use may also reflect the chunk sizes we use and where in a hierarchy of ideas they fall. Understanding language in this way will help you immediately in everyday communication. In negotiation or selling you will typically need flexibility within the whole spectrum, from vague to specific, big chunk to small chunk.

For example, in negotiating, by chunking up you will more likely gain agreement, even if only that 'Both parties want a mutually beneficial outcome', or that 'Both parties agree to a "fair" negotiation', or that 'All stand to gain by finding agreement', or that 'We all want to settle the matter as soon as possible'.

Then, by chunking down, you may isolate any obstacles to agreement, and the particular issue that needs addressing. This may hinge on a single clause in a contract, or it might turn out to involve, when isolated, a very minor concession. You may also need to chunk down when any plan or agreement needs implementing, as generalities will not suffice at this stage. Laterally, you might compare with another deal you have done, or an *example* of the particular issue under consideration.

You may need to use all three approaches, and each has its own language patterns. To chunk down, ask the question: 'What provides an example of that?' Keep repeating the question and see how far you can go. To chunk up, ask the question: 'What does that exemplify?' or 'What purpose does that have?' Again, see how far you can chunk up any word or concept. Laterally, 'What provides *another* example?' or 'How many can you think of?'

Just by *exploring* the issue within a hierarchy of ideas – the big picture, the significant detail – you will access more ideas and insights.

Let's imagine a typical business negotiation in which the parties have to agree on price, terms and conditions. How would chunking apply?

I'm sure we both want to conclude a mutually profitable deal. (up)

Let's spend some time on that retention clause. (down)

This formula worked well on the Saudi contract a couple of years ago. (sideways)

OK, can you spell out the remaining sticking points? (down)

We both want to get away for the weekend. (up)

How did you arrive at the £800? (down)

That's the way we have always worked with other suppliers. (sideways)

We both want this to go well. (up)

It seems we just have to agree on the scheduling, then a couple of minor things. (down)

What if we brought the second instalment forward in exchange for the 15%? (further down)

There's nothing either of us can do about the interest rate (up) but what if we cut part of the management fee? (down)

What if we get John to manage it personally? (down)

I'm sure we could start by the 20th if that will help your people. (down)

Chunking up can take attention off a difficult but minor issue and regain consensus, however generally. Chunking down can focus on the relative insignificance of the items left to negotiate. Whenever you risk losing rapport, chunking one way or the other will tend to restore the other party to a more consensual state of mind. Note also that we each have a pre-ferred approach – an eye for detail, or a broad-brush approach – so you can also direct your chunking to match the other party or parties. Don't forget the rapport skills you learnt on Days 4 and 5. As ever in NLP, what you have already learnt remains valid as you add new learning.

Uptime and Downtime

In using ideas and language we continually switch from the general to the particular. This suggests both a continuum (as in Figure 8.1) and a hierarchy (as in Figure 8.2). In an organisation hierarchy, you may not find a very marked dividing line between the people who manage and the people who actually do the work. 'Managers' and 'workers' do not slot into neat, black and white categories. In the same way the hierarchy of ideas involves a continuum of thinking and a whole network of relationships.

You have already seen how our thoughts represent things both from the present, external world of the here and now, and also from our inner world of memories and imagination. This also forms a thinking spectrum, or continuum. At one end of the spectrum we think and act with alertness and focus externally, as when in conversation with another person. At the other end we enter our own thoughts, daydreams and inner world of reality. The former we term uptime, and the latter downtime, of which dream sleep (or, in the extreme, a coma) provides an example.

We constantly move up and down this thinking spectrum. At one moment we relate to everything around us and respond very consciously to sensory representations. A moment later we may reflect on something, recalling a memory or imagining a future scenario and thus go into downtime. Even when driving a car or doing something that appears to require great concentration we can enter a down-time world of our own, running on 'autopilot' and relying on habitual, unconscious behaviour.

Miltonian vague language patterns, which we cover on Day 9, reflect downtime – associated with the state of trance. Meta Model language, on the other hand, covered on Day 10, *responds* to most of the Milton patterns, drawing out *specific meaning* and recovering some of the 'deep structure' of the language. This tends to bring us back to the here and now, and reflects the uptime end of the thinking spectrum. Much of the time, of course, we operate somewhere in between, partly aware of the world around us, yet preoccupied to some degree with our own thoughts.

Managing uptime and downtime means gaining better control over what we do and achieve. Sometimes we need to remain very alert and in uptime, using the 'sensory acuity' or 'noticing' skills we have already met. Listening skills, for example, involve a lot of uptime concentration. People often find such activities draining, as the conscious mind seems to work very hard. On other occasions we need to get into downtime, more associated with relaxation and usually more natural and enjoyable. In fact downtime mental processing does not seem like 'thinking' at all, such as when we daydream. In this mode we access our unconscious mind, the source of special insights and creativity. Today, and on Days 9 and 10, you will see how language and the uptime–downtime thinking continuum relate to each other.

NLP concerns choice. And the choice *to think what you want to think* has special importance. From this fundamental choice so many others follow. In particular, you can choose to *manage* your personal thinking spectrum, and to enter uptime or downtime whenever you wish. Part of that 'thinking management' involves language and how you use it.

TURNING WORDS INTO OUTCOMES

We know from the first presupposition, 'The map is not the territory', that we each construct different meanings or representations about the world in which we live. That includes what people say to us and what we read. Yet, even when we take the trouble to choose our words carefully, language still offers a very crude tool to convey thoughts and ideas. This applies especially to abstract words (or what we call 'nominalisations').

Searching for Meaning

Take a simple statement like 'Lorna is a very intelligent child'. (Notice the ubiquitous 'to be' verb which 'labels' Lorna.) To understand the meaning of this statement we need to know precisely what 'intelligent' means. So we check it in the dictionary. Under *intelligent*, we get referred to the noun *intelligence* and its various meanings – *wisdom, capacity, comprehension, understanding, intellect, reason* and so on. We also find words like *news, information* and *report* and quickly realise this means 'intelligence' as in MI5 and spies. So we can safely ignore those references.

But the other words present a problem. Take *comprehension*, for example. We really need to check the meaning of this word as well. We then find the words *understand* and *know*. We met the word *understanding* earlier, so it might pay to check on that one. Not surprisingly *know* turns up, but also words like *intelligible* which means we have got back to where we started, more confused than enlightened. A final check on *know* takes us into *belief* (and I don't think that covers Lorna's description, but can't say for certain now), and *friendship* and *association* which presumably relate to knowing someone such as a work colleague.

So much for using a word like 'intelligence' precisely, by understanding its dictionary definition. But just about any abstract word will throw up the same problems when we try to tie it down to a specific meaning. At best we get back to where we started, and at worst finish up going round in circles. This highlights the limitations of symbols (in this case words) in conveying thoughts and ideas.

Paradoxically, communicating in language (with all its

unique benefits to humankind), adds a further thick barrier between external reality (what precisely Lorna said or did) and what registered as understanding on the neocortex of the hearer as Lorna's 'label'. But, however flawed, language remains the best tool of communication we've got and places us at the pinnacle of intelligent life. So aim to get language on your side. Understand its character and limitations, and use it as a sculptor uses a favourite chisel to produce something worthwhile.

Choosing the Right Words

Note that we have used abstract words or nominalisations, like 'intelligence', to illustrate these language limitations. Not all words give us the same trouble. Verbs, or certain verbs, get us a lot nearer to deeper meaning.

Sensory verbs

For instance, a sentence like 'Brian cut the cake into four pieces' doesn't send us running for the dictionary. We can *imagine* 'Brian', 'cutting' and 'cake', converting the words into sensory representations. In other words we can 'see ourselves' or others doing the thing so that it (literally) *makes sense.*

As we have already discovered, we don't see and hear so much with our eyes and ears as with our minds, where electro-chemical changes translate sensory inputs into meaning. The precise super-camera we call the eye, or the triple wizardry of the inner ear, do not directly create feelings. But the *electro-chemical* changes in the brain, once the sights and sounds register, certainly do, just as if we had pressed a light switch or swallowed Prozac. Action verbs tend to create vivid mental pictures, rather than hazy abstractions.

Let's go back to Lorna. A few statements about Lorna will tell us what she does or can do. She can do long multiplication; she has a bronze medal for swimming; she can cook an omelette, for example. With this basic information we can understand her better. We can then *choose* to call her 'intelligent', or whatever, or not risk using a label at all. We still understand Lorna imperfectly, however, and in practice words can never convey the full meaning lodged in the 'deep structure' – the neural networks of a human brain.

So, what could go wrong with the straightforward statement 'Brian cut the cake into four pieces'? Well, Brian might 'be' a sea lion, cutting a four-foot cake of peat with a chainsaw or laser-cutter. So we can still create the wrong mental picture, however vivid and sensory the verbs help to make it.

Now try saying the statement out loud, *emphasising* different words in turn – *Brian, cut, cake, four*. Notice the different meanings this allows you to convey, beyond the words themselves, such as, '*Brian* [not John or Peter] cut the cake' or 'Brian *cut* [not made or ate] the cake'. Hence the importance of the way we use words and the deep structure upon which we base them.

For effective communication, we need enough words to give us meaning. But we don't need so many that we get bogged down with too much deep structure (which could render all normal communication impossible).

Hierarchies of verbs

Although more 'concrete' than abstract nominalisations, verbs vary a lot in the preciseness of their meaning, forming their own hierarchy of preciseness or vagueness. The verbs 'travel', 'imagine', or 'have', for instance (sometimes as vague as abstract nouns), may beg a lot of questions. For instance, 'He has travelled widely' does not tell us much about the nature of his travel. On the other hand, 'He once rode a bike from Paris to Calais, whistling and waving his arms' uses more sensory verbs to make the meaning clearer. So, under such a verb hierarchy, 'travel' will support 'walk' which will in turn support 'stroll', 'saunter', 'march', 'hike', 'ramble' and 'stride'. Then we can march quickly or slowly, and take a long or short hike. This illustrates the language continuum

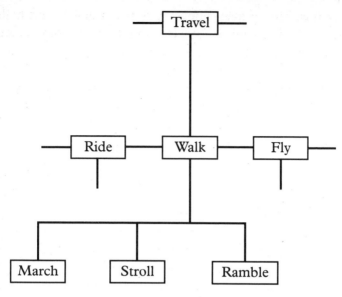

Figure 8.3 Hierarchy of verbs

between big and small chunk, and between Milton language vagueness and Meta Model precision.

As a rule, 'doing' words associate with the precise, specific end of language and small chunks, whereas abstract words or nominalisations associate more with high-level generalisations or big chunks. We can therefore describe a nominalisation as a doing-word turned into a noun, for example:

relate (v)	relationship (n)
communicate (v)	communication (n)
love (v)	love (n)
respect (v)	respect (n)

To be or not to be?

We have already seen the special significance of the verb 'to be', as we used it in 'Lorna *is* a very intelligent child'. The use of the verb 'to be' seems to throw up as many problems in understanding as the use of abstract nouns. You can easily

check this. Find a magazine or newspaper article and high-
light uses of the verb 'to be'. Remember all the tenses, and
the singular and plural uses – *be, was, were, been, will be, am,
are, being* (not forgetting apostrophes, as in 'she isn't').

Now *reword* those sentences to exclude the 'to be' verb in
any way you can, attempting to maintain the full meaning.
You will find some easy. 'She was lonely' might become 'She
felt lonely'. 'He is a fast walker' becomes 'He walks fast', or
'He usually walks fast'. In particular, the passive voice,
disliked in any case by many journalists and fiction writers,
disappears. Some you will not find so easy. On the one hand
you will have to think outside a very familiar pattern of
words. But you will also raise questions of real meaning by
removing the offending language. For example, *was* she
always lonely? What does the speaker mean by 'lonely' – what
does she *do*, how does she *feel*, what *happens*? Would she agree
with the 'lonely' description, or does it just tell us what somebody else thinks?

Deletions, generalisations and distortions

A nominalisation or 'to be' word provides 'surface' understanding. Replacing the 'to be' verb usually raises questions
about the deeper structure of meaning. Specifically, it
identifies the ubiquitous deletions, generalisations and distortions in our everyday language.

The brain deletes, generalises and distorts as it filters the
vast amount of input that would otherwise overload it. You
met this in the NLP model on Day 1. As a linguistic process,
it provides us with a vital survival strategy. Our conscious
mind registers a tiny percentage of the million and one bits
of information impacting on it at any moment, yet salvages
enough information to survive.

At the same time, however, all this provides a recipe for
misunderstanding and miscommunication between people.
Everyone's private sample of 'reality' differs. As we have
already seen, 'The map is not the territory.' Any individual
can only perceive a minute part of the story. This realisation

typically creates curiosity about other people's maps, and – we hope – a new tolerance of difference. If we accepted that none of us could claim 'totally rightness', much of the conflict in the world would disappear.

Now that you have this background knowledge of language, you can start to learn patterns from both ends of the language continuum. The Milton Model (covered on Day 9) allows you to use vague language purposefully. And the Meta Model (covered on Day 10) enables you to recognise and respond to common language patterns in order to get more precise understanding. Both provide powerful tools in your NLP armoury to make you a better communicator and goal achiever.

PRESUPPOSITION FOR TODAY

> **People make the best choices available to them.**

Making choices comes naturally to human beings as part of our inbuilt tendency to achieve goals, or to have a purpose. The flexible approach of the four-stage success model (see Day 2) assumes more than one way of doing something, or more than one viewpoint on any problem, behaviour or situation. So, inevitably, we have choices. NLP also says, 'Choice is better than no choice.'

Generally, the more choices you have, the more you can control a situation and bring about your desired outcomes. But you can only choose within your present knowledge and resources – if you like, according to your own map of reality. Other people's behaviour can therefore seem strange or misplaced from where you view it. However, *their* behaviour probably reflects the best choice available to *them* at the time from their personal vantage point. You can then change behaviour, your own and other people's, by identifying more and better choices.

TODAY'S TO DOs

- Experiment with chunking, following the examples given. See how far you can chunk up any word or concept. You can do this on your own, jotting down the words that come to mind and so forming hierarchies of language. Otherwise, get a patient friend to help you. This exercise will give you linguistic fluency and the ability to understand how different chunk levels fit different situations.

- Think of a word that seems to fit a person you know well – such as 'self-confident', 'loyal', or whatever. Then write down some statements about the person: what they actually say or do, using action verbs. Then check whether the abstract word reflects reality – whether it represents the right 'label'.

- If you did not do the exercise earlier, find a magazine or newspaper article and remove all the 'to be' words you can find. Note how the prose changes and any questions that the exercise raises about the exact meaning. (See pp. 126–7.)

- Take a paragraph or two from any book or magazine and E-Prime it – remove all references to *be, been, were, was, will be, am, are, is* and *being*, while keeping the meaning clear. Experiment with different ways to express the meaning you think the writer wanted to express. You can do the same exercise with your own writing, such as a report or article, and you may find it produces clearer, more readable language. In fact it may change your thinking.

DAY 9

The Value of Vague Language

This chapter covers:
- **Milton language patterns**
- **Rapport and utilisation**
- **Using the patterns**

'Have you got the time?' A closed question like this one grammatically invites only a yes or no answer. Yet in practice it invariably elicits the time – the outcome or intention, no doubt, of the wrongly worded question. Interestingly, it usually gets a better response than the more precise 'Would you please tell me the time?'

Likewise, 'Can you move to the left a bit?' produces a similar action response, instead of the yes or no answer it literally requests. And how many times has a salesperson got an appointment by asking 'Shall we make it Thursday or would you prefer earlier in the week?' The customer tends to focus on the apparent choice, when they really didn't want to commit to any date.

These common examples illustrate the way vague or general language can bring about successful outcomes in situations where more precise, correct language might fail. Often, we use such language patterns, unaware of their linguistic vagueness but instinctively aware of the likely response they will get. Today we will consider a range of such language patterns that you can use *purposefully* (or deliberately) to bring about communication outcomes.

The Milton Model comprises language patterns that Richard Bandler and John Grinder, the founders of NLP, modelled from Milton Erickson, probably the most successful hypnotherapist of all time. Erickson used what he termed 'artfully vague' language patterns to communicate more effectively.

As we have seen, we use language in many different ways to achieve a communication outcome. Sometimes we have to get across detail and specific meaning. At other times, general or abstract language fulfils our need. For example, if you want a person to use their own imagination rather than direct them specifically, the less you direct their thinking the better. Or you may want to appeal to their emotions rather than their reason. In other cases you may wish to bypass objections by not dwelling on specifics, or by deliberately omitting what has no part in the desired outcome of your communication. You can also use this kind of language to pace and lead a person's reality, as on Day 5. Milton language engages or distracts the conscious mind, allowing access to the unconscious mind and all its resources.

Although these patterns turn up all the time in everyday language, Milton Erickson used them to induce trance in his patients. But we all spend much of our time in trance, or 'downtime', and trance has its uses well beyond hypnotherapy, such as accessing your unconscious mind, described on Day 3. It also forms part of the 'right-brain' approach to creativity, problem solving, memory improvement and much more. Due to the origin of the language patterns, some of today's examples refer to trance induction in a therapeutic situation. But you can use the patterns in everyday communication, especially to leapfrog the conscious mind in order to avoid objections and achieve a desired communication outcome.

MILTON LANGUAGE PATTERNS

What language patterns do you need to recognise? We have listed some patterns below, with examples of how to use them. Don't let the titles put you off – some may sound very technical. You might prefer to invent your own names for the ones that give you trouble. Otherwise, concentrate more on the patterns themselves, which you will no doubt hear examples of in your professional and day-to-day life. You will find the language patterns both relevant and useful. We have left some 'to be' words in the actual patterns as they reflect actual spoken language usage. They also add to the vagueness, so in this case they have a positive role to play.

On Day 10 you will learn how to question these patterns and obtain specific information. You will thus have language tools that you can use both vaguely and specifically, depending on your purpose, or desired communication outcome.

Mind Reading

Claiming to know the thoughts or feelings of another without specifying the process by which you came to know the information, e.g. 'I know that you are wondering . . .'

Lost Performative

Value judgements, omitting the performer or holder of the value judgement, e.g. 'And it's good to remember . . .'

Cause and Effect

The implication that one thing causes another. We commonly use implied cause and effect statements, such as 'If . . . then . . .', 'As you . . . then you . . .'. Other cause–effect words include 'because' and 'make'. We often accept cause and effect statements without questioning the logical relationship.

Complex Equivalence

When two things have equivalent meanings, e.g. 'You are old. You can't relate to young children.' Or, 'You've been going for hours. You must be tired.' One thing *means* something else.

Presuppositions

The linguistic equivalent of assumptions. 'You are learning a lot . . .'. You assume the presupposition true. We cover these in more detail on pp. 141–3.

Universal Quantifiers

A set of words which have a universal or absolute character (see p. 139). 'And *all* the employees . . .', or 'You will *never* . . .'.

Modal Operators

Words which imply possibility or necessity, and which form our rules in life. 'You *can* learn . . .' (possibility). 'You *must* come . . .' (necessity). 'You *should* learn . . .' (implied necessity). Parental or educational conditioning tends to reinforce modal operators of necessity, e.g. you must, you need to, etc.

Nominalisations

Process words which have frozen in time thus turning into nouns, e.g. '. . . provide you with new *understandings*.' (Meaning: 'You will understand [verb]'). Credible, respectable words like education, independence, respect, relationship, insight, may fall into this common category. Attempting to define nominalisations using a dictionary soon indicates their potential for vague, but purposeful communication.

Unspecified Verbs

'And you can . . .' The process word (verb) lacks a complete description. What, how or when you can remains unspecified.

Tag Question

A question added after a statement, designed to displace resistance, e.g. 'Can you not?'

Lack of Referential Index

A phrase which does not identify who or what the speaker refers to, e.g. 'One should, you know.'

Comparative Deletions (Unspecified Comparison)

Where the comparison has no attribution – you do not know what or who it relates to, e.g. 'And it's more or less the right thing.' Or, 'That's not so bad.'

Pacing Current Experience

Where you describe the person's experience (verifiable, external) in an undeniable way, e.g. 'You are sitting here, listening to me, looking at me.' This simple device can help to create rapport.

Double Binds

This pattern creates the 'illusion of choice', e.g. 'Would you prefer to make that change now or simply let it happen as we talk?' Or, 'Your unconscious mind is learning something else and I don't know whether you'll discover just what you've learnt . . . now, in a few moments from now, or some time later . . .'. In the first illustration the attention focuses on the presupposed *choice* (now or later), not questioning the presupposition (to change). In the second illustration the attention focuses on when you will discover what you have learnt, not questioning the presupposition that you will learn something else.

Conversational Postulate

The communication takes the form of a question, inviting either a 'yes' or a 'no' response. It allows you to choose to respond or not and avoids authoritarianism, e.g. 'Could you just look up for a moment?' Or 'Can you move a little to the left?' We tend to look up or move to the left, rather than answer yes or no.

Extended Quotes

'Last week I talked to Tony who told me about the exhibition in Birmingham when he talked to someone who said . . .'. A series of contexts called 'chaining' tends to overload the conscious mind and dissociate the speaker from what he or she says. As well as depersonalising a communication, a quote can have an impact out of all proportion to its 'pedigree', as public speakers and other influencers know well. And 'chaining' quotes and anecdotes can enhance this effect.

Selectional Restriction Violation

A badly conceived, illogical statement that does not make sense, e.g. 'A chair can have feelings.' (Only humans and animals can have feelings.)

Ambiguities

Phonological
Juxtaposing *homonyms* (e.g. 'Hear', 'Here') can cause confusion and direct attention unconsciously to the out-of-context meaning (i.e. 'Hear, hear' used after a speech).

Syntactic

When you cannot determine the function (syntactic) of the word in a sentence from the immediate context, e.g. 'They are visiting relatives' ('Visiting' – a verb or an adjective?). Or, 'They are training consultants' (Training – a verb or an adjective?).

Scope

When you cannot determine by linguistic context how much one portion of a sentence applies to another portion, e.g. 'Speaking to you as a child . . .' (Who does 'as a child' refer to? The speaker or hearer?). Or, 'The disturbing noises and thoughts . . .' (To which does 'disturbing' relate?).

Punctuation

(a) Run-on sentences:

' . . . want you to notice your/hand/me the glass'

'Notice your watch/what/you are doing'.

(b) Pauses: 'So you are feeling . . . better now?

(c) Incomplete sentences: 'So you are . . . If you can change that, then perhaps . . .'.

Utilisation

Using spoken words or immediate happenings around in your communication, e.g. '. . . and the sound of the traffic in the distance . . .'.

You will find some of these Milton patterns self-explanatory. Others need further explanation and examples. Some do not constitute 'proper grammar' but this usually goes unnoticed in speech and need not reduce the effect of a communication. We discuss some of the patterns below and apply them to situations you will easily recognise. But first, we need to remind ourselves of some basic communication principles and add a few practical tips that will help when using the patterns.

RAPPORT AND UTILISATION

To take a person into trance or 'downtime' using Milton language patterns, it helps to have good rapport. Everything you have learnt so far about communication still applies. The process requires you to *pace a person's reality*. That means understanding, respecting and matching. You have already met the idea of matching experience to gain rapport (see Day 4). 'Purposely vague' language patterns encourage a person's agreement. 'Chunking up' to general or abstract thoughts, you will recall, did a similar job in negotiation (see p. 120). Once relaxed and in rapport, a person will tend to follow your lead. In some cases the patterns themselves help rapport. In other cases you will need to establish and maintain rapport in the way you have already learnt.

For instance, you can use your pacing skills (see Day 5) to pace the person's 'reality'. Utilise anything going on around you. For example, you can weave an otherwise disturbing sound, such as a door slamming in the background, into what you say. 'As you hear the slamming of distant doors and the traffic noise far in the distance, consider . . .'. This helps to induce or deepen trance.

In the same way you can often utilise words the person has used themselves to reflect their reality and similarly deepen trance. 'That's right, your mind seems to wander, and as you think about . . .'. Or, in a business meeting, 'I think that's John coming back [hearing car approach or door close]. We can agree on this before he joins us at two.' We call this technique *utilisation* because you make use of any current experience in your communication.

The language patterns above tend to induce 'downtime' or trance, an altered state in which a person operates more from their unconscious mind. Such patterns tend to bypass the conscious mind and allow the person to go 'inside'. A presupposition that would not stand logical scrutiny may thus gain immediate acceptance. In some cases you can access an empowering memory experience and any learning that it will provide. Appealing to the unconscious, the language may 'leapfrog' rational objections and obstacles to the communication. Thus, in some situations, you can bring about an outcome not possible with precise, 'uptime' language.

As we have seen, language covers a continuum and you will hear many applications of Milton language in everyday situations not usually associated with trance. We have already referred, for instance, to chunking up in negotiation, which tends towards generality or sometimes vagueness. We all experience light trance on a day-to-day or even moment-to-moment basis when preoccupied or daydreaming. You will find this a receptive state for some forms of communication. Children quickly enter a trancelike state, when addressed in 'Are you sitting comfortably? Once upon a time . . .' language. Adults, similarly, respond readily to anecdotes, metaphors, quotes, presuppositions, and the vaguest of language. Again, as we have seen, the communication response or outcome takes precedence over the language or medium. Hypnosis relies on a deeper state of trance but follows the way the mind works naturally.

Because a Milton statement omits specific detail, the conscious mind, in order to make sense of the statement, has to draw on resources stored in the unconscious mind. In searching for meaning, the unconscious mind 'scans' the memory and accesses options unavailable at a conscious level. Remember that most of our 'thinking' takes place at the unconscious level. Sometimes change will only come in this way, as a person finds new and highly creative solutions to specific problems. Language just stimulates existing mental resources.

Once familiar with Milton language patterns, you will start to notice them everywhere. Advertising firms, for example, frequently employ these sorts of language devices in their slogans. Politicians, preachers and inspirational speakers all use their own versions of hypnotic or 'artfully vague' language, even though they may not *intentionally* create a trance-like state in their audience. In fact this language skill might account for much of their success as communicators. Their messages go straight to the unconscious mind and affect people's behaviour without the barrier of the conscious mind.

USING THE PATTERNS

We discuss some of the more popular patterns below, giving examples of how you can use them for better communication.

Cause and Effect and Complex Equivalence

Sometimes these overlap. Cause and effect, however, has a time implication – effect follows cause in time. In the case of a complex equivalence, the equivalence exists in parallel or concurrently.

For example: 'She makes me laugh', 'He is driving me to drink' and 'Poetry inspires me' all deal with cause and effect. In other words, A causes B, and B follows A.

However, 'She turns up late, so she must be disorganised', 'She smokes, so she can't be health-conscious' and 'He must be clever, he got an A grade' all deal with something having equivalence to, or meaning something else. Note that 'be' or 'is' implies *total* identity. You can communicate equivalence, if useful for your communication outcome, using these artfully vague language patterns.

Universal Quantifiers

A whole range of 'universal' words suggest this pattern – 'all', 'every', 'none', 'nothing', 'no one', 'nobody', 'never', 'ever'. These words give no room for exceptions, however inaccurate the implication, e.g. 'You *always* say that' or 'You *never* appreciate what I do.' Because the pattern usually contains one of this shortlist of 'universals' you will easily spot it.

However, sometimes a universal quantifier *implies* universality even when we do not use the actual words. For example, 'Teenagers are lazy' implies or could certainly suggest that *all* teenagers 'are' (a 'to be' verb 'identifier') lazy. 'Fast driving kills' provides another example. These imply a universally true statement. Thus, deliberately vague language can bring about a worthwhile outcome (in the above case, not to drive fast).

These implied universals come in many shapes and sizes. They may not actually involve 'universal' words, so you will need more skill to recognise them. By the same token, when you use them 'deliberately vaguely', the more you can conceal the language pattern, the better. To fulfil your purpose you need to make the statement appear to stand up to logical analysis. For example, the statement 'Achieving budget means promotion' might well motivate a junior salesperson. (Did you also spot the complex equivalence? In fact, one phrase may comprise several Milton patterns.) On the other hand, 'Achieving budget *always* means promotion' might not stand up to logical analysis. It might therefore set off alarm bells, failing to convince and motivate.

In general, you may well find that a statement incorporating a presupposition or implication avoids an otherwise negative response and loss of rapport. Thus you can bring about your communication outcome without objections.

In fact, you can use both *expressed* and *implied* universality as a powerful communication tactic. For example:

'We *all* win'
'*Nobody* loses'
'It *always* works'
'It happens *every* time'
'You can't [implying *ever*] fail'
'*Everybody* can do it'
'Japanese cars [implying *all*] are reliable'

and so on. *Purposeful* generalisation or vagueness, often a description of Milton patterns, can thus bring about your communication outcome. The *outcome*, of course, rather than the language used (or the process), determines effectiveness. Or, in terms of the communication presupposition you have already met, 'The meaning of a communication is the response it gets'.

Presuppositions

Language abounds with presuppositions and in practice we could hardly carry on ordinary communication without presupposing all sorts of things. We can use them more positively, however, for more effective communication. We use surface-level language all the time, essential for 'economical' everyday language and 'getting things done'. In a similar way presuppositions, as well as making for grammatical economy, help us to get things done – achieve outcomes.

First you need to spot them, and what they mean – what the speaker or writer presupposes. For example:

'When you give this more thought you will agree.' (presupposes that you have already given it some thought)
'Jean telephones me every week.' (presupposes you don't telephone enough)
'You are as stubborn as Fiona.' (presupposes Fiona is stubborn)
'At least he did his best.' (presupposes not good enough)
'Eli flapped his wings.' (presupposes Eli is a bird or winged object or being)

Note that a single statement may contain several presuppositions. In the last case, for example: Eli had wings to flap; he owned them; he had two or more wings; he belonged to the male gender; and so on. The more presuppositions you can embody in a communication, the greater the possibility of achieving your outcome by artful vagueness. You can also incorporate (or watch out for, if receiving a communication) other Milton patterns in the same statement. For instance, whose wings did he flap? Does the statement refer to a man-made flying contraption, an insect, or an angel? Did he flap once or continuously? On terra firma or in the sky (ambiguities *if not presupposed*)?

We will cover this further on Day 10. For the moment, check through a magazine or newspaper article and see how many presuppositions you can spot. Once familiar with their universal power in language, you can begin to use presuppositions deliberately, as part of a communication strategy. Similarly, when receiving a communication, recognising a presupposition allows you to question for further specific meaning, as we shall learn from the Meta Model on Day 10.

When you use presuppositions skilfully your listeners or readers tend to accept the presupposition in order to make sense of the sentence. Bypassing resistance in this way enables you to jump several rungs of the ladder towards your communication outcome. Often the specifics or deep meaning do not add to the purpose of the communication in any event, and might in fact obscure it. So, paradoxically, your vague language has a greater effect. Milton language enhances this effectiveness by addressing the unconscious mind, especially when your desired outcome involves a change in attitude or long-standing behaviour.

A sales manager on our practitioner training admitted he had trouble with his monthly sales meeting. His sales team did not enjoy the meeting and he could not work out how to improve it. After learning the Milton Model on the NLP training programme, he returned to work and ran his most successful meeting ever, with excellent feedback from his team. A colleague of ours attended that meeting and reported that the sales manager had used 'pure Milton language'.

This kind of language, comprising the patterns listed above, tends to relax the listener, encourages creative thinking and influences at a much deeper level than more rational, specific language. People often look on trance with suspicion, believing they will 'lose control' or that someone else has taken charge. However, hypnosis really means *self*-hypnosis, in the sense that people only go into trance when willing to do so. Although influenced by the language, they will only make decisions or act in line with their own values and desires. When achieving outcomes by using Milton language, bear in mind the need for ecology. Check back if you need to. Win–lose communications, such as may happen in negotiation or selling, at best give short-term advantages, and can end up spoiling relationships.

PRESUPPOSITION FOR TODAY

People work perfectly.

The human neuro-physiological system operates as a truly awesome resource. In fact it works *perfectly*. As it happens, we have a choice as to what outcomes we programme into this cybernetic, goal-seeking system. But the system works just as well whatever the inputs. Even when we witness socially or morally imperfect behaviour we can usually detect some inner positive intention (or meaning) efficiently carried out in the form of the person's behaviour.

The system does not differentiate between a conscious or unconscious intent; it just needs a target or purpose. And it operates as impressively as it does in carrying out inbuilt body functions like temperature control and breathing. You and I may not understand another person's map of the world, but it nevertheless comprises that person's best perception, and reflects their resources of knowledge and experience. *Given their outcomes*, it serves them well. In every case people work perfectly.

TODAY'S TO DOs

- Listen for examples of Milton language patterns today. To start with, you don't need to put them in the right category and remember the labels. Rather, just begin to spot examples similar to the ones given above. We suggest that you start with only a few patterns, so that you can focus your learning better. And start with the easy ones, building on existing skills and knowledge rather than stretching yourself too far too fast.

  For example, you will recognise universal quantifiers by the all-inclusive words (or 'universals') used, like 'never', 'always', 'every', 'all'. Or you might listen for cause and effect or complex equivalence examples – situations where you might ask, 'Does that really mean this?' or 'Does this follow from that?' Choose other patterns that take your fancy, or that you think work colleagues will unknowingly adopt. Don't *speak* the patterns at this early stage. You have done well simply to recognise them.

- Look through magazine advertisements for Milton language patterns. Extend this to a couple of paragraphs of an article or other piece of prose. You may miss patterns the first time through, so you will need to check carefully.

- Experiment with more leading in your rapport work. Check back on pacing and leading (see Day 5) if you need to.

- If you did not do this earlier, find a magazine or newspaper article of a few paragraphs and see how many presuppositions you can spot. Almost certainly, the first run-through will not capture all of them, so you will have to go through the piece more than once.

Remember, as explained above, that a single statement may contain several presuppositions. Again, notice any kinds of written material which seem particularly heavy or light on presuppositions.

- Think about today's presupposition and list all your resources, inner attributes, values and latent capabilities as well as more visible ones. Then think about changes you would like to make in your life and how you can utilise your personal resources to bring them about.

DAY 10

Getting Down To Specifics

This chapter covers:

- **The Meta Model – deep structure and surface structure**
- **Meta Model questions**
- **Using the questions**
- **Applications for change**

The Meta Model comprises language patterns first identified by Bandler and Grinder, the co-founders of NLP, based on modelling Virginia Satir, an outstanding family therapist. Satir had a certain way of gathering information, using language to clarify language in order to reconnect the words people use with their experience. In terms of what you learnt on Day 9, the Meta Model *recovers* the lost meaning in the Milton language. It reflects the other side of the language coin, or the other end of the general–specific continuum. Now established as an important element of NLP, the Meta Model can help clarify both our language and our thinking.

You can use the Meta Model to gain a more accurate understanding of other people's 'maps'. It probes the 'deep structure' of language, by questioning the 'surface structure'(or the language we use in ordinary communication).

THE META MODEL – DEEP STRUCTURE AND SURFACE STRUCTURE

To understand the Meta Model we first need to look at how thoughts translate into words. Our thoughts encapsulate infinitely more meaning than language can ever express. Yet even given this limitation, language does exist at a deep level in our neurology and, when necessary, can express considerable detail which lies behind what we say. We term language accessed at this deep level, 'deep structure'.

In everyday life, however, our language does not reach this deep level. We effectively précis language into 'surface structure'. The sentence 'Lorna is a very intelligent child' illustrates surface language. All the additional information about Lorna and her intelligence (in what way, compared with whom, who says so? etc) forms the deep structure of the surface statement, before any deletions, distortions or generalisations. In the same way that we filter the mass of information taken in by our senses, we create surface structure from deep structure by continuously distorting, deleting and generalising language.

The Meta Model categorises common language patterns into these three main types: deletions, generalisations and distortions. It then gives standard responses in the form of questions that help to elicit the deeper meaning behind the words used.

All our sensory representations (not just language) involve short cuts, approximations and 'sensory guesses' (in other words, the generalisations, distortions and deletions or omissions). The Meta Model 'responses', which you will meet today, address most of the Milton patterns you met on Day 9. Specifically, Meta Model responses or questions:

- Expose generalities
- Reveal ambiguity
- Recover deletions
- Correct distortions

- Clarify vagueness
- Elicit specific meaning
- Induce conscious 'uptime'
- Recover the 'deep structure' of the language

Figure 10.1 simplifies this language distinction. All the time, when communicating, we generalise, distort and delete in order to bring to the surface different levels of meaning.

The idea of distortion and deletion need not suggest anything sinister. In fact this process, both useful and necessary,

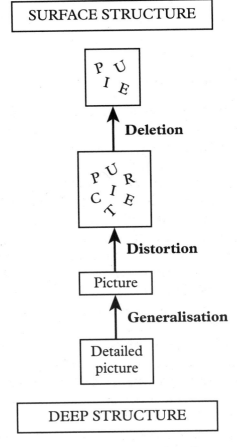

Figure 10.1 Deep structure and surface structure

enables us to handle the vast amount of information potentially available to our brains at any given moment. We tend to use language intuitively, naturally 'releasing' only what seems right in the context and for the purpose of our communication. In fact we do most things (not just communications) habitually and 'without thinking'.

Individual differences abound, of course. For instance, a talkative, communicative person will tend to provide a lot more of the deep structure than a non-talkative person, more at home with monosyllables. But even the non-stop talker only utilises a small fraction of the information theoretically 'available' for any communication. So everyone uses generalisation, deletion and distortion, and the Meta Model helps us recover the meaning lost in this universal filtering process.

Language Short Cuts

In the vast majority of situations a statement like 'Mary had an accident and will take sick leave for a couple of weeks' will form an acceptable 'surface level' communication, especially in a work context. Indeed, if the listener receives all the information the informer has about Mary, they will soon find themselves overloaded, if not bored or annoyed, e.g. 'Mary, a 27-year-old wife and mother of two children named . . . who grew up in . . . Her toe was in plaster for three weeks and a day . . .' and so on and on. For a typical everyday 'surface level' communication we have megabytes of back-up information (deep structure). But we *assume* (albeit not necessarily consciously) that we do not need it for the purpose of the communication. So we omit it, or lump it together in a few general words.

In different situations, however, you might need far *more* information. This will depend on the *understanding* you want to get across to the other person – the *purpose* of your communication. For instance, in the case of Mary, you may wish to communicate from a medical point of view, from the point of view of sickness benefits, or from the point of view of arranging office back-up cover. In each case you will draw on the detail of deep structure language to say specifically what you want to say, depending on the desired outcome of your communication – what you want to achieve.

However, we sometimes use shorthand or surface structure regardless of the needs of the parties involved. These short cuts again take the form of generalisations, deletions and distortions, illustrated by the Milton Model (covered on Day 9).

Under these circumstances, we can easily misunderstand even apparently straightforward messages. This happens as often in a family or social situation as in a company or an organisation. In effect, we *overdo* the short cut, convinced that the other person 'should have known', 'did not listen', 'must have realised', etc. We assume that the person's perceptual 'map' mirrors our own, and therefore do not see the need to spell things out. All too soon, however, we realise that we cannot mind-read and that our maps do indeed differ.

The Meta Model takes the form of a series of questions that seek to reverse and unravel the deletions, distortions and generalisations inherent in all normal language. A lot of meaning tends to disappear somewhere in the journey from thought to language, from deep structure to surface structure. The Meta Model questions can recover and clarify this missing or suspect information. The remaining language will more closely reflect 'what was in the person's mind', and allow better communication and mutual understanding.

The specifics of Meta Model language tend to involve the 'uptime' end of the thinking spectrum. However, you can also use the Meta Model to tap into *unconscious* resources but in a different way to Milton language. Meta Model questioning can access the unconscious level of the mind where it *translates* deep structure into conscious meaning and purposeful, rational behaviour. In effect it *trawls* the unconscious mind for specifics relevant to what you want to understand.

So where the nature of your communication requires more external 'uptime' focus and alertness, the Meta Model will help.

Use each language tool to fit the need. Sometimes, for instance, you need to incubate a situation for unconscious processing. In this case you need to *bypass* the conscious mind. The 'artfully vague' Milton patterns (covered on Day 9) will do the job. At other times you need to act with alertness and logic, and the Meta Model patterns stimulate this.

We saw, on Days 6 and 7, that a person's way of internally representing things in terms of modalities and submodalities reflects their whole identity and personality. Similarly, the way we each use and respond to language opens up another area in which we can match personalities and merge our mental maps. As you begin to recognise the linguistic generalisations, distortions and deletions a person habitually uses, you will get to know their unique mental map of the world – their reality. This process can therefore create rapport in any communication, and in turn the sort of long-term relationship that depends on a 'coming together of minds'. Quite simply, the better you understand the other person's map, the better your communication.

It follows that, if communication outcomes form part of your hierarchy of goals, you will start to get what you want and live the kind of life you aspire to. If your desired outcomes don't include communication ones, you will still need communication *skills*, such as the Meta Model, to achieve your outcomes *through* people. As with the Milton Model, you need to familiarise yourself with Meta Model language patterns so that you can eventually use them with unconscious competence.

META MODEL QUESTIONS

For each Milton Model language pattern, we suggest a question or comment that will recover the 'deep' meaning. We refer to these fairly standardised questions as Meta Model responses. You will probably think of other responses as you become familiar with the process. The more specifics you can elicit, the more 'deep structure' meaning you will reveal.

Distortions

Mind reading
'You don't like me.'
How do you know that I don't like you?

Lost performative
'It's wrong to criticise.'
How do you know it's wrong?
According to whom?
Who says it's wrong?

Cause and effect
'You make me angry.'
How does what I'm doing cause you to choose to feel angry?

Complex equivalence
'You're always shouting at me – you don't care about me!'
How does shouting at you mean I don't care?
Have you ever shouted at someone you care about?

Presuppositions
'If my boss knew how overworked I was, he wouldn't ask me.'
How do you know he doesn't know?
How do you know you're overworked?

Generalisations

Universal quantifiers
'She never listens to me.'
Never?
What would happen if she did?

Modal operators of necessity
Words to watch for: 'should', 'shouldn't', 'must', 'must not', 'have to', 'need to', 'it's necessary':
'I have to finish this tonight.'
What would happen if you didn't?

Modal operators of possibility
Words to watch for: 'can', 'can't', 'will', 'won't', 'may', 'may not', 'possible', 'impossible':
'I will not pass this exam.'
What will prevent you passing it?
What would happen if you did pass?

Nominalisations
'Communication around here is non-existent.'
Who fails to communicate with whom?
What do you want to communicate?

Unspecified verbs
'He hurt me.'
How, specifically, did he hurt you?

Simple deletions
'I'm fed up.'
With whom? About what?

Lack of referential index
'They don't care.'
Who, specifically, doesn't care?

Comparative deletions
Words to watch for: 'good', 'better', 'more', 'less', 'most', 'least', 'worse', 'worst':
'He's the worst boyfriend.'
Compared to whom?

USING THE QUESTIONS

When learning the Meta Model not everyone finds the different labels easy to remember. In fact, as with the Milton Model, you do not need to remember these, provided you can recognise the *patterns*. More importantly, learn to ask the right sort of questions to get the precise meaning.

When learning the Meta Model it will help if you:

- Listen to what the person says
- Repeat it to yourself
- Ask yourself, 'What have they missed out?'

As you become more familiar with all the different responses or challenges, you will realise that in many cases more than one could apply. The skill includes knowing in what context to use the patterns.

You can ask yourself some more questions as you become more skilled, such as:

- What caused or causes this limitation?
- What direction does it need to go in?
- What should I direct my challenge to?
- If I use this challenge what result will I get?
- Can I think of any other useful questions?

As with other NLP techniques, you will tend to use them at first in a prescribed, structured way. Then, as your skill increases, you will act in an increasingly instinctive and creative way as you become *unconsciously competent* – one of the characteristics of excellence (see Day 1). Each conscious intervention potentially improves your unconscious skills, in which you will begin to trust. Having said this, you will still have the choice, any time you wish, of *consciously* noticing language patterns and intervening for the purpose of fulfilling your outcome. Choice at this level has special value, as you can fundamentally influence a communication and its outcome.

Presuppositions

On Day 9 we expanded some of the Milton Model patterns with fuller discussion. All those comments still apply of course in understanding the *reverse* role of the Meta Model. Today we will add a few further comments about presuppositions and help to develop the skill of spotting them.

In order to make sense of a phrase or sentence the listener must assume the presuppositions inherent in it. In effect they set up the neurological network, or mindset, that the presupposition entails. Mentally, they 'make real' the thing presupposed. Language that presupposes something often brings about the behaviour or occurrence presupposed. So, using the Meta Model approach, you can identify and recover the meaning bypassed by the presupposition, and *also* influence behaviour.

Although part of linguistic distortion, the continuous use of presupposition probably adds to the efficiency of everyday language. We saw on Day 9 that, used *purposely*, it can bypass resistance and help you reach a desired outcome quickly. Using the inverse Meta Model, you can now learn to identify the presuppositions and recover the meaning *without* the language distortion.

Presuppositions fall into different categories and we have suggested seven below to start you thinking about them. You will notice some familiar language categories like 'cause and effect'. In fact a presupposition may comprise *several* 'embedded' language patterns. You may also notice, as we saw on Day 9, that in some cases the 'to be' verb fulfils a role in allowing you to bypass specifics.

1. Existence
'I wonder how old it is?'
To accept this sentence, you must presuppose that the 'I' and the 'it' exist. Most statements include existence presuppositions.

2. Possibility

'I wonder how quickly you will learn to play chess?'

This presupposes that you have the ability to learn to play chess. The mind then addresses 'How quickly'.

3. Cause–effect (sequential presupposition)

'If you practise cooking you will soon become skilled.'

This statement presupposes that one thing will follow another, or cause another.

4. Complex equivalence

'Travel the world – broaden your mind.'

This presupposes that one thing means or has equivalence to another.

5. Time

'Next time you try this it will be easier.'

This presupposes the effect that time has and that a 'next time' will occur. The mind then addresses 'easier', 'leapfrogging' the question of possibility.

6. Ordinals

'Pork was the third dish on the menu.'

This presupposes a sequence or order, as well as a first and a second dish.

7. 'Or'

'Would you like it gift-wrapped or just as it is?'

This presupposes that you have decided to buy it in the first place.

Soft Front Ends

People often remark that Meta Model questions seem very challenging and might cause offence. How can we maintain rapport while asking this type of question, especially in a non-therapeutic context?

The secret lies in using what we term 'soft front ends'. This means introducing your question in such a way that you do not cause any offence or provoke argument. The

American television detective Columbo has mastered this 'soft' technique. He has the knack of asking the most probing questions whilst appearing guileless and unwilling to cause offence. To use this technique, simply adapt your question or 'frame' it in such a way as to disguise its depth and relevance, always maintaining good rapport. You need to 'come across' as transparent, non-threatening, trustworthy or even naive in order to gain the information you want and, most important, maximise rapport in the process.

Examples of commonly used soft front ends include:

'I'd really like to understand this, so what exactly do you mean by . . .?'
'I'm just wondering how x means y [specify]?'
'This is new to me. Is this always the case?'
'Can you imagine, just for a moment, what would happen if . . .?'

Practise Meta Model questions with and without a soft front end and notice the difference in the responses you get.

APPLICATIONS FOR CHANGE

These NLP language skills provide you with powerful instruments for change. With practice, you can use them confidently in just about any context. When not aware of the change process, or your 'intervention', people will show little resistance.

As we have seen, the Meta Model *reconnects language with experience.* You can use it to:

- Gather information
- Clarify meaning
- Identify limitations
- Open up choices
- Form better outcomes

- Break or sometimes gain rapport
- Create better relationships
- Solve problems
- Gain insights

Some of the illustrations we have used today, and on Days 8 and 9, suggest further applications. And you can try them yourself and monitor the results.

For instance, you may find, when using Meta Model questions to discuss a person's problem, that the problem (from the subject's point of view) seems to solve itself. Or rather, the *person* solves it him- or herself, experiencing the give-away 'aha' insight. In fact they create new neurological networks which, triggered by your stimulus questions, provide new meaning. The person sees things from a different perspective, or in a new light. So you can adapt the Meta Model as a problem-solving technique. Simply apply the questions to the 'problem statement'. Or apply the responses to the goals you set on Day 2, as a further test of their 'well-formedness'. Use the model with others, or yourself.

PRESUPPOSITION FOR TODAY

> **There is no failure, only feedback.**

People often take some time to grasp the language models and develop skill in using them. If they do not get them right straight away, less successful memories replay in their heads, registering yet another 'failure'. In fact 'not getting it right' forms part of the learning process (especially while honing our newly learnt skills to a level of unconscious competence). So use this presupposition in such situations of doubt. If what you do doesn't have the effect you want, at the very least you will gain useful feedback information.

The principle applies universally, not just in communication. If you change your behaviour so that you get a different outcome, and in due course the outcome you want, it changes the whole meaning of what at first appeared as failure. It forms part of the essential *process* of success. This presupposition supports the four-stage success model (see Day 2):

1. Decide what you want.
2. Do something.
3. Notice what happens.
4. Change what you do until you get your desired outcome.

The model implies that you may not get what you want at the first attempt, but you can treat 'failure' as useful 'feedback' to help you reach your ultimate goal. The Meta Model has the advantage of generating plenty of feedback.

TODAY'S TO DOs

- Make a list of occasions in the past when, according to how you felt then or now, you failed. Then think about what you learnt from those experiences and how it could help you achieve your present goals.

- Choose some Meta Model patterns you think you will easily spot and start to notice them throughout your day. As with the Milton patterns, don't try to remember the labels initially.

- As soon as you start spotting patterns, form a response in your mind using the examples above, but adapting them to the context. Don't say anything out loud at this stage. Relationships can come to an end because of premature, over-enthusiastic Meta Model questioning! First build up your knowledge of the patterns and responses, and your confidence will increase.

- Think of any problem or issue you need to resolve. Write it down in simple language as a 'problem statement'. Now apply the Meta Model questions, adapting them where you can, or passing on to the next if one doesn't seem to fit. Imagine responding to someone who has presented you with the problem in real life. Notice how the issue becomes more and more specific, and the problem better defined. Get ready to receive insights, perhaps after a period of incubation, when you put the matter out of your mind.

DAY 11

Once Upon a Time

This chapter covers:

- **Simple and complex metaphors**
- **Metaphor as a tool of communication**
- **Metaphorical caveats**
- **Generating a complex metaphor**

A metaphor denotes something else, or represents some other meaning. Essentially it helps us understand one thing in terms of another – often something unknown or lesser known in terms of something familiar. For example, 'Sheila is a brick' tells us something about Sheila. 'The baby is as pretty as a picture' tells us something about the baby. For present purposes we will forget our school grammar and lump metaphors together with similes ('Sheila is *like* a brick'). We know Sheila and the baby better because we know something about bricks and pictures. Metaphor also gives another perspective on a situation or behaviour. Today you will learn about metaphor and its very powerful role in communication.

SIMPLE AND COMPLEX METAPHORS

In NLP, the term 'metaphor' includes similes, analogies, allegories, jokes, parables and stories. You can use any of these devices for better communication, as well as for solving problems, spotting opportunities and other useful outcomes.

'Sheila is a brick' exemplifies a *simple* metaphor, as does 'The tutor is a dream' or 'The course was a marathon'. These can save lots of words and make a comment more graphic and memorable. A well-chosen metaphor can also motivate or demotivate someone, as they associate with the mind picture it conjures up. In short, metaphor can help produce a more effective communication outcome.

Many simple metaphors and similes have turned into clichés, so they no longer help us communicate. 'White as a sheet', for example, has its origins in the days of universally white sheets. It thus has little metaphorical power, and for young people the association may not make sense. Similarly, 'raining cats and dogs', or 'can of worms', whilst quite acceptable to those familiar with the clichés, would have alarming associations for anyone not conversant with such nuances of language. However, with this proviso, clichés can add to your metaphorical communication armoury, making your language more vivid and colourful. Whatever language tools you use, keep focused on your desired outcome.

NLP deals more in complex metaphors – analogies, allegories and stories. In particular, it uses stories with many levels of meaning. These do not usually convey a specific meaning, but rather unlock otherwise inaccessible resources in the hearer. They stimulate the mind. In some cases they uncover problems unknown to the story-teller (communicator) as well as the listener, because of the way they access the unconscious mind. A story can easily distract the conscious mind and engage 'downtime' thoughts. It avoids premature criticism or rationalising.

In a therapy situation, metaphor helps in communicating with someone in a trance, or to induce trance. In everyday communication, metaphors, whether simple or complex, can convey meaning without causing offence or provoking objections. In other situations they can trigger extraordinary levels of creativity and help to solve otherwise intractable problems. (Harry Alder's book *Train Your Brain* – see Further Reading – focuses on these aspects of metaphor in more detail.)

Metaphor stimulates right-brain, holistic thinking. Unlike abstract language patterns and nominalisations, it stimulates the imagination, and converts easily into visual and other sensory images. You can see, hear and feel a brick. But you cannot so easily *imagine* 'reliable', 'trustworthy', or other nominalised descriptions of someone's personality. Metaphor helps to bridge our mental 'maps'. We all have different associations, but we have a better chance of common understanding if we use sensory-rich words. The oft-quoted test 'Can you put it into a wheelbarrow?' illustrates the way metaphor puts language into concrete, sensory terms.

We also associate metaphor with unconscious thought, and in particular with what happens when we 'incubate' a problem or issue outside our conscious mind. This usually happens when we think about something quite different. The unconscious mind seems to associate or relate a present issue or problem to anything in our extensive life database which may offer meaning. The metaphor acts as the link or catalyst. It seems to 'resonate' in this mysterious thinking process. It 'presents' insights to the conscious mind that can bring about change and reveal solutions.

Do not underestimate the importance of metaphor, not just in literature but in many areas of 'human excellence'. The great teachers and communicators throughout history have used simple stories to convey profound truths, to influence, inspire and motivate. In many cultures the oral story-telling tradition has special prominence, amongst adults as well as children. And metaphor has triggered some of the world's greatest scientific discoveries and inventions.

Sadly we have lost the art of metaphor and story-telling in recent decades. Television and video and a more hurried way of life have taken their place, especially in Western society. However, anyone can relearn the art of metaphorical story-telling. In metaphor we have a tool for better communication and learning, and bringing about change, as well as entertainment. The phrase 'Once upon a time' takes most people into immediate trance, opening up the unconscious mind in a way that a more objective form of communication never can.

METAPHOR AS A TOOL OF COMMUNICATION

When communicating, you can use metaphor for:

- Simplifying
- Depersonalising
- Stimulating creativity
- Enlightening
- Matching
- Personalising
- Getting attention
- Overcoming resistance
- Creating vivid memories
- Introspection and insight
- Identifying problems
- Generating emotion

Simplifying

As we have seen in the simple example of 'Sheila is a brick', a single word can transmit a lot of meaning. You can make a communication both more *efficient* (economical in words and other input) and *effective* (in bringing about a communication outcome). In particular, a metaphor can *simplify* meaning by using a concept already familiar to the other person. It acts as a bridge between mental maps, however far apart, helping you communicate very complex matters simply and effectively.

Scientists and philosophers, as well as artists and writers, need metaphorical ideas to aid their thinking. Just as important, they can often communicate their thoughts better when they use analogies and metaphorical figures of speech. Often the breakthrough in an invention or other creative act comes when we identify the right metaphor, typically drawn from the world of nature. It sparks off creativity. But it also forms the basis on which the creative person can communicate the idea to other people. It usually produces the 'aha' moment that signals understanding. So you can use metaphor as a *simplification bridge*. This allows for the interchange of the most complex, rich meaning between mental maps. It results in better communication, with all the benefits it brings.

Depersonalising

You can also use a metaphor to depersonalise an issue in any communication. Sometimes communicating something directly causes offence or embarrassment. Or it may provoke immediate objections. Using an intermediate story involves a less direct communication, although the other person can easily draw the appropriate message from the story.

Thus, 'I heard of someone the other day . . .' can get a point across sensitively, provided the story has some bearing on the person's circumstances or behaviour. Even when the person knows you have directed the story at them, they will probably not take offence at a mere story or third-person quote. 'If the cap fits [they will] wear it.'

The metaphor allows you to stay personally outside the issue. You will thus achieve your outcome more easily, because you have not provoked their instinctive defence mechanisms. After all, why get angry or upset about a story about somebody else? Once you have created another way of thinking, you will probably succeed in stimulating some change.

Stimulating Creativity

Metaphor tends to associate with right-brain processing. It accesses the unconscious mind, and can thus draw on all the person's inner, creative resources to identify and solve problems. Even without attempting a solution, you can help a person gain an insight and bring about change. A metaphor which has associations with their situation will do its own job. Sometimes metaphors simply plant the seed of an idea. Sometimes they help a latent idea to flower. Sometimes they unlock the insight that turns an idea into an innovation.

Metaphors have provided the key in cases of extraordinary creativity. Einstein used the sunbeam metaphor when he conceived his theory of relativity. Moreover, he actually took part in the story (just as a little child would), going for a cosmic ride at the speed of light. He *entered into* the metaphor. This ability to *associate* with a metaphor, using all the senses, makes it a powerful tool of creativity.

Enlightening

The metaphors we use tell us a lot about ourselves and others. Some people, for example, use a lot of military terms, like 'in the firing line', 'winning' and 'losing', the 'troops', getting 'shot down', 'targets', 'ammunition', 'plan of attack' and so on. This tells us a lot about their map of the world and their likely values and beliefs. It also gives us opportunities to create rapport by matching experience (which we learnt about on Days 4 and 5). Sometimes a person's attitude and behaviour creates negative feelings. But, in terms of their metaphorical world (military, sporting, gardening, or whatever), it starts to makes sense.

In other cases, metaphors might indicate, for example, a 'win–win' approach; the idea of 'fate'; or values such as 'strength', 'co-operation', 'independence' or a 'pioneering spirit'. The metaphors we live by tell us a lot about ourselves, just as the sensory predicates we use reveal our sensory preferences (see Day 6). Start to identify the metaphors you relate to, and the people you communicate with most. The new self-understanding you gain from this will inevitably help you win rapport and develop better relationships.

We may not *subscribe* to a certain way of thinking and the concepts people use. But we can certainly *relate* to the person by adopting their kind of metaphor. It makes sense to do this *for the purpose of achieving a communication outcome* and for the sake of nurturing an ongoing relationship.

Matching

The use of metaphor offers another area of possible 'likeness' in communication, another opportunity to match the other person's values or interests. It bridges mental maps. For instance, you can use a military, win–lose type of metaphor but with a win–win outcome (story ending). In this way you may well bring a military person round to the logic of win–win, and to the sort of change in strategy that will bring it about. *Pace* their experience through metaphor, then *lead* them to another option.

We reveal our values through metaphors. Matching values a person holds dear can help you achieve rapport. Metaphors offer a direct line to their inner world. You can join a person's story world by using their story language.

Personalising

We saw earlier that we sometimes need to depersonalise communication. When speaking for an organisation, however, you may want to do the reverse. An organisation can seem faceless and impersonal. So you may want to communicate with human qualities rather than as a legal entity. At a company level, metaphors frequently reflect and support the culture and mission of the organisation. A corporate language evolves based on the dominant metaphors applied to the business.

For example, you could ask, what if our company was: A car? A brand of clothing? An animal? A book? A film star? A tree? A place to live? A movie? A holiday destination? A type of food?

You might choose as a place to live a thatched cottage or a lofty castle; a tree might bring to mind a slender birch, a weeping willow or an ancient, stately oak. Try creating your own analogies. These images can sometimes personify a company in a way that words cannot. Lots of examples may come to mind. For instance, you can draw on nature, man-made artefacts, real or fictional characters, as you wish.

As a corporate exercise, this process tests out consistency of perception between managers and staff and, if possible, between company people and customers and competitors. By identifying appropriate metaphors and *personalising* an otherwise inanimate organisation you can start to work on your positioning in the marketplace (or customer perception and the characteristics you need to support it).

You may then want to *change* your perceived corporate personality, a process described in detail in *Corporate Charisma* (Paul Temporal and Harry Alder, Piatkus). Some companies have used metaphor in this way to set their mission statements. The following sorts of descriptions might emerge:

A. A friendly and reliable person who prefers family life and old-fashioned values.

B. A young, ambitious and contemporary person who loves freedom and fun.

C. A visionary, innovative and intellectual person who takes pride in their state-of-the-art knowledge.

Such a 'corporate personality' will evoke the desired characteristics and behaviour more realistically (in 'picturable representations', sounds and feelings) than abstract words such as 'excellent', 'best', 'reliable' or 'responsive'. The company – through its people – can then align its policies and nurture its culture in a more understandable, measurable and effective way.

If a business acts congruently with a metaphor which attracts their customers, the metaphor has its own brand effect. It allows the company to focus and co-ordinate their mission, strategy, and promotion. This contrasts with the faceless, grey image of many large companies that fail to capture the public imagination. So we can extend the use of metaphor to business and organisations for a more personal communication.

Sometimes you may particularly wish to personalise an issue. A person may say they understand a problem clearly, but fail to see their part in it, let alone that they may have caused it. In this case you will want the person to apply the metaphor or analogy *personally*. The skill here involves getting the person to associate with a metaphor which by the end of the story mirrors part (or all) of the problem.

The choice and use of metaphor will depend on the nature of the communication – for instance, one-to-one, a group presentation, a chairperson's comments or a more formal conference-type speech. At one level you can incorporate simple metaphors that intuitively occur to you. We use these all the time, as you will see from the following examples:

put down roots   branch out   turn over a new leaf
in the mire   plain sailing   lay the foundations
an uphill climb   all downhill from here   she's a star
he's a wily old fox   a whipping boy   reap what you sow
water under the bridge   get your wires crossed
blaze a trail   change gear   spare tyre   peter out
under a cloud   silver lining
which side your bread's buttered on   in the soup
have your cake and eat it   make mincemeat
a taste of your own medicine   career ladder
glass ceiling   up against a brick wall
paint yourself into a corner   open door   blind alley
easy road   put the brakes on   counting the pennies
having your back to the wall   on the carpet
spanner in the works   nuts and bolts   loose screw
baby with the bath water
milk them for all they're worth   odds on

hedge your bets   on your high horse   rein in   nest egg
ring fence   switched on   switched off   burnt out
frozen out   eye to eye   neck and neck
feet under the table   hand in the till   tongue in cheek
knuckle under   Achilles heel   take it on the chin
heart on his sleeve   heart in my mouth
pulled the wool over his eyes   put her foot in it
put your heart into it   let your hair down
splitting hairs   hand in glove   finger in the pie
head in a noose   head over heels   toe in the water
gloves off   no holds barred   game, set and match
long shot   own goal   level playing field   sticky wicket
on the back foot   on your toes   back to base
through the roof   up in smoke   two-edged sword
sabre rattling   big guns   tighten your belt
shoot from the hip   no stone unturned   down and out
countdown   all sewn up   cobbled together
for the high jump   one more hurdle   carry the torch
in at the deep end   eye on the ball   head in the sand
watertight argument   cast-iron case
gold-plated engineering   tin-pot   battle axe

In addition to these sorts of simple metaphors used in everyday communication, both formal and informal, a complex story-type metaphor may go down well in a speech, as part of a seminar, or in a therapy situation. The famous hypnotist Milton Erickson used stories to extraordinary effect. A puzzled client would leave him wondering just what he had paid fees for, yet find his problem mysteriously solved. The secret lay, of course, in Erickson addressing the unconscious mind, where so many simple problems lie, without conscious left-brain interference.

From the earliest age people can easily relate to metaphors because they require sensory rather than intellectual, abstract processing – you can see, hear or feel them. A multi-sensory metaphor especially, such as a person or an animal, can translate an otherwise abstract idea into something easily imaginable or 'picturable'. Multi-sensory representations can have additional emotional impact and we tend to remember them better. 'Picturable' representations usually figure somewhere in cases of outstanding feats of memory. And well-chosen metaphors usually get the best communication results.

A simple story can create choice and new perspectives, and almost inevitably the hearer will take the 'message' on board. Yet even when 'the cap fits' it remains a metaphor, so you don't appear as a self-appointed adviser or problem-solver. You therefore need lose no rapport in recounting the metaphor. In fact, the more obscure the association, the better. The *conscious* mind often will not spot the link. The 'message' of the metaphor goes straight to the unconscious mind and has its influence without conscious resistance. Strangely, neither the story-teller nor the story take credit. The problem-holder 'owns' his or her insight personally.

Getting Attention

Metaphors get and keep attention, whether of an audience of one person or a thousand. Somehow the mind cannot resist a story or anecdote couched in direct, sensory language. Listen to a 'charismatic', 'easy to listen to' or entertaining speaker and you will find they use metaphors a lot. Or compare a standard textbook with a fast-moving novel to check how the novelist keeps the reader's attention. One may contain better, more logically constructed English, with more profound concepts. But the other, full of metaphor and sensory language, may have greater impact and stay longer in the memory. Again, aim to achieve your communication outcome.

Overcoming Resistance

You can't fight a metaphor. It doesn't argue or try to persuade, so it does not arouse opposition or objections. It overcomes resistance without the person knowing. When problem-solving, you can tell a story in a way that depicts the problem and ask the person (problem-owner) to finish the story. By association with the story or symbolism, an 'insight' often occurs. It seems an answer lay in the problem-owner's imagination all along, but *surfaced* in the story ending. Importantly, the problem-owner both conceives and 'owns' any insight or solution, and thus has the motivation necessary for successful resolution.

Creating Vivid Memories

How often do you forget the main subject of a speech, lecture or presentation but find you can remember a story or anecdote from it years later? Metaphors make extensive use of all the senses, conjuring up sights, sounds and feelings. They bring a communication to life. A speech composed of abstract, non-sensory language does not register in the mind in the same way and has less effect. When you use metaphors your hearer identifies personally with the sights and sounds of the mental pictures you create. They 'register' the message and remember the communication. The skill involves choosing or constructing the metaphor (see below) and communicating it appropriately.

Introspection and Insight

You can also use metaphor as a powerful self-development and therapeutic tool. Asking 'What if I were . . .?' helps you communicate with your own unconscious mind. This can happen in many ways. For example, the metaphor can involve an *object* or *entity*, such as a tree, a building or motor car, a character in a well-known story, an animal, plant or whatever. The intuitive ideas triggered by this process will tend to reveal your unconscious intentions and values. You can thus access your right brain through the metaphor.

Alternatively you can use a natural *process*, such as shedding leaves, hibernating, or the rise and fall of the sun; or a more mechanical process, such as a train ride or building a dam. Otherwise you can tell a story in which the hearer easily identifies with the main character. The story need not have an ending, or could have an ambiguous one. You don't need to provide an answer or a solution. The power lies in the association the other person makes with the metaphor.

In a similar way you can develop a metaphor or even a single word another person has used, as in the military examples quoted earlier (see p. 166). By adopting a metaphor which reflects a special interest, you will also create rapport. As we have already said, you don't need to *apply* a metaphor. Nor need you suggest any 'solution'. The individual's unconscious mind makes its own interpretation and application, 'owns' any solution, and poses any new questions. Utilising a person's own metaphor acts like pacing their experience (see Day 5). It builds rapport and helps you resolve seemingly intractable issues.

Identifying Problems

A complex metaphor can resolve many issues without the speaker ever trying to find a solution, or even recognising the problem. For instance, it might address a work problem today, then provide an insight a few days later into something concerning the family, or a personal matter. The metaphor draws on *your* resources and addresses *your* problems. So it does not limit you in rich, stimulating insights. More often than not, the metaphor helps to *identify*, rather than solve a problem. Having exposed the *real* problem, a solution follows close behind. Using a single metaphor when addressing a group illustrates this. Several different insights can solve the various problems of the group at the same time, however different the people and their concerns. The interpretation or self-application of the metaphor, rather than the eloquence of the communicator–story-teller, creates the breakthrough – 'Yes! I can see the problem now.'

For example, the authors worked in an organisation at one time that had become uncomfortable through overcrowding. It had grown like Topsy, delighted with its success but without any forward planning. Parts of the company seemed fragmented and chaotic. Without any explanation Beryl told the story of a plant given to her that grew so much it had outgrown its small pot, and badly needed nourishment, cascading all over the place and beginning to shrivel in places. She did not know just what to do to ensure the plant's survival and health. So she asked the participants to come back the following day with a positive ending to the story.

The participants came up with a variety of endings. The naively simple story had clearly engaged them at an unconscious level. The stories told by the participants led to some very creative suggestions about improving the company and solving their current problems. The process totally bypassed the low morale and cynicism that had previously accompanied any discussion about the state of the company. Moreover, the company executives, rather than the consultant, had come up with and thus 'owned' the solutions.

Generating Emotion

Because they access the senses, including feelings, metaphors can generate emotion. A short story, told with congruency and feeling, can trigger tears and laughter in a way that even the best non-metaphorical prose or public speaking cannot. And emotion means motivation. It often forms the basis of decisions – to buy, to change, to act. The deciding ingredient in a successful communication, it captures the imagination, appealing to heart rather than head.

METAPHORICAL CAVEATS

People readily understand the general meaning of a brick, a lion, a tree, or whatever metaphor we might use. But our unique meanings may differ a lot. A wild animal, for instance, represents an object of love to some people and hate or fear to others. If 'Sheila is a brick', the way we think of Sheila depends on the way we think of a brick. As we have seen, a metaphor will tend to draw very effectively on the other person's unconscious resources. But the result will not necessarily fulfil *your* outcome – what you wanted to achieve. You have no idea what association any metaphor will have for another person.

However, you can sometimes create a *direction* with a metaphor. The form that direction takes depends upon the unique interpretation and creativity of the listener. So, in choosing and presenting a metaphor to give direction, the more knowledge you have about the person, the better. The better your choice of metaphor, the better you will 'fit' their perceptual map and achieve your desired outcome, for instance when persuading or influencing.

Metaphor will usually have *an effect*, cause a reframe and bring about change. But it may not produce the effect you wanted. The good communicator brings about an *intended* effect, a desired outcome, not just the arbitrary result of the other person's unconscious mental processes. When using metaphor to enhance a purposeful communication (to inform, warn, motivate, etc) you need to choose the best metaphor to address the person and issue in question. You will thus find a knowledge of the person's thinking charac-teristics or 'meta programs', such as sensory preference, invaluable (see Day 6).

The skill therefore lies in making the metaphor neither too obvious or realistic, nor too difficult to associate with the idea you want to communicate. First check your metaphor for possible associations, however indirect or 'lateral', with the 'presented' issue, problem or insight you want to communicate. Keep it simple, and communicate it with congruence. Get *into* the story, and envision what you want others to envision.

As with any skill, this takes practice. Start by consciously choosing and using metaphors in everyday conversation. Then gradually extend your range and use of them, to form *habits* of graphic, imaginative communication. Do *more* of what works and drop what doesn't. You have an almost infinite variety of metaphors to choose from. Start to create your own, or use popular metaphors in a different, surprising context.

One word of warning: don't talk yourself out of rapport like a salesperson who loses a sale by appearing over-zealous. You can ruin a communication (like a watercolour painting) by putting in too much detail. Communicate economically, and go for *perceived reality* rather than technical accuracy.

Also, remember to match your metaphors to the person and the context. What works in an after-dinner speech may not work in an intimate, one-to-one communication. What works with a complete stranger may not work with a person you know well. What works for a sporty person may not work for a bookworm. One person requires the merest hint of a metaphoric suggestion, whereas in other cases you may have to paint a whole metaphorical picture.

Finally, watch out for clichés. People no doubt used metaphorical expressions like 'My hands are tied' in negotiation before they entered everyday language and lost their edge. Hackneyed versions of once powerful metaphors no longer evoke much emotion. And a metaphor with a too-well-known meaning will not help a person to find their *own* meaning through associations in their unconscious mind. So, choose and use metaphors creatively. Vivid or even bizarre ones can, almost literally, *capture* the imagination.

GENERATING A COMPLEX METAPHOR

Everyone uses metaphors so you don't need training in that sense. However, to generate an appropriate complex metaphor, a few ground rules may help. First you need to consider the situation. List:

- The elements
- The relationship between the elements
- The present problem or situation
- The emotions and other effects of the situation

These give you the 'plot of the story'.
  Next, list:

- Reasons to change or solve the situation and some possible options
- Ways of choosing and/or experimenting with solutions
- Useful lessons en route and/or helpful beliefs to reinforce success
- Good conclusions and possibilities for the future

These offer the possibility of goal solutions.

Next transpose these factors to a different situation that might parallel the problem. Don't make the connection so obvious that you create a conscious association. At the same time don't make it so remote from the problem or issue that no creative associations occur. Use your intuitive rather than logical skills, and trust your creative mind to throw up ideas. This may happen as you make your list. Alternatively, ideas may come to you after a period of incubation, so you may need patience. Metaphors do not follow rational problem-solving wisdom, and nor does the process of generating them. Rules do not apply when choosing metaphors.

PRESUPPOSITION FOR TODAY

> **Resistance is a comment on the communicator and may be a sign of insufficient pacing.**

We tend to blame the other person if our message does not get across, or if they do not respond in the way that we expect. Today's presupposition places the responsibility for a communication squarely on the communicator.

You have learnt how simple matching can help create rapport and bring about better communication. In a conversation, we can easily forget to pace the other person and maintain rapport through matching, especially when emotions come into play. Take the trouble to achieve and maintain rapport through pacing. The other person will tend to listen better, respond better, and co-operate more. Otherwise, you may win an argument but fail to achieve your communication outcome. When faced with resistance, rather than using a stronger argument or louder message, take it as a signal that you need to use more pacing to build better rapport.

TODAY'S TO DOs

- Think of a current problem you have. Then, to test your skills, think of a natural metaphor to illustrate it. You have the whole of nature to choose from! If it helps, work through the alphabet – avalanche, beaver, cloud and so on. Now relate your problem to the metaphor and the metaphor to your problem. Just 'freewheel' in your thoughts. Note how you feel about your problem after the exercise and consider now what you might do to change things.

- Think of a metaphor that describes *you*. If you want to change in any way, what metaphor might describe the *new* you. Consider how the metaphor might help you make the needed changes.

- Experiment with metaphor in everyday communication. Take a little time to consider anything you have not communicated well, such as something you have tried to persuade a colleague or boss about, or perhaps where a personal relationship has reached an impasse. Think of metaphors and apply them to these situations. Notice how your perspective changes and ideas arise that you can use next time you communicate with the people concerned. Change starts with you, of course, but it will soon affect the people you thought created the problem. Check back on the many ways metaphor can help communication, such as simplifying an issue, and explore as many of these as might apply in your situation.

DAY 12

Getting Another Perspective

This chapter covers:
- **Different perceptual positions**
- **What position to take**

Much of NLP involves looking at things in a different way to get a different perspective. This enables us to understand other people's maps of reality and to enrich our own. Thus we gain greater mutual understanding, create rapport and achieve better communication, with all its associated benefits.

You met the terms 'associated' and 'dissociated' on Day 7. In an associated experience you see through your own eyes and it feels like actually experiencing the event yourself. In a dissociated experience you see yourself as an external observer would. These two perspectives represent *subjective* or *objective* ways of thinking about something. They relate respectively to the first person ('I') and third person ('he, she, them') forms of speech we use in everyday language. And we term these different viewpoints *perceptual positions*.

DIFFERENT PERCEPTUAL POSITIONS

You can look at any experience in at least three ways.

First Perceptual Position

The first position, or 'associated viewpoint', represents your own subjective point of view – 'How does this affect me?' When remembering an experience in this way you will see things as if through your own eyes. In particular you will recall the inner feelings associated with it.

Try it. Think back to an important event in your life, such as meeting someone for the first time, starting a new job, or whatever. *Associate* with the memory, using all modalities (see Day 6).

When describing such an experience we tend to use appropriate first-person language, such as 'I feel', 'the way I see things', and so on. This perceptual position equates to personal 'consciousness'. Do you know, for instance, whether the colour 'red' means the same to somebody else? Objective scientists usually mistrust this subjective state (which partly explains the slow progress in cognitive science and understanding the human mind). Conversely, we cannot think wholly objectively from an associated, first perceptual position.

Second Perceptual Position

The second perceptual position views an experience from the position of the other party to a communication or event – an interested party. From this perspective, you start to understand how the other person feels. In any communication or mutual experience people perceive things differently. We saw this in the presupposition for Day 1: 'The map is not the territory.' By projecting yourself into the other person's map of reality you get an important new perspective.

To do this, imagine stepping inside someone else's skin and experiencing the world as they do. Listen to 'you' and notice the response. We associate this perceptual position with empathy, or 'putting yourself into the other person's shoes'. The skill of taking second position will give you far more accurate information than just *wondering* how a person feels.

Conflict in a communication or a relationship usually calls for a second perceptual position on the matter. When you understand better how the other person sees and feels things, your own feelings will probably change. Your changed attitude to the person will then tend to increase rapport. So they will also change. And the increased rapport will in turn make it easier for you to see their point of view.

A perceptual position 'switch' can start a positive spiral of better communication. Behaviour that seems wrong or strange can take on new meaning when you perceive it from the other person's point of view. In fact most of the time each of us believes that we act rightly, sensibly, normally – with good *reason*. To genuinely take on a second-person position means that you begin to understand the validity of perspectives different from your own. You can also begin to understand the real purpose behind another person's actions or words (which they themselves may not have identified). And this might give the key to the right communication to bring about your own outcome, through them.

Of course, we can never fully understand the subjective consciousness of another person. NLP does not offer psychic gifts. But it can take you a long way towards seeing things as another person does, whether you agree with them or not. To take different perceptual positions requires an imaginative 'as if' skill that anyone can develop, with practice. Even very small children use their fertile imaginations to empathise with suffering siblings and friends. For most of us, the skill of taking the second perceptual position involves removing mental blinkers and *unlearning* long-established thinking patterns. But, with practice, we can all revive some latent, natural empathy.

Third and Nth Perceptual Positions

When using the third perceptual position to view an experience, you act as a complete outsider or third party, and not as a direct party to the communication – like the classic, wholly objective, independent, 'fly on the wall'. You take the disinterested scientific viewpoint, the role of the impartial observer. You distance yourself from the action and the key players, stand back and observe.

This position can represent *any* perspective other than those of the parties to the communication. For example, you could adopt the viewpoint of a consultant, parent, casual observer, school teacher, and so on – to the nth degree. Ask yourself: 'What would it look like to so-and-so?' This way, you can open up *infinite* viewpoints.

WHAT POSITION TO TAKE

Each position has its own importance. It simply differs from the others, giving different meaning in different contexts and circumstances. Together, the viewpoints will give a comprehensive perception of any experience.

Although identified as distinct perceptual positions, in practice we tend to move from one to the other without consciously doing anything other than 'thinking about' an issue. Having said this, some people will have a preference or aptitude for one way of thinking. A person who tends to view things in a detached, objective, impersonal, abstract way will feel at home with the third perceptual position. A person who can easily empathise with another person and 'feel for them' will naturally take a second-person position. And a person who seems to dwell only on their own subjective experience instinctively takes the first perceptual position.

You can extend your skills to develop all three perspectives, match those used by other people, and thus create better rapport. Experienced salespeople, negotiators and counsellors readily use each position in their work.

As well as the communication benefits, adopting these different perceptual positions can enable your mind to come up with creative ideas and solutions to difficult problems. By thinking in this way we open up new brain networks. The unfamiliarity or 'difference' stimulates the brain to give special attention. Insights and intuitions suddenly occur to us when we adopt unfamiliar perceptual positions. So the benefits apply to far more than communication, improving every aspect of your thinking.

Perceptual positions form part of an approach, termed the *triple description*, developed by John Grinder and Judith De Lozier in their book *Turtles All the Way Down* (see Further Reading). In essence, we can better understand our own mental maps and the maps of others by freely moving between these three positions. We can taste the rich differences in perception. Practise taking different perceptual positions. This skill will help you create the vital rapport you need to bring about change in yourself and others.

PRESUPPOSITION FOR TODAY

Learning is living – we cannot not learn.

Any parent knows how fast children learn in the days before school. Life then seems like one big adventure. Sadly, once a child associates learning with school (often with painful overtones), the rate of true learning may well decline. We can't restrict learning to the classroom: it simply means the way we, as human beings, survive and achieve our desires.

Every time we 'miss' a target, try something else, and finally get what we want (and even the tiniest children can do this well), we learn. And, as long as we have to make sense of all the sensory stimuli that constantly bombard us, we operate in learning mode. We do not always associate this largely unconscious process with learning. Nevertheless, the system carries on working perfectly anyway – we cannot *not* learn.

TODAY'S TO DOs

- Think about a person you have difficulty getting on with and try taking second position. See, hear and feel as they do. Note how you change your attitude to the person, as well as your behaviour.

- Think of something that arouses very negative emotions in you, and try taking third perceptual position. You can wear different observer 'hats', if you like, such as wise adviser, grandparent, five-year-old child, respected mentor and so on. Note how the issue now seems less emotive, you seem more distanced from it, and interesting new angles open up.

- Consider a real interview or one-to-one meeting in which you will participate in the future. Choose an event about which, although you want to achieve an outcome, you have some doubts or anxiety. Set up simple props like table and chairs, as if in an actual face-to-face meeting, sit in 'your' chair and silently rehearse in your mind what you will say (first position). Then move to the other person's chair, step into their skin, and listen to yourself asking for what 'they' want (second position). Return to your own chair, recount the other person's response, and consider what you may need to change to get a more positive response.

- Now move to the other side of the room and take on the role of 'film director' (third position). Run through the scene in your head and evaluate, as director, what needs to happen to improve it and get the results you want from the meeting or interview. From this more objective position, you may come up with totally different insights and change your plan accordingly. You don't have to 'act out' perceptual positions in this way, but it may help as you acquire the skill.

- Think of a past experience in which you consider you failed, and would like to remove the memory altogether. Think of three ways in which the experience has proved useful, or may prove useful in the future. Note what learning you can squeeze out of a painful event or circumstance. Use your creativity. Start to expect further learning and benefit even from distant memories. Notice what perceptual positions you adopted.

- Think about what different kinds of written material illustrate these perceptual positions. Which kind of writing do you understand better? Which affects you more? How can you incorporate these perceptual positions into your written and verbal communication?

DAY 13

Taming Time

This chapter covers:

- **Coding time**
- **Time and different cultures**
- **Through time and in time**
- **How to identify a timeline**

A number of NLP writers and trainers have used the concept of a timeline to describe the way we record and store experience over time. The way we behave and identify ourselves depends upon our unique past experiences – a collection of memories. These time–space experiences make us unique. They give us what we call consciousness and personality. Our experience happens over time, of course, and we have very old as well as recent memories. At the same time we sometimes look into the future. So a person's timeline represents this unique chronology of experience. It forms our memory coding – past, present and future – as the brain stores it.

CODING TIME

We know very little about the neurology of memory. But the idea of such a timeline process, or a chronological sequence of life experiences, makes sense. We must, for instance, have some way of knowing whether something happened five minutes ago or five years ago. Or, for that matter, that something we imagine about the future hasn't already happened. After all, we use the same sort of sensory inputs (sights, sounds and feelings), whether we think about the past or the future.

Sights, sounds and feelings, on their own, do not seem to contain any kind of time coding. In some cases, for instance, distant memories involve very vivid recall, almost as though the event happened yesterday. Conversely, we may have difficulty conjuring up a far more recent memory. The coding seems to happen at the *submodality* level (see Day 7).

Setting all these experiences in chronological order appears to require another dimension of understanding – a neurological process that makes sense in terms of time. We know little about this aspect of our thinking as a brain process. But the idea of a time *line* (rather like a river flowing from its source to the sea, or a road on the journey through life), provides a useful metaphor.

In a quite literal sense your unique present-day identity reflects your personal timeline. It includes, for instance, all the decisions you have made in the past and which have brought you to the present – your individual history, in hours, days and years. This personal time 'record' provides important personal knowledge, which can help us understand ourselves better. But it can also bring about change. You can decide to use time in a different way.

Certain techniques based on the idea of a timeline enable you to alter the very neurology of past memories. You can manipulate them, in the best sense of the word, to achieve your present outcomes. You can *choose* to change them (just as you changed memories, on Day 7, by switching submodalities to change the way you feel).

We each have a unique timeline. Consider, for instance, the way we all think differently about time, even though it comprises standard units on a clock. Some people seem to have 'all the time in the world', while others never seem to have 'enough hours in the day'. And this, it turns out, does not necessarily reflect your job or what you actually achieve with your time. Rather it reflects your personality or thinking style, and specifically the way you *code* time. The old adage 'If you want a job doing, ask a busy person' illustrates this well. The way you perceive time internally determines the effect it has on you and how you use it.

According to timeline theory we *all* store time in a *linear* way. Things happen in a line, in sequence, one event after another – something that happened a year ago happened before something that happened a week ago. But there the similarity ends. As individuals, we code this time distinction (or store it in our brains), in different ways.

How, then, do we 'manage' time in our minds? You can get some clues by the words people use in everyday communication, just as you learnt on Day 6 how to tell from predicates their likely sensory preference. Expressions like 'You will look back on this and be grateful', or 'You will look back and see the funny side', suggest that we can store past memories as if *behind* us. Similarly, we talk about *looking forward* to an event that has not yet happened. Again, we instinctively use metaphors of space and direction. But now let us consider some cultural differences concerning time.

TIME AND DIFFERENT CULTURES

These different time expressions seem fairly insignificant until we learn that different cultural norms apply to speaking or thinking about time.

Anglo-European and Arabic Time

So-called 'Anglo-European time' follows the linear model of time in which one event follows another *in a line*. For instance, some people describe time as going from left to right, with the distant past to the far left and the distant future far off to the right.

Using this linear concept of time, diaries and appointment books take on special importance. If you have not finished your meeting by four o'clock you have to 'get a move on' because you 'have another lined up' and 'time will not wait for you'. You have got to fit all the events in your life into this linear process. Time seems like a moving conveyor belt and everything you do has to keep pace with it. If not, the world will leave you behind, work will not get done, and you will have lost time forever. Time seems like a river, endlessly flowing from its source to the ocean.

So-called 'Arabic time', on the other hand, presents us with a different notion. It applies not just to Arabic people but also to people in many tropical or hot countries. In cultures with such a timeline, time happens more in the present. It always happens *now*. So you can turn up for an appointment at any time because time has not gone. It resides always in the here and now. Such people seem to 'live in the present'.

These different concepts of time can infuriate someone from another culture or timeline type. Anglo-Europeans may consider it discourteous not to keep an agreed appointment to the minute. On the other hand, someone who works according to Arabic time may consider it discourteous not to give full attention to their present guest, however long it takes, and whoever they keep waiting. As well as values, the very concept of time differs.

These concepts of time affect many millions of people at a deep cultural level, impacting on every aspect of their lives. It follows that, if time happens now, we have no concept, or a different concept, of the future. And this may account for what seems to Anglo-Europeans a fatalistic attitude, or lack of foresight as to what might happen tomorrow, amongst Arabic timekeepers.

Individual Differences

We also find these cultural stereotypes in individuals, whatever their cultural background. Many Western people, for

example, seem to have the same carefree attitude characteristic of Arabic time. Sometimes a husband and wife will have
different attitudes to time – one extra-punctual and meticu-
lously organised and the other easy-going and *laissez faire*.
So, even within cultural norms, large variations exist.

For instance, a difference exists between, say, the southern
states and the bustling cities of north-eastern America. And
in many countries we find a time difference between country
and town people. Then, within these common geographic,
national or cultural norms, we find many individual excep-
tions. In some cases a person has a sort of 'split personality'
and will act differently at work to the way they act at weekends or when on holiday. Or a person may change their attitude to time with age and experience. More starkly, this can
occur on becoming aware of a terminal illness. In each case
we use a different way of coding time. So neither culture nor
nurture provide the full answer. It happens in the brain, as a
unique neurological process.

THROUGH TIME AND IN TIME

As we have said, the words and expressions we use give clues
to our personal timeline, or the way we store memories. But
we can also express the timeline metaphor spatially. If I asked
you to *point* to the past, then to the future, where would you
point? It may seem like a stupid question. But, assuming you
disregard its stupidity and *instinctively* point, what might it
tell you?

It turns out that we often represent time by a *line*. It typically runs from left to right (past to future) or sometimes right
to left. In these cases all your memories, as well as the present
and future, lie somewhere *in front* of you, as if within your arc
of vision. Thus you can 'see' the past as memories and at the
same time 'look into' the future – the same expressions we use
in talking about time. We call this 'through time', and it illustrates what we described earlier as Anglo-European time.

We can also represent time by 'In Time', more character-istic of Arabic time. In this case time stretches from front (future) to back (past) with part of it 'inside' us. Whereas a Through Time timeline lies completely in front of you, part of the In Time timeline lies behind the plane of your eyes.

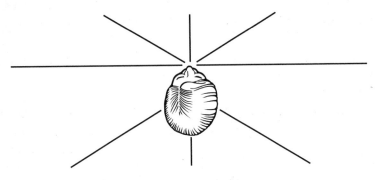

Figure 13.1 Timelines

Let us describe these important distinctions further. We have already said that 'through time' people have an awareness of time, and get upset when others do not. For them time takes a continuous and uninterrupted course. It should not have unexplained gaps. It may pass quickly or slowly, but 'through time' people take account of *duration*. Usually such a person *dissociates* memories, so they in effect see themselves in the memory. You recall that their whole timeline lies within their imagined field of vision. As well as positively planning for the future, looking to the future might mean worry and anxiety. And, as well as the past providing important lessons, it may also mean regret or remorse. So these common personality traits can stem from a person's timeline.

The way the person perceives everyday things reflects all this. For example, a 'through time' person will tend to value services (say of a consultant), on the basis of time spent. That, to them, means value for money. Typically, they will want more time for the same price because time, of itself, has value. An 'in time' person, by contrast, values a consultation simply for the results it gets, even if it involves hardly any time at all.

Stereotypical 'in time' people will concern themselves less about punctuality, often turning up late to an event. They tend to 'savour the moment'. They only see things immediately in front of them. The future lies ahead, beyond or *behind* the next immediate event, and therefore out of sight. So they may have little interest, for instance, in forward planning or looking back at the past. Nor will they dwell on the past.

If you recognise in yourself characteristics from each type, you probably store time in both an 'in time' and 'through time' way.

If you start to notice these different concepts of time and how they affect different people, it will help you achieve rapport with people of a different timeline to your own. You can also experiment with changing your timeline – either in the short or long term. For instance, you may want to match someone you work with (for rapport), or to change how you perceive time to better achieve your outcomes. Each timeline serves the individual 'perfectly'. Rights and wrongs do not exist. However, it may help to have the *flexibility* to change your attitude to time at will. In each case we first need to identify a timeline.

HOW TO IDENTIFY A TIMELINE

You can identify a person's timeline using the following simple questions:

1. Can you remember something that happened a week ago?

2. As you do, can you notice where it seems to come from?

3. Repeat the process for questions 1 and 2 for one month ago, one year ago, five years ago, and ten years ago.

4. Repeat the process, but imagine something happening in the future. Do this one month in the future, one year in the future, five years in the future, and ten years in the future.

5. Do the locations of these past memories and future imaginings imply a line or some linear arrangement of your memories?

The words the person responds with may indicate confusion or uncertainty. So watch for where the person *looks*, and their body language, especially pointing or gesticulating in a certain direction. The conscious, rational mind might not readily offer verbal answers. But the unconscious mind might well provide reliable physiological indicators. In the event of negative answers, try the approach: 'If this memory *did* have a location where *might* it lie?'

You could also try using a memory with an actual location – for instance, involving a house the person once lived in or a place they worked at. You can suggest a linear timeline, just as you used metaphors on Day 11. But do not direct the person in any way as to the arrangement of the timeline. They will always have *some* system of time, whether immediately identifiable or not. So you don't have to create it. You should respect it, as you would respect any aspect of their mental 'map' of reality.

You can easily apply the same process to locate your own timeline. Choose a relaxed time when you feel you can think instinctively rather than logically. Stay sensitive to what your unconscious mind seems to say. Or ask a friend to go through the process with you.

You will immediately gain several benefits from this short introduction to Timeline Theory:

● It enables you to consciously focus more or less on the past or future. You have the choice. Thinking less about the future usually means less worry, for instance. And thinking less about the past may mean fewer regrets and unhelpful post mortems. Remember, however, you don't need to focus on what you want to forget, but on new thoughts – what you want.

- You can understand how other people think about time and get better rapport.

- You can 'reframe' any problem or issue just by putting it into a different time context (e.g. 'How will I feel in five years?').

- You will understand yourself better, and control your feelings and behaviour accordingly.

You can learn more about Timeline Theory from a book of that title by Tad James and Wyatt Woodsmall (see Further Reading). They give a full account, not just of the principles of the theory, but of its many applications such as goal-achievement, personal change and therapy.

PRESUPPOSITION FOR TODAY

> **There is a solution to every problem.**

According to some research, when you believe a solution to a problem exists you have a better chance of finding it. Often the initial or 'presented' problem does not identify the main or root problem. When you identify the real problem it usually throws new light on the situation. And the original problem, as such, frequently disappears. This supports Day 10's presupposition: 'There is no failure, only feedback.'

The presented problem, however, may form part of the learning that eventually takes you to your goal. Although it may constitute an obstacle on the road, you can circumvent, remove or climb over it. Or you may discover another road to take. Looked at in this way, any problem forms a stepping stone to your next and ultimately your final destination. As many successful business people assert, every problem presents an opportunity. It just depends on how you view it.

TODAY'S TO DOs

- Using the above guidelines, identify your own time-line – Through Time or In Time? Draw a picture of where it lies in space in relation to you.

- Listen to people you work with or meet frequently and notice their attitude to time. As well as the words they use, how might their behaviour indicate their timeline?

- Memorise today's presupposition. List a few problems. Then, accepting the presupposition, *imagine* a number of solutions. Consider in what direction they may lie, who might hold clues, how you can influence solutions yourself. Also imagine each problem as already solved, enjoying all the sensory evidence.

  This exercise, and the presupposition, will help when you come to reframing on Day 15 and changing behaviour on Day 21. The presupposition will get you into a positive, expectant state of mind, and the techniques you learn will powerfully reframe the problems.

DAY 14

Choosing Where To Change

This chapter covers:
- **Relating behaviour to neurological levels**
- **Neurological levels and organisations**
- **Alignment**

A lot of NLP work concerns personal change. And change usually involves not just outward behaviour, but some other level 'below the surface'. It involves our beliefs and values and 'parts' of us that we don't always recognise. Our behaviour results from all these inner representations – at many different levels. Unless change takes place within a person's mind, change (or at least lasting change) will probably not occur.

A 'meaningful life' tends to have congruence between these different levels of thinking. We also term this 'alignment'. This means that each *part* of the *total person* goes in the same direction. Inner misalignment can cause inner conflict between different levels of the mind. Lasting personal change requires an understanding of these different levels of the mind.

The anthropologist Gregory Bateson originated a model of neurological levels, later developed by Robert Dilts as shown in Figure 14.1.

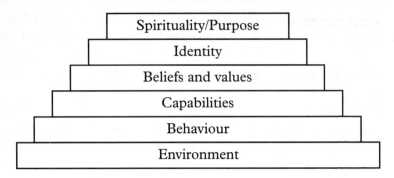

Figure 14.1 Neurological levels

Each level organises the information for the level below it. The rules for changing something at one level differ from those for changing a lower level. Changing something at a lower level *can*, but does not necessarily, affect the upper levels. Changing something at the upper levels, however, will *always* make a difference at the lower levels – rather like a cascading waterfall in which the upper levels always flow down to the lower levels. In the neurological levels model, if you change what you believe, you will tend to change what you do. Conversely, a change in behaviour will probably not last unless some belief or value (a higher level) supports the new behaviour.

Not surprisingly, research has shown that confusing these neurological levels tends to create problems. By understanding and identifying the levels and the way they affect us, however, we can bring about change.

RELATING BEHAVIOUR TO NEUROLOGICAL LEVELS

To understand how these levels apply in your own life, start at the lowest level – environment, and work your way up to the higher levels. We have listed some examples below.

Environment

Think for a moment of the world you live in – where you operate, the things and people around you (at home, socially, when doing sports and hobbies or at work).

Behaviour

Think of a specific behaviour that you excel at – for example, listening, making lists or drawing up schedules.

Capability

What overall capability does this behaviour form a part of? For example, relating to people, organising or planning.

Belief

What does it say about you? What must hold true for you to have this capability? What do you believe about yourself? For example, do you believe in the importance of people, the importance of health, or the importance of personal development?

Identity

What statement might indicate your identity (who you 'are') – for example, 'I'm a people person', or 'I'm a natural organiser'.

Spirituality

What symbol or metaphor represents your spiritual connection or some higher ideal you espouse? Perhaps a dove, a deep ocean or a secluded garden?

Applying the Neurological Levels Model

Following these examples, apply the model to a behaviour you excel at. To further test the model, do the exercise again, choosing a different behaviour.

Note how each level feeds down into the next in a logical hierarchy. For example, your belief about the importance of people feeds down into your capability in relating to people. This capability in turn feeds down into your listening skills. Conversely, your listening skills *support* your 'people' capability and your beliefs about people.

Imagine what would happen in the case of a change at a high level (say belief or identity) and also one at a lower level. Which would have the greater effect on your life? Which change would last longest? Which change would you find hardest to implement?

You can use this model when addressing problems or important issues needing decisions. Start by identifying the *level* of the 'presented' problem – the one that first occurs to you. Then think about its root or cause, also in terms of the levels. See if you can trace the issue to each level and think about what it means in terms of personal change.

To use a common example:

Environment: My desk is untidy.
Behaviour: I don't put things away.
Capability: I don't understand the filing system.
Belief: We need creativity rather than too much order.
Identity: I'm a disorganised person.

The 'problem' might *present* itself at any of these levels. For example, you might identify an environmental issue, a skill weakness or a limiting self-belief. In this case the lower-level, related problems appear as the effects or results of your problem. In any event, the solution usually lies at a higher level.

You can change most minor behavioural issues one or two levels up. In this case, we have omitted the spiritual category. A major personal issue, on the other hand, would probably have its root at a higher or 'super self' (spiritual) level.

You can apply the model to all forms of self-development, as well as to solving problems. It also helps in understanding and communicating with others. These neurological levels illustrate the mental maps and neurological filters we met on Day 1.

NEUROLOGICAL LEVELS AND ORGANISATIONS

All but the highest neurological level can easily translate into the context of an organisation:

Identity = Mission and vision
Beliefs = Philosophy and culture
Capabilities = Skills and knowledge
Behaviour = Customs and practice
Environment = Equipment, surroundings and location

In some cases the equivalent of the highest 'spiritual' level does apply. This happens when the organisation, often a non-profit-making one, pursues a cause bigger than itself, such as a charitable, health or environmental concern.

These neurological levels also illustrate the way companies motivate their staff, or bring about change:

Mission and vision
The work force identify with and gain inspiration from the company's mission. They have a collective sense of direction and purpose. People take pride in working for the company. The company has a distinct personality of its own.

Philosophy and culture
The company respects different values. People give loyal service because they feel that respect. Common belief affects 'how we do things round here' and the company applies values in considering staff, customers and systems. They set clear policies on such things as rewards, training and welfare.

Skills and knowledge

The management conveys information and understanding. The work force respond to demands because they understand the situation. The management implement training and other policies. They keep staff up to date with new technology and they run efficient systems. They empower staff to use their discretion and staff can contribute to higher-level decisions.

Customs and practice

The organisation rewards and punishes individual behaviour. Staff participate in discretionary training and make suggestions. Staff adhere to accepted norms of the company.

Equipment, surroundings and location

The company provides good facilities and working conditions. They tend to manage by exception – they concentrate only on what does not conform to their plans.

Each of these levels needs congruency with the level above to have the greatest change impact. Most of us will have come across an organisation or a person who boasts a particular mission or belief that does not match their behaviour or environment. They live a lie, and will probably not succeed. Furthermore, such incongruence may well breed resentment and cynicism. By contrast, alignment fosters empowerment and means the whole organisation, like a single person, moves in one direction.

ALIGNMENT

When considering a specific problem, asking the following sorts of questions will help to identify the neurological level at which it exists:

Spirituality/purpose	Who else?
Identity/mission	Who?

Belief systems and values   Why?
Capabilities   How?
Behaviour   What?
Environment   Where?

Use the following exercise to align the neurological levels in your own experience. You will then, in effect, have all your cylinders firing together to reach your goal. Let your imagination go to work. Do not underestimate the power of this process to change your life, however simplistic it may seem:

1. Choose an empowering state (such as mastery, confidence, creativity, peace, etc). Identify where and when you want to experience it. You can call that state x.

2. Arrange the neurological levels, from spirituality to environment, in line on the floor as locations. Sheets of paper will do to position the levels.

3. Stand in the 'environment' location with your back to the rest of the levels. Think of *where* you want to experience x. Describe the environment to yourself in your head.

4. Step back into the 'behaviour' location and ask: '*What* do I want to do in that time and location?' Notice your posture, gestures, expressions, the sound of your voice, your feelings. Notice, in your imagination, other people and their reactions, comments and behaviour.

5. Step back into the 'capability' location and ask '*How* do I behave like this in that environment?' Notice what you say to yourself, the skills and knowledge involved, and how you imagine or 'code' this setting in your mind.

6. Step back into the 'beliefs' location and ask *why* you do what you do. Or: 'What do I believe that allows me

to use those capabilities, and take those actions, in that environment?'

7. Step back into the 'identity' location and ask: '*Who am I that I would have those beliefs?*' Think of a living metaphor for your identity – perhaps a symbol, a colour, an animal, a plant – whatever your unconscious brings to mind. We covered this in the chapter on Metaphor, Day 11.

8. Take a final step back into the 'spirituality' location and ask: 'What overall vision or purpose am I pursuing in my life?' Or: '*Who or what else* motivates me at the deepest (or highest) level?' Notice how your vision or purpose transcends all the levels of personal transformation before you.

9. Maintaining your clarity of vision or purpose, step forward into the location of identity and feel them merge.

10. Bring both the vision and identity into the level of your beliefs and feel them all merge.

11. Bring your vision, identity and beliefs into the capability location and feel them all merge.

12. Bring the vision, identity, beliefs and capability into the level of behaviour and feel them all merge.

13. Bring your vision, identity, beliefs, capability and behaviours into the level of environment and feel them all merge.

14. Enjoy a new sense of alignment and know that you have all these resources at your fingertips whenever you want to use them.

You can use the neurological levels model to:

- Identify and clarify problems, whether personal or organisational

- Identify the best level at which to make changes
- Understand yourself better, your goals and motivations – 'what makes you tick'
- Understand other people better – 'what makes them tick' – and create better rapport and relationships
- Solve problems
- Clarify the goals you set on Days 2 and 3
- Establish a sense of purpose in everything you do
- Get *perspective* on your life by understanding issues from different perceptual levels

PRESUPPOSITION FOR TODAY

> **I am in charge of my mind and therefore my results.**

The mental 'map' we met in the very first presupposition means *my* map – *your* map. *You* can think what you like. *You* can choose what has importance. *You* can change your beliefs and values, and the way you react to people and circumstances. No outward circumstances can rob you of these basic human choices. 'You are what you think', so you can take charge of what you do and achieve. Whatever your past, you can start to control your present and future. This presupposition can help anyone improve their effectiveness, particularly results-oriented people.

TODAY'S TO DOs

- List some problems you face, either at work or in any area of your life. Allocate each one to a different neurological level. For example, perhaps you consider your study too tiny? Or you need another bedroom? Or you have outgrown your personal computer? Classify this sort of problem as environmental. Classify a language, writing or other skill that has let you down as behaviour. A problem that involves managing people, organising your work or speaking in public would probably fall into the capability level, and so on.

- Then think about these problems in terms of different levels. For instance, how might your behaviour affect your environment? And how might your identity or self-image affect your capabilities? This will help you get to the root of the problem, and suggest at what level you need to make changes.

- Now consider how you can apply the same process to an organisational, 'political', or systems problem at work or in your business.

- If you did not do it earlier, try the alignment exercise (see pp. 202–4).

DAY 15

Thinking Outside The Box

This chapter covers:
- **Frames and reframing**
- **Reframing for results**
- **Meeting frames**

FRAMES AND REFRAMING

Much of what you have learnt so far has concerned change – particularly changing *perceptions* (the way you think about things or the way you 'see' things). *Frames* form part of the system of filters through which we represent things internally. They act as mental templates or patterns, into which we conveniently slot the billions of sensory messages we continuously process. The 'frame' you set, consciously or unconsciously, reflects the way you perceive something, or the way you look at it. *Reframing* means changing the frame of reference around a behaviour, statement or event, finding another meaning or interpretation, seeing things in a different light.

It seems that, as humans, we need to order things in mental pigeon-holes or frames. Sadly, however, we get stuck in the rut of certain ways of thinking – mindsets. So we miss out on new ways to solve problems or perceive issues. When you

do go outside your present frame, or change it, you *reframe*.
More an attitude than a skill, reframing requires a whole
new, creative 'out-of-the-box' way of thinking.

> **The meaning of any event depends on the frame in which
> we perceive it.**

When you expect a welcome visitor you will probably perceive (or 'frame') a knock at the door differently from a
knock late at night when you expect no one. Your frame of
reference differs, and so does the meaning. Changing the
frame means changing the meaning. And changing the
meaning means changing the effect of a communication,
behaviour or event.

You can use reframing in all sorts of situations. Although
essentially a mental process, it can bring about immediate
change in behaviour. You may find it difficult to change
another person's behaviour, or indeed your own. But you can
always change the way you think or the way you see things –
even if just a bit at a time. Reframing changes the way you
feel and therefore what you do.

REFRAMING FOR RESULTS

Reframing brings fast results, and has thus gained popularity among practitioners of NLP. It has many applications – in
business, personal development, communication and therapy. It offers a powerful problem-solving tool in its own
right, with scores of techniques based on the simple principle of 'changing the frame'. It stimulates so-called lateral or
'outside-the-box' thinking. In conflict situations, reframing
can have a far greater effect than persuasive oratory or
weight of argument.

Content and Context Reframes

Reframes can affect the *context* of the situation. For instance, you can change the place or time. Just think of another context in which the behaviour might seem positive or useful, or where the behaviour would appear in a different light.

Or you can change the essence or actual *content* of the situation. For instance, you can change the behaviour or circumstances, or simply give something a different meaning.

Most humour involves some sort of reframe. The punchline of a joke instantly changes the meaning and the emotion that goes with it. An unexpected change of content or context turns the meaning on its head, and the resulting surprise and unfamiliarity creates humour. For instance, the late comedian George Burns frequently used one-liners that incorporated humorous reframes. Examples include: 'By the time you're 80 you've learnt everything . . . You just have to remember it.' or 'Take my wife . . . any time.' The metaphors we covered on Day 11 offer endless reframes. The new story context places familiar problems or issues in unfamiliar surroundings, giving them a different meaning.

As we saw from the NLP model on Day 1, we can only ever experience a filtered version of reality. So we *unconsciously* distort things all the time. Changing the meaning, whether through the context or content, means changing the way you react and behave. Taking another perspective can instantly change how you feel, thus indirectly affecting your behaviour and outcomes. Reframing therefore offers a *low-effort* route to results.

Get into the habit of asking: 'What could this mean?', 'In what circumstances would this appear different?' or 'In what context might this behaviour seem positive and useful?' Several reframes may quickly come to mind.

Controlling Your State of Mind

You control the reframing process and it need not depend on external events or circumstances. For example, imagine your teenage daughter comes home later than expected. Your feelings and behaviour while waiting for her will depend upon how you 'frame' the situation. Has she had an accident? Has she wilfully disobeyed you? Has she tried to telephone? Reframing has no limits. And you can *choose* how you interpret the situation. Thus, the way you frame things can affect your behaviour, your blood pressure, and, in the longer term, your health.

So far, the way you frame the behaviour or situation has not affected your daughter. However, it has certainly affected *you*. Even if you remain calm, trusting and seemingly unaffected, that reflects the way you have framed the situation. The frame you adopt determines your state, because it determines your perception.

Our brains have to give *meaning* to things; they cannot bear to leave anything unexplained. So we put everything into a mental pigeon-hole. Unfortunately we often 'file' things instinctively in the most obvious, comfortable or convenient frame, rather than representing them realistically or rationally. This tends to happen quickly and sometimes unconsciously, making you feel strongly about something without knowing why.

Reframing, in effect, 're-files' experience to better reflect present 'reality', or your *choices* as to possible reality. You can always choose to reframe. You have the choice of *thinking* differently. Using reframing techniques, you can begin to *choose* your state of mind.

The Habit of Seeing Things Differently

In the case of the teenage daughter a parent might respond: 'Easier said than done.' Yet, like swimming or riding a bike, once you have established an unconscious skill as a habit you really *do* find it easy. Thinking skills can also become thinking habits. And this includes the invaluable mental skill of reframing.

Once familiar with the process, you can reframe an otherwise negative or emotionally unpleasant behaviour to make it empowering, purposeful or useful. Just *recognising* choices can put you in a better frame of mind to handle a situation or make a decision. You have a way out – light at the end of the tunnel. Reframing can solve major problems with what seems like a miraculous insight. But always aim for choice. If you can perceive *several* frames, you have already created choices. And choices represent resources that enable you to respond effectively. Reframing probably involves less skill than pacing and leading. But, to acquire the habit of reframing, you need to apply it continually in everyday life. An open, flexible, creative mind will bring extraordinary results with minimum effort.

Improving Relationships

In due course, the way you reframe will affect other people, of course. Any parent knows how a teenager reacts to their 'jumping to conclusions', not trusting, or worrying unduly. Spontaneous behaviour, reacting to a single, rigid frame or interpretation can soon escalate out of all proportion to the original words or circumstances – turning into the stuff of divorce, conflict and war.

Reframing a person's behaviour will not *directly* change it. However, the process will almost certainly affect your *perception* of that behaviour – how seriously you take it, how far you let it affect you emotionally, and the way you interpret it. We know that the way you think or feel affects your own behaviour, including the things you say. So your behaviour will no doubt *indirectly* affect the other person. You cannot insulate yourself from the effect of feelings. Or, to misquote another presupposition, 'You cannot not communicate.'

You don't have to communicate *consciously*. On Day 4 you met the presupposition 'The meaning of a communication is the response it gets.' If you have an effect on anyone because of what you do or don't do, say or don't say, you communicate something. Silence, a misinterpreted look, or a communication intended for another person, can all create an outcome or effect. Our whole physiology, as well as the words we say, continuously conveys 'messages' to others. *We cannot not communicate.* And it pays to accept this sobering reality. Simple awareness of this fact can give us more control over the effect we have on others, and the outcomes we achieve with and through them.

Creative Problem-Solving

Sometimes a problem simply disappears when reframed. On other occasions it changes, perhaps to an effect rather than a cause. You thus identify its root. In other cases a reframe suggests a completely novel solution that abandons old mindsets. Reframing often means shaking yourself out of a mental rut.

Clearly, some reframes seem to have more practical use than others. They might, for instance, more closely reflect the 'actual' situation. In this case the 'viewpoint', if you like, moves only a few degrees. However, the less radical or creative the reframe, the less likely that it will resolve the problem or issue. So don't go for a 'sensible' interpretation. The problem-owner has probably already addressed the problem from many points of view, but with a mindset of 'filtered' experience. To get out of a mental rut, you will need something more.

A major or bizarre reframe may at first seem contrived and silly. But, once you have developed this thinking process, you will start to recognise its advantages. Give it a try. Think of three current problems, whether to do with work, home, friends and social life or whatever. Then apply at least three reframes to each. Do this quickly and intuitively. No doubt you have already addressed any real, current problem in a logical, rational way or it would no longer constitute a 'problem'. So, as a good test for reframing, choose a real problem you consider intractable.

Paradoxically, when we *try* to solve problems we often miss the best solutions. Reframing does not mean logically matching or modelling a situation, but rather breaking free of a restrictive model or mindset. The 'problem' concerns the mental rut rather than the 'content' of the presented problem – what the rut contains. Another person may see a problem as an opportunity, or a curse as a blessing, simply because they have placed it in a different frame. Although we so often blame our environment or circumstances, the real difference lies in our respective mental maps. By shifting your perceptions, you create choices for empowering, useful actions that will help bring about your outcome. You act as the main player.

Reframing in Practice

Let's say a colleague at work has a habit of running you down in front of others and not appreciating the effort you put into assignments. His abruptness and general attitude upset you. How might you reframe the situation?

- He has a painful medical condition.
- He feels insecure and on the verge of a nervous break-down.
- He gets similar treatment from *his* boss.
- Continuously henpecked at home, he can only survive by venting his feelings at work.
- He has earmarked you for special promotion and needs to test your metal for the sort of harsh management environment you will have to face.
- He does not know how his behaviour affects you.
- Others feel he treats them in just the same way.
- He suffered terrible abuse as a child.
- Three months ago he lost his older brother.
- He has suffered three break-ins at home in the last year.
- He has a terminal illness.
- His wife and children adore him.
- He gives you the most difficult assignments because you produce the best work. So, logically, you get the most stick.

- How would he act in a social setting, while pursuing a hobby or interest you shared, or at a dinner party?
- He knows of impending company problems but cannot share them with staff yet.
- Imagine him as your brother-in-law.
- Imagine he has left you a fortune in his will.
- Imagine he has a long white beard.
- Imagine he loves you but has difficulty showing it.
- Imagine the situation will only last for two months/two weeks/two days.

Once you get used to the process, you will come up with plenty of your own reframes. But so far you have not brought yourself into the equation. For instance, you could ask yourself:

- What if I had a thicker skin (like so-and-so)?
- What if we swapped jobs?
- What if I thanked him for each observation?
- What if I giggled at every communication?
- What if I bought him a nice pen?
- What if I had a job offer from another company?
- What if I won the lottery?
- How does this person affect my major life goals?

Note that a reframe does not need to have logic, feasibility or even common sense. It acts in a similar way to the metaphors you met on Day 11. It simply disturbs existing mindsets and opens up new, creative neural networks. So you have more choice about how you feel and what you can do. Common sense and logic, however, usually appear in hindsight.

MEETING FRAMES

Reframing offers an excellent tool in communication, as in training or counselling. All the rules for a good communication, including a well-formed outcome (see Day 2), stand. In particular, you will need to maintain rapport (see Day 4). You do not need to *articulate* a reframe for it to have effect. It can stay in your mind.

When you *do* communicate it, for instance to help someone solve a problem, the skill lies in reframing in such a way that you maintain rapport. Always match values and experience. When you have rapport, a person (in a sincere quest for a solution) may respond positively even to the most 'lateral' reframe. Aim, however, not to shock or to display your wisdom, but to stimulate in the other person the creative 'aha' breakthrough. What seems like a perceptive insight into a person's inner world can establish excellent rapport.

As an example of the wide application of frames, you can apply this technique to meetings of any kind. You will probably recognise some of the frames we have listed below. We have added some questions to illustrate the frames and show how you can use them for more effective meetings.

As with the many other language patterns you have met, you do not need to concern yourself with terms, or even strict definitions. In some cases the terms will help (as with the self-explanatory 'As if' frame). In other cases, you could try coining your own labels. Try to recognise *patterns*, and the sort of questions that stimulate reframing.

Outcome frame

A procedure at the beginning of the meeting as a whole and at the beginning of each agenda item that identifies and gets agreement on the outcome of that item. (The work you did on goals/outcomes in Day 2 concerned setting outcome frames.)

Question: 'What specifically do we want from this meeting/item?'

'As if' frame

A technique that helps people project themselves into the desired outcome and identifies the sensory-specific evidence of success. You think 'as if' the outcome has happened.

Question: 'Imagine you have already achieved this outcome. What do you see, hear and feel that lets you know you have achieved the outcome?'

Contrast frame

Here you compare different options to assess their relative value or to improve the decision-making process.

Question: 'What's the difference between what you have described and what we have now?' Or 'How does this compare with/relate to so-and-so?'

Agreement frame

This frame uses any points of agreement to match, pace and lead to a required outcome. It builds on common ground. For example, 'I agree that we need **x**: and you might find it useful to add some **y** as well.'

Relevancy challenge frame

A procedure to keep the meeting on track and challenge irrelevant meandering or time-wasting. This can apply particularly where you have already agreed on outcomes or fixed an agenda.

Question: 'How does what you say relate to the outcome for this item?'

Back track frame

A technique of summarising the points discussed in order to clarify decision-making, or summarising the decision made to check agreement. This avoids later disagreement, facilitates recording of minutes, and ensures that the relevant person understands the action required.

Question: 'So we have decided . . . does everyone agree?' Or, addressed to an individual, 'Let me see if I understand you correctly . . .'

You can use any of the above frames as appropriate at any time in the meeting. You may wish to use them as a guide to positioning agenda items or as a checklist for the chairperson. But any member of a meeting can improve the meeting's effectiveness by incorporating these framing patterns. Notice also the use of soft front ends which we covered on Day 10. You can mix and match all these techniques.

As well as meetings, you may find frames useful in any type of communication, such as interviewing, counselling and mediation, negotiation, training, preaching and education, as well as in family and social communication. You should find it easy to adapt the different frames to the circumstances of a communication.

PRESUPPOSITION FOR TODAY

> **Whatever you think you are, you are always more than that.**

This presupposition highlights the amazing capacity of the human mind–body system. It embraces the limitless subconscious mind which controls so-called unconscious competence or autopilot-type functions that account for so much human excellence. You can take control of your mental filters *just by thinking*. This means that your brain capacity need not dissipate into disempowering thoughts and unwanted behaviour. The adage 'If anyone can, I can' opens a world of potential excellence. Today's presupposition places that infinite potential squarely inside you, as a basis for motivation and self-esteem. Accept it as a neurological reality.

TODAY'S TO DOs

- If you did not do the reframing exercise above, have a go today. Think of any three problems or issues you face and think of at least three reframes on each. The work example on pp. 213–14 shows how you can let your imagination loose. It doesn't matter if your reframe does not seem 'realistic' or 'feasible' (your 'logical' left brain may think your ideas irrelevant or stupid). But even nonsense reframes can change the way you feel about a situation, and that usually means the beginning of real change.

● As you go about your work today, start noticing and reframing behaviour around you. You will invariably put an instinctive meaning or interpretation on what you experience, but start to ask: 'What else might this mean? How can I reframe this statement, question, behaviour, information or event?' Notice how differently you feel, and how differently you act (or don't act).

● Experiment with taking different perceptual positions (see Day 12) throughout the day, and notice how your feelings change.

DAY 16

The Key To Personal Excellence

This chapter covers:

- **Strategies for success**
- **Feedback systems**
- **Identifying and using strategies**
- **The TOTE model**
- **Strategy chunks**

People get results because of what they do and the way they do it. Excellence requires excellent strategies. Incompetence results from incompetent strategies. In NLP the term strategy usually means 'a prepared mental programme, or sequence of representations, leading to a specific outcome'. This may sound very technical – but it will get clearer as we go along. Like following a recipe, you have to use the right ingredients in the right order to achieve success. A strategy means the way we think in order to achieve something.

STRATEGIES FOR SUCCESS

Most people can hardly imagine doing anything at all unless something motivates them or they *think* that a certain course of action will prove worthwhile. You *expect* that what you do will achieve a particular outcome. Your mental strategy may start, for example, with an appraisal or test of whether you should even bother. You then need a strategy for the motivation to get started, followed by a strategy for actually doing something. Like the combination number to a safe, a mental strategy works consistently, time after time. So, understanding how to install and change strategies gives you the basis for personal excellence.

Strategies as Neural Networks

The idea that 'You are what you think' can extend to the fact that we also tend to *do* what we think. Or at least, we do what occupies our thoughts. NLP emphasises these *internal* representations which inevitably produce behaviour that in turn produces desired outcomes. Within your brain, these strategies constitute awesomely complex neural networks.

Human life comprises an unending series of representations, both internal and external. We constantly see, hear and feel, as we live out our lives and relate to our immediate environment. In this sense we inhabit two worlds – an outer world, and an inner world of memories and experience, beliefs and values. Strategies embrace both.

Strategy Levels

Strategy extends from large 'chunks' of behaviour down to the very detailed thought submodalities described on Day 7. You need a strategy for roofing a house or selling a company, for example. And a strategy may take the form of specific words or a mental image that motivates you to do something.

For instance, you need a strategy for: getting out of bed in the morning, deciding what you want to eat, breaking an egg, frying it, eating it and enjoying it, feeling anxious about something coming up that morning at work, doing sums in your head, tying your shoelaces.

Each of these examples comprises smaller strategy chunks, right down to the level of the submodalities you learnt about on Day 7. Higher-level strategies may include scores of smaller chunks. Note, however, the different levels of activity. And variety. You can smash an egg in many different ways. And people make decisions or motivate themselves in all sorts of different ways.

We carry out these strategies largely unconsciously, of course. But NLP allows us to consciously identify and change them for the better. So far you have learnt how to change your outcomes, and change how you feel. You can now start to change the strategies you adopt for achieving your outcomes. And this will give you more control over the way you feel, your attitudes, values and beliefs.

Strategy Syntax

To succeed, you need to think and act in a particular order or sequence. You have to get the elements of your strategy right (just as you have to choose the right words for a sentence to make sense). But you also have to get the *order* or syntax right. This applies to any strategy for any activity, behaviour or skill. You will soon realise that even the simplest habits involve complex strategies that consistently work for our benefit.

FEEDBACK SYSTEMS

We achieve outcomes through a *system* of strategies. Once you know how the system works, it will produce the same results consistently. This system broadly follows the four-stage success model we met on Day 2:

- Decide what you want
- Do something
- Notice what happens
- Change what you do until you get your desired outcome.

To carry out this cybernetic or goal-oriented approach, you need:

- A specific target.
- The ability to do something towards achieving it.
- A means of knowing by how much you have missed your target.
- The ability to keep changing what you do until you reach your target.

We all possess these system requirements – so it only remains to *harness* our resources to best effect.

Setting Your Target

Electro-mechanical or robotic-type systems provide examples of feedback systems. The *target* may range from a temperature setting on a central heating system or dishwasher, to a city at which a ballistic missile aims, or an operation a robot has to perform. Such mechanical feedback systems surround us. But we do not always associate human behaviour with them. In some very important cases, we set and achieve goals unconsciously.

For instance, our physical 'system' consistently achieves all sorts of inbuilt survival goals, from maintaining our body temperature to healing wounds on our skin. In these vital cases we just *trust* the system. We unconsciously 'know' that it works.

Fortunately, NLP allows us to tap into this same inbuilt cybernetic or goal-achieving ability for *conscious*, purposeful goals. You have to begin by deciding what you want (the first stage in the four-stage success model). Much of this *process*, however, remains unconscious – like learning to talk and walk as a child, or the ability to mimic someone else's skill. Whether conscious or unconscious, you need a specific target or outcome. So the well-formed outcomes you defined on Day 2 provide the essential targets in this dependable feedback system.

Reaching the Target

Staying with the four-stage success model, you then have the ability to **do something** (stage 2), using your amazing total neuro-physical system – your mind–body. Your clever 'system' also has the ability to **notice what happens** (stage 3) through your senses. You can further develop this skill by what NLP terms sensory acuity. (A central heating system achieves this calibration or 'noticing' by means of a thermostat which senses how far the room temperature 'misses' the 'target' we have set.) Finally, you can **make changes** (stage 4). The boiler in a central heating system turns on or off to adjust the temperature – and thus gets nearer to its target. Not surprisingly, the human 'boiler' works with far greater sophistication than any man-made device. We have an awesome neuro-physiological system to do the job. Numerous autopilot behaviours rely on this inbuilt feedback system, producing what we call unconscious competence.

IDENTIFYING AND USING STRATEGIES

You may wish to elicit someone's thinking strategy for several reasons. For example:

1. To model excellent behaviour. As well as copying the behaviour, we need to understand how the person *thinks*. They may not know the thought processes that produce their excellent behaviour ('I just do it'), so you will need to 'elicit' their strategy.

2. In a therapeutic situation, knowing someone's strategy allows you to undo or 'scramble' it, making it ineffective. If you scramble a strategy that leads to a certain behaviour, the person can no longer do that behaviour. The phobia cure, a popular NLP process described on Day 21, works in this way. So you gain important information which you can then use to bring about change.

3. If you learn a person's motivation strategy and you have built a rapport (see Day 4), you can 'play it back' and motivate them. Similarly, if you know a person's decision-making strategy, given rapport, you can play it back and they will make a decision. So the ability to match someone's thinking strategy gives you a very powerful tool for selling, negotiating and influencing.

4. Once you identify an 'excellent' strategy, you can start to use it yourself – to achieve your own outcomes.

In addition, you can start to identify your own strategies. If you wish, you can change them to achieve different outcomes, or achieve the same outcomes more easily and enjoyably.

THE TOTE MODEL

NLP has adopted the TOTE computer model as a guide to eliciting strategies. This may appeal to readers who have met it in an engineering context. But the simple four-stage success model above does a similar job, and you can stick to that if you prefer.

TOTE stands for:

Test/trigger
Operate
Test
Exit

Test/trigger
The first Test acts as the stimulus, cue or trigger that begins the strategy. Let's say, for example, you want to buy a sweat-shirt. In the first Test you may see a picture in your head of the sweatshirt you want, with you or somebody else wearing it. We annotate this as 'Vi' or 'visual internal'. You met this sort of notation on Day 7.

Operate

The Operate stage accesses the data by remembering, creating or gathering information from the internal or external world. In this case it comprises what you do to find a sweatshirt. It will no doubt include some 'Ve' (visual external), as you look around externally; then, perhaps, some Ad (auditory digital), as you talk to yourself about the possible options and pros and cons; maybe some K (kinaesthetic), the feelings you get.

(Second) Test

The second Test compares some aspect of accessed data and the criteria established by the first Test. Here you compare the sweatshirt you had in your mind with the one you have now seen. Does it live up to what you wanted? Here you see externally (Ve), and also see internally the image you fed forward as your criterion (Vi). And you *feel* either positive or negative about the comparison (K). You compare the two choices in the same representational system, like for like, whether visual, auditory or kinaesthetic.

Exit

The Exit or decision point represents the result of the Test. If you have a match then the strategy exits and you buy. If you have a mismatch, and follow the strategy, you will not buy.

The strategy may then recycle (or enter a loop) by:

- Changing the outcome or redirecting the strategy ('I'll buy shoes instead').
- Adjusting the outcome or chunking laterally ('I'll put the money towards a holiday').
- Refining or further specifying the outcome ('I'll hang on for a better-quality winter sweatshirt').
- Accessing more data ('I'll shop around some more').

In the case of a mismatch, the strategy recycles to the first Test/trigger phase, or to the Operation phase. If you make a purchase, your buying strategy has ended. If unhappy, you might keep looking around, thus repeating the Operation stage. Once you get a match you will buy and Exit. Alternatively you might Exit not deciding to buy. In this case you might start the whole process again. This time you might change your first Test/trigger, perhaps imagining something different, more realistic. Or perhaps you just have a (literal) change of mind.

We give two further simple illustrations of the TOTE model below.

Making a Cake for Tea

(First) Test
I decide I want a cake for tea – the *trigger*.
I visualise the finished cake – a chocolate one – and this becomes the test to feed forward to later in the strategy.

Operate
I go through questions or actions in my head: 'Do I have the ingredients in my cupboard to make a chocolate cake?' I see in my fridge or cupboard eggs, margarine, sugar, chocolate, etc.

(Second) Test
The ingredients fulfil the requirements to make the visualised cake.

Exit
I exit the thinking strategy and begin the behaviour of making the cake.

Weeding the Garden

(First) Test
My garden needs weeding – trigger.

Operate
I run through my schedule for the week and conclude I have no time for the weeding.

(Second) Test
My garden still needs weeding. At this point, instead of exiting, I recycle, as the second test did not turn out satisfactorily. I have not achieved my desired outcome.

Operate
I decide to telephone a gardener in the neighbourhood to ask if he can help me out with the weeding.

Another (Second) Test
If he agrees, the weeding will get done.

Exit
I exit the thinking strategy and make the phone call.

Identifying Strategies Using the TOTE Model

Using the TOTE model, you can use simple questions to elicit a person's strategy:

(First) Test
How do you know when to . . .?
When did you begin . . .?
What let you know the time had come to . . .?

Operate
How do you do it?
How do you recognise alternatives?
How do you generate alternatives?

(Second) Test
How do you know when your operation succeeds?
How do you determine acceptability or satisfaction?
How do you evaluate the alternatives?

Exit

You have completed the strategy. If questions remain you will either keep testing (second test), carry out further operations, or go back to the start of the strategy.

You can begin to understand the other person's mind by carefully watching their eye movements. Remember that they carry out their strategy unconsciously. They do not think about thinking, or even, in the case of an 'autopilot' activity, doing. However, immediate questions (as the strategy runs) may elicit the strategy as it happens ('I hear myself say', 'I see a picture of . . .'). In this case their eye movements will *confirm* the representational systems (see Day 6) in operation.

STRATEGY CHUNKS

Where does a strategy start and end? A buying strategy, for instance, may start when you become motivated to buy something and finish when, having made the purchase, you know you have made the right decision. Whether buying a house or a loaf of bread, you often have to handle 'chunks' of information. So you may decide on smaller, more convenient 'chunks' for your strategy as follows:

- Motivating
- Decision-making
- Convincing
- Reassurance

The earlier examples illustrate these strategies. On Day 17 you will cover the 'convincer' strategy in some depth.

Eliciting and annotating a long operation can involve very complex processes. First you have to break down a strategy into what appear as discrete parts. You can then make comparisons with other contexts. For example, you may well find that a person's motivation strategy applies to many contexts other than buying. Similarly a decision-making strategy applies to many different kinds of decision. You can thus use the strategy in many more ways, from deciding how long to set the microwave oven to who to marry!

The Size of Strategy Chunks

Your outcome may concern a large, extended operation – like planning a conference or organising a wedding. In such a case you will need to deal in big chunks. But you will also need to understand certain *aspects* or phases of these long complex operations, like how to pin a flower to the best man's lapel. So you will 'chunk down' accordingly.

Treat important decisions (e.g. whether to do something yourself or hire someone to do it for you, whether to do it now or wait, whether to replace some old windows or change your car) as stand-alone strategies. Similarly, a strategy for getting and staying motivated will form part of a task or project that calls for motivation.

In some cases you will need to go into detail in order to *understand* the strategy, before you can change it or use it yourself. This may involve submodalities as well as modalities (check back to Day 7). For instance, what do you see, feel or say to yourself when you make such a decision? You may need to isolate thinking patterns and behaviour at a micro level in order to understand macro strategies – for instance, changing your job or writing a short story. Make sure the strategy chunk size reflects the level at which you want to understand and need to change behaviour.

The Number of Strategy Chunks

The chunking decision will affect the number of elements in the strategy sequence. As a guide, one or two chunks might mean you have not elicited the whole strategy. More than six or seven, on the other hand, might mean you have spanned more than one discrete strategy (perhaps combining motivation and decision-making) or that you have recorded a loop. A loop (see the TOTE model above) simply means that you repeat (or recycle) part of the strategy before exiting.

PRESUPPOSITION FOR TODAY

> **If one person can do something, anyone can do it.**

Anyone can use the four-stage success model you met on Day 2. We all have standard brain hardware. You can use your brain as you like, and programme it with 'software' thoughts. People we associate with excellence (or even genius) simply use their brains more effectively. In the areas in which they excel, they have successful strategies. Although not magical formulae, these strategies do comprise particular sensory *representations* in a particular *order*, as we have seen. Often the person does not know what specific thinking or even behaviour brings about their success, or so-called unconscious competence. Hence the need to elicit strategies. Once you can identify a strategy, you can change it – or copy it. In the words of today's presupposition, if one person can do something, anyone can.

TODAY'S TO DOs

- Try eliciting the buying strategy of a close friend or relative. They will soon understand the principles themselves and may help you to identify your own buying and other strategies.

- Choose a strategy you use a lot, whether at home or at work (such as writing a report, making a sales call, preparing a meal) and break it down into as many component chunks as you can. Note the internal as well as external processes. Start to think about the way you think in these internal strategies. Can you identify which modalities (or 'rep' systems, see Day 6) you use?

DAY 17

Strategies For Success

This chapter covers:

- **The convincer strategy**
- **Spelling strategy**
- **21 tips for identifying strategies**

Today we address two types of strategy. The 'convincer strategy' formed part of the buying process you met on Day 16 but applies widely to different behaviours involving convincing. So we will cover it in more detail.

THE CONVINCER STRATEGY

What NLP calls 'the convincer strategy' relates to the number of times a person runs through the decision-making sequence, how long they need to make the decision, and the characteristics of the strategy they use to convince themselves fully. For example, how many different products does a person have to see or handle before deciding to buy? And how long do they take to make up their mind?

We have listed four main convincer strategies, or 'buyer personalities':

1. Automatic
These people see something or hear about it only once and can decide straight away – a salesperson's dream!

2. Number of times
These people need to compare several products, or get friends to accompany them to a number of shops, try on different clothes, etc, before deciding.

3. Consistent
These people have to go to every possible shop, read all the technical magazines, consult consumer guides, etc – the salesperson's nightmare.

4. Period of time
These people need *time*. They will think it over, sleep on it, and perhaps leave the decision for a few days before they feel convinced.

The convincer strategy affects a person's decision strategy and it may form a separate chunk when considering the overall buying strategy:

- It may precede the main or final decision strategy (Consistent).
- It may represent the number of times a decision strategy runs (Number of times).
- It may only concern the time factor (Period of time).
- It may reflect a strong motivation strategy that jumps quickly to action with no apparent decision process (Automatic).

We have used buying, as a familiar example. However, a convincer strategy can apply in any situation where convincing takes place. For example: hiring staff, choosing a supplier or consultant, deciding on a policy, moving furniture round a room or choosing a life partner.

So this strategy gives you very useful information about a person when you want to predict or change behaviour. It also provides invaluable self-knowledge which you can apply to achieving your goals or outcomes.

However deep-rooted these strategies, you can still change them. This makes strategy elicitation a powerful tool for personal change. For instance, someone with an 'automatic' convincer strategy may wish to interpose an Ad (auditory digital – 'speak to yourself') test, like 'Do I really need this?' or 'Can I afford this?' A slow, 'many times' convincer, on the other hand, might choose to use a different Ad element, such as 'Do it now'. And a 'period of time' person may resolve to make a decision within a specific timescale.

Understanding your convincer strategy provides very useful self-knowledge. And you can use this to change the way you make decisions. Understanding other people's strategies will help in selling, negotiation and other many other types of communication. It affects all sorts of decisions, from changing a job or moving to another country to choosing a car. Knowing your own and other people's convincer strategies opens up choices. You might decide to abandon a strategy that has served you well, especially when under pressure from others. Or you may decide to change your strategy to bring about a change in some behaviour, and achieve a current outcome. If you want to convince someone, for whatever reason, knowing their convincer strategy gives you a key to success.

SPELLING STRATEGY

We each have different strategies that work for us in our different skills. These often apply to us uniquely. Each person does what they do in a different way. The variety and ingenuity of people's strategies continue to surprise us as we encounter them in seminars. In some cases, however, like spelling, common elements may occur more generally. Here we can identify 'standard' excellence strategies. Based on important work in this area carried out by Robert Dilts, NLP offers useful strategy guidelines which almost invariably improve spelling skills. The research concludes that the best spellers predominantly use the visual, rather than, as one might expect, auditory sense. Anyone whose spelling falls below par can benefit from using the following simple strategy:

1. Look for a few moments at the word you want to remember how to spell.

2. Look away from the word. Then, moving your eyes up and to the left, visualise the spelling. Look back at the original image (in the book or wherever) to fill in any missing letters and correct any part of the word. Repeat the process until you can easily visualise the correct spelling in your mind. It may help to position the image up and to your left, a little away from you. You can, if you wish, imagine the word written in felt-pen on a flip chart, in big plastic or neon letters, or whatever. Choose a visual representation that makes an impact for you and that you can easily remember. Make it a dynamic, moving image if you wish, seeing yourself actually writing, complete with any sounds and feelings.

3. Look away again, look up at your mental image, and write the word down. If incorrect, go back to step 1 and repeat the process.

4. Try looking at your mental image and reading the spelling backwards (something almost impossible to do phonetically), to test the process.

Get into the habit of learning to spell words in this way and you will notice how easily you can recall them. You will find further specific tips on spelling in *NLP for Managers* by

Harry Alder (Piatkus). Other memory skills, such as mental arithmetic, also use the visual sense a lot, although the sub-modalities or characteristics of the visual images vary a lot from person to person.

21 TIPS FOR IDENTIFYING STRATEGIES

Identifying strategies forms an important part of the modelling process you will cover on Day 18. The skill will demand all your sensory acuity, and we have listed some further tips to bear in mind when eliciting someone's strategy:

1. Stay in uptime (see Day 8).

2. Establish rapport (see Day 4).

3. Set the frame (see Day 15).

4. Identify the context of the strategy – for example, to do with the children, a career matter or a health decision? If buying, for instance, will the person use their own money or somebody else's? Do they see it as a consumable or major lifetime purchase? Many strategies apply in different circumstances and parts of life. Others may not, but, in any event, identifying the context may well simplify the elicitation process.

5. Associate (see particularly Day 7). Ask: 'Can you see yourself from the outside? If so, step inside yourself and see the experience through your own eyes.'

6. Anchor the state (we cover anchoring on Days 19 and 20). Sometimes you may have to revisit the strategy and it helps to anchor it so that you can easily recall and fine-tune it. A strategy may only apply spasmod-ically. For example, once in a while you make an impulse purchase that you later regret. Once a person has vividly recalled such an occasion, anchoring it

enables them to quickly recall the same memory so you can elicit more of their strategy.

7. Speak in the present tense. Thus, for example, in eliciting a buying decision strategy:
'You're in the shop, what do you do first?' Then, 'So you look at the dresses . . . what happens next?' Or, 'So you *are looking* . . .' This helps get the person into an associated state, to 'relive' the experience. The present tense characterises the intuitive, unconscious mind for which time does not make sense, so it helps to stimulate otherwise lost memories. When accessing memories, you may find yourself tempted to use the past tense (e.g. 'What did you do next?'). However, when addressed in the present tense, the person will often answer in the same tense and actually run the strategy again.

8. Use eye accessing cues (see Day 6) to identify the representational systems used.

9. Explore strategies using basic who/what/where/how questions:
How do you know?
What happens first?
What happens next?
What happens just before?
How do you know that you've finished?

10. As these last questions suggest, you need to move forward to get at the connecting parts of the strategy. For example, you may get a comment on what sounds like an exit. In this case, take the person back to the trigger or get them to run the strategy.

11. Backtrack 'frame' if necessary (see Day 15). This just means going back over what you have elicited by way of summary, to give an opportunity for any correction. 'So, let me see if I've understood this correctly.

First you . . .' Run their strategy and watch their physiology which will confirm that you have got it right.

12. Watch out for loops. You will probably identify a clear
     cycle of the sort you met in the TOTE model you met
     on Day 16, but smaller loops can easily happen. For
     example, a *feeling* might create negative inner *dialogue*
     (Ad), which reinforces the *feeling*, and so on, in a
     repeat mode. In real life, although we may run many
     loops or re-tests, we would not do anything at all if we
     did not exit each strategy cycle. So you may have to
     run through the strategy a number of times to identify
     it. Once you have the person associated and running
     their strategy in front of you, their eye movements will
     tell you the representational system used. Their pred-
     icates and the descriptive sensory words they use will
     reinforce this. Remember that people's strategies
     operate unconsciously. They will tell you what they
     'think' they do, but your observation may provide
     more accurate information.

13. Make sure you have the main functional pieces or
     chunks. Part of strategy elicitation involves identifying
     where a strategy starts and ends. A high-level strategy,
     like buying a house or giving up smoking, made up of
     many smaller chunks, might take a long time. By con-
     trast, a strategy that involves a quick decision or intu-
     itive action can happen in seconds. Decide on the
     chunks you want to elicit. You then have a better
     chance of asking the right questions and guiding the
     person into re-running their strategy.

14. Watch out for so-called 'auditory markings': voice
     tone, pauses, emotion in the voice, confidence or hes-
     itance in responses, and so on.

15. Elicit all the major representational modalities until
     the strategy seems complete. The following illustrates
     a house-buying strategy:

Trigger	*V internal* plus list of criteria
Operate	*V external* compare *V internal*
	Ad self-talk re: value for money – Can I afford it?
	K Feel good
Test	*Ad K* Do I consider my criteria fulfilled?
Exit	To buy or look further

16. Use *unspecified predicates* ('How do you think about . . .?').

17. Use multiple-choice questions, e.g. 'Do you see a picture, or hear something, or have a feeling about it, or say something to yourself?'

18. When you think you have the sequence *feed it back* to the person and calibrate (see Day 5). In other words, using your sensory acuity skill, notice whether the person's non-verbal language fits what they say. Then, using the backtrack frame (see point 11 above), try to get confirmation of the whole strategy (rather than doing an interim re-cap). The feedback might go something like: 'You see the dress on the rail, compare it to the picture you had in your head, ask yourself if it represents good value for money, and if you get a good feeling you buy it – have I got that right?' In this example, you have elicited the sequence: Ve, Vi, Ad, K. If correct, the person's face will light up and they will nod assent. If not, they will look confused or unhappy, or shake their head. Or they will correct you as they re-run the strategy internally.

19. Elicit the submodalities (see Day 7) for added emphasis. You will note that the strategy or modelling notation (Ve, Ad, etc) does not take account of submodalities, just modalities (VAK), and the internal/external distinction. However, whether a visual representation appears bright and clear or very dim may well form a critical part of the strategy. And

the same can apply to any other submodality, however innocuous it may seem to you. Ask the person, for example: 'So you see a picture in your mind ... what sort of picture? Bright? In colour? Do you see yourself in the picture? Or do you see as if through your own eyes ...? Can you hear a voice inside ...? What does it sound like?' (These questions will help elicit the associated/dissociated distinction covered on Day 7.)

20. Elicit as much information as you need to achieve your goal – to identify the person's strategy. Use open who/what/how questions (which encourage answers other than yes or no). Remember that more information might come from the person's body language, voice tone and eye movements than their words.

21. Test your work.
   a. Can you run the strategy yourself and get the same or a similar result?
   b. Use a different example of the same sort of strategy – for instance, buying something else, reading something else, making a different important decision, and so on, to see if it follows the same strategy. Ask: 'Does it work with a different subject-content?'
   c. Test whether the strategy 'collapses' if the person *omits* one or two elements or changes the syntax or sequence. Aim to identify the key elements without which the strategy will not work.
   d. Check whether the strategy works in another *context*. Strategies do not always cross contexts but they may do. For instance, a successful strategy might transfer from a social or family context to work, or vice versa. If you find the same sequence running in a different context, you have good evidence that you have identified the strategy.

PRESUPPOSITION FOR TODAY

> **Choice is better than no choice.**

One choice amounts to no choice; two choices may present a dilemma; but three or more choices will give you a lot of control over your outcomes. This presupposition resembles the Law of Requisite Variety: 'The system with the widest range of variables will constitute the controlling element'. The flexibility of behaviour inherent in the four-stage success model (see Day 2) also assumes choice. The human imagination creates choices, and can reframe problems and situations to generate alternative ways of seeing things. Vertical or left-brain thinking stops at the first reasonable solution. But right-brain or lateral thinking does not stop – it assumes a better way exists. Start to think outside the box of conventional thought and create new choices.

TODAY'S TO DOs

- Assess the convincer strategies of people you know well. What does the knowledge you gain mean for you in your communication with them?

- If you want to improve your spelling skills try the spelling strategy on p. 235. Experiment with difficult words from a dictionary just to prove to yourself the effectiveness of the strategy. Add to the strategy, element by element, to see if you can improve its effectiveness. For instance, you may want the word to 'feel' right as well as retaining the visual image. Or you may say the word to link the pronunciation with the visual image. Or you might want to experiment with colours.

- Practise Meta Model responses (see Day 10), extending your repertoire of recognisable patterns and

responses. Don't speak responses out loud until you
have practised them mentally in real-life situations.

- Think about a present issue or problem you face and
  try to generate five or more choices. Can you choose,
  for instance, to feel differently, to interpret things differently, to act differently or to learn something from
  the situation or experience?

DAY 18

'If Anyone Can, I Can'

This chapter covers:
- **Modelling**
- **Capability and skill**
- **The modelling process**
- **Strategies that work**

Having learnt how to elicit strategies, you can now start to copy or 'borrow' them (NLP refers to this process as modelling). With this technique, otherwise ordinary people have an extraordinary route to personal excellence.

MODELLING

Modelling lies at the very heart of NLP. Indeed NLP owes its origins to modelling, applied mainly to eminent therapists who got remarkable results without knowing exactly how they did it. Not surprisingly, modelling has remained central, although its applications go well beyond therapeutic work and extend into sport, business, government, selling, negotiation, family, relationships and personal development of all kinds. To acquire a skill, initially you only need to find somebody who can do what you want to do. Then, using the effective, practical tool of modelling, you have a short cut to excellence.

We understand excellence by observing it in people. This need not suggest that we ordinary folk require superhuman geniuses as our models. Rather, every individual exhibits his or her own excellent behaviours, or skills. We need to recognise and focus our interest on these. In other words, find excellent *behaviours* rather than excellent *people*. Anyone can qualify as a 'model'.

For instance, you may discover a wizard at mental arithmetic. You may not, however, choose the same person to model, say, getting out of bed in the morning or keeping a tidy desk. Similarly, an athlete's or sportsperson's 'excellence' may involve highly specialised physical skills developed over a lifetime of training, but in other areas they may offer little help.

You and I have skills that we carry out automatically, with what NLP describes as unconscious competence. And wherever we find such skills or behaviour, we find plenty of other people who would like to carry out those skills with such ease and to such a level. In fact we all work *perfectly* all the time. Or at least the *system* does, whatever the outcome. But we still have to translate so-called talents or natural skills into outcomes – in other words, to get results.

We soon notice special skills and talents. Thus a person who excels, say, in art, sport or business, may earn their living from that skill. If not, they may nevertheless achieve worthwhile goals and find pleasure in what they do. In either case you might want to emulate their *skill* rather than copy them as *people*. Modelling excellence in people means modelling *aspects* of a person's behaviour or skills rather than the whole person. You model what the person can *do*. This, as we have discovered, involves their thinking strategies. And their thinking strategies include the beliefs and values that underpin and motivate their behaviour.

Nature or Nurture?

People who display special skills often exhibit them from an early age and you will probably know of examples of extraordinary skills among children. Such cases support the argument that these things boil down to genetics, and we should content ourselves with whatever talents the cosmic lottery has doled out. But rarely do we meet a top performer who does not put his or her success down to endless training, application and sheer hard work. In other words, raw talent, whatever its source, requires nurturing, developing and in most cases technical training before the world recognises it. Even so-called child prodigies receive encouragement and absorb talents around them in a sort of early hothouse of belief and expectation. For example, the great composer Wolfgang Mozart displayed extraordinary talent from the earliest age, giving piano recitals in the courts of Europe at the age of six. But his father Leopold nurtured his talent, imposing on his young son an extremely demanding regime of keyboard practice.

Nurture and nature only tell part of the story. We also need to consider some key aspects of modelling:

Strategy

As we saw on Day 17, people with a skill actually have a *strategy* (conscious or unconscious) for what they do. If they think about it, or if someone observes and remarks on their natural talent, they may then acknowledge a hitherto unconscious skill. Once revealed, it turns out that no magical element exists at all. Despite perhaps appearing strange or different, like any strategy it simply involves sequence or syntax of (VAK) representations. Remarkably, as you learnt on Day 1, you can reproduce almost any strategy you wish.

Motivation

Success may result from a person's motivation, commitment and perseverance rather than their inherent talent. Nature sometimes seems to provide remarkable aptitudes but not always the desire that keeps us going. But we all experience high motivation in certain areas of our life, and on certain occasions, however limited. So you can transfer motivation (another strategy) from one area of your life to another (see switching submodalities in Day 7). Or you can 'borrow' (model) someone else's strategy if you find it works better. As a rule, we have all the resources and skills we need (like motivation), but may not have applied them beyond limited areas of our experience. Early environment often accounts for a dogged determination to succeed.

For instance, following his father's imprisonment for debt, the young Charles Dickens' mother put him to work in a blacking factory, while she lodged with the rest of the family in the prison. But, on his father's release, and already psychologically scarred, Charles, again at the insistence of his mother, continued to work in the factory. Throughout his life Charles hid these dark, painful memories even from his wife and close friends. However, these childhood experiences seemed to contribute to his creative energy and probably help account for his preoccupation with alienation and betrayal in novels like *David Copperfield* and *Great Expectations*. Even much less obvious obstacles in early life can motivate a person to extraordinary achievement.

Experience

Don't expect that modelling will get you any Olympic medals, or help you topple some business rival with your new-found acumen. This would ignore the need for actual experience, and in particular the many 'failures' (or feedback) upon which success depends. Similarly, physical conditioning, diet and lifestyle may also contribute to physical accomplishment. Furthermore, your models have no doubt had many years' start on you.

However, taking into account your late start, or physical build, you can emulate a strategy to a high degree. If you don't become the world's best, or join your country's team, you may well play for your town or county. You can excel *relative to where you now stand*, measured against your own standards. Using the modelling process, people have achieved remarkable results.

Outcomes

Another major factor concerns the 'well-formedness' of your goal or outcome (see Days 2 and 3). This includes the mixture of 'secondary gain' and ecology that also dictate what we achieve. 'Excellence' has to have an outcome. And the pleasure of achieving the outcome has to make the effort worthwhile. This sort of evaluation takes place unconsciously as part of our early nurture. But, whatever the source of our very different desires and motivations, we should not underestimate the possibilities. Only your imagination can limit you. Your innate, neuro-physiological resources know no such limit. So, for present purposes, you can forget both nurture and nature. A well-formed outcome has a far greater effect on what you do and achieve. 'If anyone can, I can' has more currency in the marathon of life than a genetic or early environmental head-start. With modelling, you have a practical tool to make the 'I can' a reality.

Other Factors

Even convinced geneticists agree that nature represents only one factor among many. We can often overtake the 'natural' talent of others through application, commitment and training. For instance, early parental encouragement, peer and cultural acceptability, facilities and actual training clearly tip the balance in terms of the factors that bring about eventual success. More to the point, we can model apparently 'natural' skills using the same process – good news for those who feel genetically short-changed. Any natural advantage may give no more than a head-start. Rather, treat *any* skill or talent, whatever the source, as a good basis for modelling.

CAPABILITY AND SKILL

When modelling, you have to distinguish between a capability and a skill. Modelling best elicits a discrete skill, rather than a capability, which probably embraces many skills. You need to treat each as a separate chunk, as we explained on Day 16. A chef, for example, needs the *skills* of whisking, carving, presenting and so on before he or she can profess cooking *capability*. Similarly, the *skill* of building rapport with an audience may not mean you have full *capability* in giving public presentations. That comprises several skills.

You may recall this distinction in the neurological levels you met on Day 14. A skill lies at a lower neurological level than a capability. And this gives us a clue to successful modelling. To model a behaviour or skill, you may need to model thought strategies at a higher level, such as confidence and self-belief.

THE MODELLING PROCESS

You can easily apply the modelling process to a physical activity, such as a craft, a specific sporting activity, or learning a new dance routine:

- First choose the skill you want to model.

- Next choose a model. You only need to find excellence in the specific skill you have chosen. For instance, the model might not impress you as a person overall, or even in the area of competence of which the skill forms a part. For example, the person may paint an excellent watercolour wash but not have very good technical draughtsmanship or sense of perspective. Or a top go-kart rider may not have passed a driving test.

- You also need to have access to the model. You need to observe carefully, perhaps from different angles and perhaps without the person's knowledge. For sport or cookery, for example, you can take advantage of good video recordings which give access to the top performers. If you can interview the model you can get them to run their strategy, observe their eye movements, and question them about the values and beliefs that underpin a particular skill.

- Watch the model carrying out the skill, simply 'taking in' the sequence of movements. Don't try too hard. Think back to your childhood – watching a friend do what you could not do and naturally copying them.

- Then see yourself as the model but in a *dissociated* state, watching yourself from outside yourself. See yourself inside the skin of the model as you watch.

- As the model runs the sequence of activities again, step right inside the model and become fully *associated*. See through your own eyes and feel all the feelings you will feel when carrying out the skill yourself. Become *one* with the model and all their feelings.

- Do all this *mentally*. Finally, and instinctively, carry out the physical activity. Don't hesitate or analyse anything – just do it. Repeat the whole process until you feel you can get 'inside' the model, confident that you have mastered the skill. Every little feedback adjustment you make will contribute to your ultimate success.

You never fully 'arrive' at excellence. In the same way you cannot make mistakes when modelling – you simply *learn*. You *cannot not learn* (Day 12's presupposition). So you may as well make a good job of your learning, and keep getting better. You can *consciously* experiment to improve a skill of your own, according to the four-stage success model (see Day 2). And in the same way you can try to make changes to the strategies you model.

Obviously you will only reach this stage of competence

when you feel you have gone as far as you can in emulating your model. At some point you will find that 'the law of diminishing returns' sets in – you will get smaller results for the extra effort you put in. From now on you can apply your own innate creativity to continuously improve in a self-generating spiral of excellence.

Let's say you model someone playing tennis, squash or any ball game. Modelling an expert will quickly get you to a reasonable level of competence. Positive mental rehearsal of your model's strategy will reinforce your skill *without the need for failures*. This will, in turn, boost your self-image as a tennis player, or whatever. However, you will soon find, perhaps by accident, that some of your own techniques work well, even though not based on your model. As you experiment with different strokes and tactics and notice what happens, you can change your strategy accordingly. In other words, do more of what works and cut out what doesn't.

Each success will boost your self-belief even further. Enjoying what you do, you will probably practise more, and take the sport more seriously, so you will get even better. You will start to interpret failures and bad days positively ('a fluke' or 'not me') – a sure sign of a self-fulfilling, upward spiral of success. Applying the four-stage success model (see Day 2), and using your mental rehearsal skills, even *unconscious* behaviour will tend to move you towards your goal. By *consciously* adding the challenge of a new, higher outcome to each success, you can ensure that you maintain your spiral of success.

STRATEGIES THAT WORK

The modelling process goes further than just eliciting a strategy, of course. If you wish not just to *know* a strategy, but to successfully transfer the skill to yourself or another person, you need to use the basic modelling test 'Can I make this work for myself?'

The strategy elicitation process you learnt on Days 16 and 17 identifies the elements of a behaviour, and the syntax (or order in which the elements occur). Here the ubiquitous 80/20 rule usually applies, and one or two elements of the strategy tend to account for its success. For example, in reading or spelling skills (covered on Day 17), the visual element usually dominates, and the most skilful people use some form of visual strategy. One person might use some Ad (self-talk) and another might get a tingly feeling as well, but their skill may not *depend* on those elements of the strategy. The same might apply to certain auditory elements in a musical skill or kinaesthetic in a sport. When transferring a strategy (or modelling), these critical or key elements make the all-important difference.

You can then learn the important skill of teaching someone else. 'Excellent' people do not necessarily *teach* well. Making their skill accessible requires extra communication skills (strategies) as well as an understanding of the strategies modelled.

Communication Skills

Apart from modelling, the other main pillar of NLP concerns interpersonal communication. The theoretical model of maps and filters has enabled people to understand the communication process much better than before. But, whatever our knowledge of the theory of communication, modelling remains the best route to actual change. Just find an excellent communicator. Then, regardless of the process that person adopts, and whether or not they fit into an accepted model, you can replicate their skill. Remember Day 4's presupposition: 'The meaning of a communication is the response it gets.'

Through modelling we extend the boundaries of excellence, as we transfer strategies from person to person. Modelling makes excellence both explicit and accessible.

Beliefs and Values

You can also model beliefs and values. They form part of the neurological hierarchy (see Day 14), in which the higher levels 'control' the ones below. Thus a capability will need to have congruent beliefs. For instance, the belief 'I'm useless at numbers' will not support a capability in maths or accountancy. In the end we need to model actual behaviour – what a person does. But we also need to address the higher-level or 'macro' thinking that controls the person's behaviour, including their motivation strategy, values and self-image.

People often reveal their beliefs and values anyway during conversation, whether explicitly or implicitly. But you have to listen. You can also ask 'why' questions, like 'Why is that important?' or 'Why did you feel that way?' These will elicit further beliefs and values. You will have to identify these beliefs and values if you want to reproduce the results of your model. They form part of their strategy. You may not hold the same values, but you will have to 'act as if' you do to produce the same quality of behaviour. Try to model the whole skill *package*, or you might miss some critical element.

Strategy Syntax

We have covered different aspects of modelling today and on Days 16 and 17. These have included experience, physiology, thinking strategy and coding, and finally beliefs and values – a *sequence* that moves up the neurological levels you met on Day 14. Your model will probably not provide the information in such a neat sequence. So it may help if you have a structure, like the neurological levels, to help you choose suitable categories and plan the elicitation process.

By using the simple modelling processes described you can acquire any skill you want. Strategy elicitation enables you to understand *how* people do what they do; and the modelling process enables you to *acquire* those successful strategies for yourself. This extends the boundaries of personal excellence to an extraordinary degree. You can, for instance, model someone's 'motivation' or 'confidence' strategy, if you need to, as you learnt in Day 7. Equally, you can model the mental and physical strategies to carry out the skills you want to acquire.

PRESUPPOSITION FOR TODAY

> **Change can be fast and easy.**

As a rule, we tend to stick to our beliefs and values and gravitate to habitual, 'autopilot' experiences we do not need to think about. The deeper our beliefs and the more ingrained these automatic behaviours, the more difficult we find it to change them. On top of this ingrained reluctance to change, cultural conditioning sometimes demands that we take the necessary medicine before getting better – no pain, no gain. As we saw, each new experience reinforces an existing 'pigeon-hole' of perception – hence the mental ruts or mindsets that we get stuck in. Our belief systems also support the *difficulty* of change. So we have some reprogramming to do.

However, a simple new perception can bring about instant change. You can choose to presuppose change as *easy*, just as you can presuppose it as difficult. You have the choice. When you address it at the right neurological level (see Day 14), change can and does happen quickly and easily. And, as you learnt on Day 15, you can reframe any situation, thus changing your brain neurology and consequent feelings and behaviour. The network of nerves that effect the change can operate as quickly as it takes you to realise that you have changed. A belief system that presupposes both the possibility and positive benefits of change will reinforce the process in a self-fulfilling way. If you want a useful, empowering belief, this one certainly fits the bill. Believe you can change quickly – and you will.

TODAY'S TO DOs

- Choose a skill you want to learn or improve and find someone who does it with unconscious competence. Model the person, using the strategy elicitation process you learnt on Days 16 and 17, and the simple modelling process above. Start with a specific skill, perhaps something lasting just a few moments and not too complex, rather than a capability (check back on the strategy chunking section in Day 16).

- Consider how modelling can help you achieve the well-formed outcomes you decided on in Day 2. Consider where a new skill falls in terms of neurological levels (Day 14) and what other level you may need to address.

- Practise some pacing and leading (see Day 5). Develop new skills.

DAY 19

Mastering How You Feel

This chapter covers:

- **Understanding anchors**
- **Getting into the right state of mind**
- **Creating an empowering anchor**

Imagine having the ability to turn on any state of mind you like. If you have ever had trouble feeling cheerful on a rainy day or staying calm when dealing with a certain work colleague or family member you will value the skill of controlling how you feel. The NLP technique of anchoring enables you to call upon empowering states of mind whenever you need to.

UNDERSTANDING ANCHORS

In NLP the term anchor refers to 'a stimulus which triggers a specific physiological or emotional state or behaviour'. The stimulus may involve a sight, sound, feeling, taste or smell.

Involuntary Anchors

For instance, a tune can bring back an instant, rich memory, and all the pleasurable emotions associated with it. The same can apply with a person's name, a person's face, a town, an item of clothing, a room or building, or a colour. These all happen involuntarily, of course, or by default. Some empower us; others disempower us. Some anchors motivate, and others induce a phobic response. Even worse, with harsh life experiences, new, unwanted anchors quickly establish themselves unknowingly. Without realising it, we spend much of our lives slavishly responding to anchors.

Designer Anchors

Anchors trigger many of the habits we would like to get rid of. So we all know the process only too well. But, with NLP, you can use anchors deliberately and purposefully. You can start to experience states of mind by design rather than by default. And you can replace those you would prefer to do without. We 'learn' most anchors at an unconscious level. But you can consciously change them and replace them with empowering *designer anchors*.

Crossing your fingers provides a simple example of a deliberate (designer) anchor. In this case a simple kinaesthetic (tactile) behaviour seems to produce, for some people, a state of hope and optimism. For many others, this and other 'hackneyed' anchors have long since lost their effectiveness. But processes such as these can still produce extraordinary, instant change to a better state of mind.

Phobic Anchors

The stimuli that trigger phobic reactions also illustrate the effectiveness of anchors – for instance, the sight of a spider, the view from the top of a building, or the roar of an aircraft engine. Phobias exemplify *negative* anchors, of course. But anchors can have both useful and not-so-useful effects. The same 'system' applies, whether it happens by default or you control it to your advantage.

Phobias illustrate the power of anchors. If you suffer from

any phobia you have proved how 'perfectly' you can use anchors. You just need to install more useful ones.

The Origin of Anchors

Each anchor has its own origins. Many psychological approaches involve dredging up distant memories, probing causes and effects. But, according to NLP, origins as such may have little significance. In some cases you may not manage to track down how the process started. And, even if you do, you may not want to erase a real experience – even a negative one. It forms part of you, a resource which you can no doubt learn from.

However, you can now *identify* and *change* disempowering, automatic behaviours, whatever their origin. Once you sort out the present, the past takes care of itself. Once you have control over the negative consequences of some past event or association, you may have little interest in digging out its origin. At the very least, you can *choose* to change any habitual, instinctive behaviour or state.

GETTING INTO THE RIGHT STATE OF MIND

We usually associate anchoring with reflex responses (like Pavlov's dogs, conditioned to salivate in response to a stimulus). Some everyday anchors produce such automatic behaviour – like an alarm bell or a red traffic light. But others change the way we feel. And we know the important part that feelings play in what we do. From the NLP model described on Day 1, you will recall that behaviour starts in the mind, and depends on how we feel, our values and so on. From the neurological levels model on Day 14, you will also recall that changing the way you think has more *influence* than making a change at the level of behaviour. Given the well-formed outcomes you developed on Day 2, you can now use anchors to get into a confident, motivated state of mind. And goal-achieving behaviour will follow.

This provides an invaluable boost to personal excellence. Often your state of mind makes the difference between success and failure, winning and losing. Sometimes you will not even embark on a worthwhile activity because you don't feel right. Or, conversely, you can ruin a job or blow a relationship because of negative, volatile feelings. Over a period of time, your state of mind can even affect your health. You learnt (on Day 7) how to change your state of mind by switching submodalities. The anchoring technique allows you to recall a state of mind *instantly*, and therefore has lots of important applications.

For instance, what if you could start the day feeling confident, energetic and optimistic? What if you could go into that interview with a sense of calm, serene confidence? What if you could walk into that office that you used to dread with a sense of self-control and self-esteem? NLP anchoring skills enable you to have the right state of mind just when and where you need it. Not only do you stay in control, but you can choose the most *appropriate* state for any activity you want to engage in, or outcome you want to achieve.

The value of anchors lies in their immediate impact on your state of mind. The volatile, unwanted feelings we experience every day frequently rob us of our goals. Many of these day-to-day and moment-to-moment states seem to occur for no reason. In some cases they result from primeval fight-or-flight responses which engage far too quickly for the conscious mind to do anything about. Physical symptoms happen in an instant, as when you have to do an emergency stop in your car, and feel your heart thumping and adrenaline pumping. It seems that you have no choice than to *feel*, emotionally, what your body tells you. Fortunately, you get back to normal in a few minutes with no significant ill-effect – grateful for the help of your automatic survival system.

However, in a work or social situation, you may already have done the damage to rapport and relationships. In some cases, as with people who get under our skin, or innocuous little events that cause us to see red, we need something better than animal responses. We need the *right* states of mind to call on at the *right* time. Anchoring provides the required technique.

CREATING AN EMPOWERING ANCHOR

We will now look in more detail at different kinds of anchors and how to create them. First you need to know what states to anchor and how to elicit those states. You can anchor a particular state of mind to use in many different situations. For most people, the state of 'confidence', for instance, will have plenty of useful applications. To install an anchor you need to recall an actual experience of the state you want, such as confidence. The more powerful the state, and vivid your recollection of it, the more effective the anchor.

Choosing an empowering state therefore forms a vital part of the anchoring process. Below, we give an outline of the overall process, which you will cover today and on Day 20:

1. Ask yourself exactly what state you want. Usually a word or two will easily describe the state (such as 'calm', 'confident' or 'in control') but make sure you know precisely the state you mean.

2. If you wish, give it a special name like the 'silver cup' state, the 'Sunday morning' state, the 'Costa del whatever' state or the 'whee-hee' state which you will immediately associate with from your memory.

3. Recall and vividly re-experience the state, just as you did when switching submodalities on Day 7. Use the following sorts of directions for recalling the chosen state: 'Remember a specific time when you felt totally . . . [e.g. motivated/calm/confident]'. 'As you go back to that time now, step into your body and see what you saw, hear what you heard, and feel what you felt . . .'

4. Choose an appropriate anchor (see pp. 264–6).

5. Set or 'install' the anchor (you will cover this final stage on Day 20).

If helping someone else to create an anchor, simply guide them through the above process. You can also use your voice tonality and your own state to encourage and lead the person into the desired state. Then use your sensory acuity to notice as the person associates into the experience. You can ask for a signal when the experience peaks.

Using Your Memory Resources

If the person does not experience a strong enough state, you can suggest that they think of another time when they experienced it and go through the same process. Remember you need not concern yourself with the actual circumstances or content of the memory. Just recall the *state* (of mind), which may well have occurred on other occasions but in different life contexts.

Perhaps they once won the sprint on a school sports day or received a rare compliment from their boss. However innocuous such memories may seem to others, they will have positive meaning and feelings for the individual concerned.

Any such memory will suffice, provided you can *relive* it, especially the feelings you had. Recent memories may come more easily, but sometimes you will find a vivid memory of many years ago just as effective. If you have only experienced the state once or twice, you will have less choice but the technique will still work. Isolated memory resources have no less value, so search them out and treasure them as personal assets.

Switching contexts

Consider your state of mind in different *contexts*. Some people have all sorts of hang-ups in work situations, yet at home or within their own small social group they have no trouble with the state in question. Or the reverse may apply.

A person may think they have no 'success memories' at all, or perhaps they cannot recall any appropriate ones. But *in some other context* they may have plenty of appropriate memories to draw upon, where they have natural talent and confidence. In this case the *state of mind*, not some clever skill, forms the essential resource.

You may want to anchor a state so that you can face job interviews, for instance. In this case, you need to choose a context in which you *do* have confidence – perhaps a weekend social activity, or a favourite sport or hobby, or even something you did as a child. You can capture that state by anchoring, and use it whenever you like.

Let's say, for example, that you have super confidence in a certain sport, but need to make an important speech without panic attacks. You can use all the inner resources you have. Treat them as useable assets and harness them to help achieve your outcomes.

Each of us has a rich memory store of both positive and negative states of mind. List the 'highs' in your memory and think of the range of empowering states you have experienced. Spend some time vividly recalling the ones that you might need in the future.

Borrowing empowering resources from others

Even with no empowering memories you can still create empowering states. We all have a natural ability to *imagine* states of mind as well as behaviours. In fact we use this all the time when we empathise with another person ('I can imagine how you must feel'). So you can ask what it *would* have felt like if you had 'confidence', 'calmness' or whatever. In this instance you can use someone you know, or a historical figure, or a film or book where you identified with a character who excelled in the particular feeling or experience you want. People with a strong imagination can bring about remarkable change, despite an unimpressive personal track record. As children we all enjoyed a rich imagination. In most cases that resource lies latent, ready to re-ignite, given a bit of encouragement.

As with several techniques of this sort, you will usually do better when in a relaxed state, when your brain pulses at a slow 'alpha' rate. Similarly, when helping someone else, try to get the person relaxed and establish rapport in the way you have already learnt.

Choosing an Anchor

You can use visual, auditory or kinaesthetic anchors. And as with any other sensory representation, you can make them internal or external. We hope you will take this opportunity to choose some appropriate anchors of your own before you proceed to the installation process on Day 20.

Visual anchors

Every day, we see visual advertising in magazines, on the television and on hoardings. However, in the case of a purposeful, 'designer' anchor, you need to have access to the visual stimulus at any time. You need to *control* the process. Unfortunately you cannot carry around your pet kitten or have that exotic sunset always in view. So you may need to establish an *internal* visual anchor.

You will need to see it easily in your mind in a moment. Consider, for instance, visualising the face of a respected mentor, an object or icon, or a motivating scene from the time and place you experienced the desired state. For example, you might anchor a state of calmness to a beautiful landscape you saw on a holiday or to some blissful, quiet retreat. Different 'mind pictures' affect us differently, so you need to choose carefully. Just ensure that you can easily recall the inner image.

You need to have access to your anchor at all times so

external images may not fit the bill, unless they form part of your 'kit'(something you always have with you). A golfer, for example, may anchor to the marking on the ball or a mark on their left shoe, for example. In this case the visual anchor will always accompany the behaviour you want to affect (the golf stroke). After reading the tips below you will easily select an appropriate visual anchor.

For the above reasons, you may find an *internal* visual anchor more appropriate. Having full internal control means you can access the state in any situation, including an emergency. And you can make it as vivid, memorable and emotional as you like. It should appear as easily and realistically as the clock on your office wall. You never know when you will want to instantly access the state. But you may have to put in a bit of practice to generate vivid, realistic internal anchors.

Auditory anchors

An auditory anchor refers to any internal or external sound. This may well take the form, for instance, of a voice speaking specific words or a phrase – for example, 'You can do it', 'Calm now' or 'Walk tall'. This can work whether internal (self-talk) or external (out loud). Just ensure that any anchor does not have *mixed associations* in your mind and so produce the wrong effect. Go for 'designer' (purpose-designed) anchors, associated with a specific state, that do not have conflicting meaning in themselves.

Decide on a *unique* sound, such as a specific burst of music, or specific words, having associations with the state you want. A word or phrase may simply name the state you want to induce. Better, perhaps, to use a special, motivating tone of voice that adds for you more meaning and uniqueness.

Sometimes imagining another person's voice works well, especially when that person tends to make you feel confident, calm or whatever state you desire. In this case the association of the anchor itself will empower you, as well as the memory it evokes. Just remember you may need to 'fire' your anchor at any time. You can always create internal representations. External ones, when you use them, should have the same accessibility. As we shall now see, this favours kinaesthetic anchors.

Kinaesthetic anchors

Most people find external kinaesthetic anchors (like 'crossing your fingers') the most powerful. However, they may give you less scope than internally generated images and sounds. Depending on your sensory preference, you may not find it as easy to generate a feeling internally. In any event, you should choose a kinaesthetic anchor you can use instantly, at any time. In this case you can use external anchors, as you can usually depend on having your body with you!

Whether internal or external, you should decide on a *distinct tactile anchor* . For instance, you could 'feel' a hand rest on your shoulder (internal), or make a circle of your thumb and little finger (external). Don't go for a 'macro' kinaesthetic 'feeling', such as 'calmness' (the very state you wanted in the first place). A simple external physical anchor will do the job.

Tips for Choosing an Anchor

Bear the following tips in mind when selecting an appropriate anchor.

- Choose an anchor **unique** to you and the state you want to elicit. As we saw, one of the most universal kinaesthetic anchors, 'Keep your fingers crossed', indicates hoping for the best or an optimistic state of mind. However, culturally hackneyed anchors like this may have gathered other associations over the years, quite inappropriate for your present purpose. In any event they will probably not associate you with the specific time, place and state of mind you want to recall. A similar but more specific kinaesthetic anchor might thus comprise simply touching your thumb and little finger or perhaps third finger (if you do neither habitually). Use *either* hand (or foot), but keep to the same one for a particular state, to maintain the unique association.

- Make it **discreet**. Friends and colleagues should not notice if you 'fire' it. Facial contortions or strange gestures adopted as anchors when summoned to the boss can summarily end a career! Bear in mind your objective: to recall the desired state instantly and anonymously, in whatever circumstances you need it. The sort of finger-anchors we have mentioned fit this requirement well. But so would crunching up your big toe (even more discreet) or gently scratching the back of your neck, provided you don't habitually scratch the back of your neck. Any internal anchor will fit the discreet requirement well, of course. You might attract attention ringing a heavy bell, switching on a loud section of a Tchaikovsky overture, or pulling out and smelling an old sepia photograph in a client's office every time you face pressure. But internally, anything goes. However bizarre the anchor, you maintain discretion.

- The anchor should, if possible, have an empowering **meaning** to you in its own right. Hence the examples of visualising people who themselves empower you, or objects or images that already have empowering meaning. What starts out as a neutral anchor, like making a circle of your thumb and little finger, will soon *take on* meaning to you, of course. But, initially at least, an anchor with existing empowering meaning can add extra impact.

- Make your anchor **portable**. Can you fire the anchor in any situation in which you might need to induce the desired state? Some external stimuli will not meet this test.

- Make it **durable**. Avoid choosing an *ephemeral* anchor. A person you once idolised can turn out to have feet of clay. The meaning changes.

You now know how to choose an anchor. On Day 20 you will learn how to install an anchor, and fire it in any situation in which you want to change your state.

PRESUPPOSITION FOR TODAY

> **The person with the most flexibility will control the system.**

This 'law' has found acceptance in systems engineering and NLP has introduced it into interpersonal communication in the form of this presupposition. Once again it reflects the four-stage success model (see Day 2) and the need to try something different, repeatedly if necessary, until you achieve your outcome. 'If what you are doing isn't working, do something else' gives a similar message. This highlights the wasted effort that often goes into repeated trying, but without changing behaviour. And it highlights the distinct advantage we have if we occupy the flexible ground within a communication, such as a negotiation or interview. Control of the system, of course, means control of the outcome, and sets us up for success. Although primarily applied interpersonally within NLP, this presupposition obviously applies to organisations as well, and illustrates the economic disadvantages of inflexibility.

TODAY'S TO DOs

- Memorise today's presupposition, and do an inventory of your personal resources. Remember that every past achievement, every empowering state of mind, everything you have learnt, constitutes a resource upon which you can draw now and in the future.

- Spend some time recalling empowering memories upon which you can base change (as for anchoring). This will increase your skill at manipulating thoughts which you can then use far more widely, enabling you to think what you want to think, see things in a different light, and adopt your true identity. The breadth of your imagination will set the only limit, and you can even restore that to childlike levels with a bit of practice.

- Decide which memory resources will help you bring about the outcomes you set on Day 2. In addressing this, check back on the different techniques you have learnt so far, which you may need to bring about the necessary changes.

- Do some revision on switching submodalities (see Day 7). You can use this skill to perfect an empowering memory which you can then anchor for future recall.

DAY 20

Instant Excellence

This chapter covers:
- **Installing anchors**
- **Using anchors**

On Day 19 you learnt how to access a desired state and choose an appropriate anchor. Today you will learn how to 'install' anchors and use them whenever you need to get into a more empowering state.

INSTALLING ANCHORS

Use this procedure to install an anchor to use yourself:

1. Find a quiet place where you will not suffer interruptions. Ensure that you will have enough time to relax and recall a memory or memories.

2. Decide on a state or feeling you have experienced in the past and that you would like to call on in the future whenever you need to. (We covered this, and the next step, on Day 19.)

3. Choose an anchor that you can use in any situation in which you might need that state or feeling. Follow the tips in the previous chapter. Make it discreet, unique and portable, and preferably choose an empowering anchor with meaning.

4. Recall a memory when you experienced the desired state strongly. Take your time getting into the experience, dwelling on each modality (seeing, hearing, feeling), separately first, then combining all the memory sensations vividly. Imagine reliving the experience. Pay attention to the details, including colours, sounds and textures, people around, voices. Make sure you *associate* – seeing things through your own eyes, rather than observing as an outsider. In particular, feel all the inside emotions you felt.

5. Once you have recalled the emotion, you can experiment with making it even stronger, doubling or trebling the intensity. For example, you can make images brighter and larger, and sounds louder. Refer back to the list of possible submodalities as ideas for experimentation (see Day 7).

6. As you approach the vivid climax of the memory fire all three chosen anchors (visual, auditory, kinaesthetic) simultaneously. Sustain the feeling. Then, before it begins to fall in intensity, release your anchor. Then come slowly back to the present.

7. Now 'change state' or 'break state' by doing or thinking about something else. Fire the anchor or anchors again and notice whether it produces the state that you experienced.

8. Repeat the process *several times*, each time intensifying and developing the memory with added sensory detail. Each time check by firing the anchors. Soon you will find it *impossible* to fire the anchors without

inducing the desired state. You know then that you have permanently installed the anchor in your brain neurology. Otherwise, repeat the process, choosing a different memory if you wish.

9. You can also check out your anchor by *future pacing*. Think of a time in the future when you will need the state. Imagine what you will experience (as a warning or cue) *immediately preceding* it (such as stepping up to a lectern or to the front of a training room, approaching a difficult client's office, or whatever). Treat this as your *cue* to fire the anchor. Now fire your anchor and notice what happens. You will recall the state just as easily when imagining an actual occasion when you will need it.

   By future pacing you can test your anchor in different contexts. Do this for several possible future scenarios to make your anchor robust in any context. Remember that your brain treats a vivid 'future pace' just like a real experience.

10. Check it again the next day. Having confirmed a permanent anchor, you will then have the confidence to call on it at any time. Then, as soon as you get the chance, use it in a real-life situation.

You can repeat this process any time you like – the more times, the better. Each success will reinforce the anchor and its associations. You can then build on your success, using any further experience in which you capture the desired state as the memory for another anchoring session.

If you use the technique regularly, for different states, you will soon learn to gauge the intensity of an experience and the best time to fire your anchor. You will also learn to quickly recall strong multi-sensory experiences. These memories provide precious personal resources that you can use to create a better future.

So far you have used all three anchors. Soon you will not

need to use all three, and by firing one anchor (the kinaesthetic one usually has most effect, but you can experiment) you will immediately reach the desired state. Before long you will not need the anchor at all. Just *thinking* the now familiar state will induce it. You now have a technique for taking control in all sorts of circumstances, and a powerful resource for excellence.

USING ANCHORS

The installation process described above illustrates how to apply anchors yourself, but you can easily adapt it to help others.

Anchoring Others

For example, you can use your skill to help a friend or colleague get into a more resourceful state. Anchoring can help especially when dealing with children and young people. Knowingly or unknowingly, they respond all the time to anchors that you and others have set. So you may as well use the same basic technique to consciously set anchors that give what both you and they want.

If you have carried out the process successfully yourself, you will find it easier to use with others. Use your sensory acuity to recognise the right point at which to get the person to fire their anchor. Establish rapport and take 'second position' (see Day 12) with the person. Put yourself into their shoes or skin – you will soon manage to do this.

The anchoring technique applies very widely, including in group situations. For example, the rattling of coffee cups will all but terminate a training session as people's minds switch to a welcome break. Likewise, two or three claps will soon have a whole auditorium of people joining in applause. Use your imagination to think of applications – we give a few ideas below.

Your Repertoire of Anchored States

You can set anchors to use in a specific upcoming situation, such as an interview, a speech, or the final of a sports event. In each case you need to choose both the appropriate state and the anchor. The process can apply to any empowering state, of course. So you can have different anchors for: calmness, confidence, assertiveness, aggression, anger, a 'couldn't care less' attitude, caring and compassion, intensity, motivation, alertness, serenity and composure, lightheartedness and fun, and so on.

Access the state in the way we have described, using a specific memory, then carry out the simple anchoring process. Some people anchor different states using different fingers. But you can use your own ingenuity in choosing an anchor, and indeed in applying it.

With such a repertoire of state skills, and the key to eliciting them, you can cope with just about anything that occurs. For example: meeting an important person, preparing for an examination or an interview, disciplining a member of staff, giving an impromptu speech, handling bad news, concentrating on a document or presentation and clinching an important sale.

Anchoring Behaviour

So far we have anchored *states of mind*. In most cases a *behaviour* change will come about, once you have control of an offending state of mind. For instance, if you feel confident in yourself, whatever your technical skills, you will probably perform better, say, in giving a public presentation. Obviously further technical training will also help, but we usually need to make mental rather than physical changes – at least at first.

Similarly, you can change behaviour associated with, say, anger, by anchoring a more empowering state. Fire the anchor when you sense the anger (for instance, when you see the face of the person who has that effect on you). You thus avert angry *behaviour*. You can check this by future pacing the situation. The person's face remains an anchor itself, but now acts as a timely 'cue' to fire your empowering anchor to associate with the better state of mind. Think about it. Most behaviour *we would like to change* involves a state of mind over which we need to have control.

Having said that, anchoring on its own will not change deeply ingrained habits such as smoking or nail-biting. These usually have powerful benefits, or secondary gains, for the person, and anchoring per se does not address secondary gain. You can identify this by using the well-formed outcomes check in Day 2 and the ecology questions in Day 3. The change techniques you will learn on Day 21 also deal with these sorts of behaviour changes more fully. Anchoring, however, will reinforce any change and help to induce the empowering state of mind you need.

Stacking Anchors

You can also recall more than one compatible state at the same time. For example, you may want to feel calm but at the same time assertive; confident, but at the same time empathetic and caring. You can therefore link several empowering states to a single anchor, as a 'hedging your bets' strategy. Simply recall the different states, applying the same anchors.

As well as 'stacking' a range of different feelings, you can anchor several empowering memories of the same state to one anchor, to increase the effect. Simply amend the process just described to include different states, or additional memories of a desired state.

Chaining Anchors

Chaining anchors involves using several anchors where one automatically leads to another. Whereas stacking acts in parallel, chaining runs anchors sequentially, one after another. This use of the technique can bring about considerable eventual change, but you need to apply the anchors incrementally.

Let's say you have a problem with anger which seems to block out any chance of rationality, let alone the calmness you really need:

- First, define the states you want to change from and to – in this case 'anger' and, say, 'serene calmness' (or calm serenity).

- Next, choose an interim state or states *between* anger and serene calmness, such as 'objectivity' or 'neutral observation'.

- Install *the state you want to change*. Then, following the installation process described on pp. 268–70, install the interim state or states, testing the anchors as we described. Do the same for the final, or ultimate, state you want to anchor.

- Now, having installed all the anchors, you can set up the chain. Fire your first anchor, which will induce anger.

- This time, apply the second anchor as you achieve the heightened state, then the third, until you reach the desired state. Each anchor needs to overlap the last for a few seconds, creating a chain effect.

- For convenient consecutive anchors, you can touch successive knuckles with a finger of your other hand. To create the chain for each anchor, overlap the pressure as you transfer your finger from one knuckle to the next.

- After a few practice runs, *the first anchor only* will immediately trigger the desired final state, as you have now created the chain effect. From now on, when you feel the anger coming on (the first state), *that state itself* will automatically run through the chain and give you the state of calmness or your desired state. The transition will happen almost instantaneously.

Technically you can set a chain as long as you like. But in practice, you will probably find more than three or four too unwieldy, and probably not necessary for results. Chaining can induce very big swings of state quickly and with a single anchor. You may find it fascinating, as so many others have done, to see how, once you have set the chain and made the neural associations, the change happens automatically and instantly. And, again, the more you practise and use the technique, the more effective and dependable you will make it.

PRESUPPOSITION FOR TODAY

> **People have all the resources they need to bring about change and success.**

We tend to blame outside circumstances, people, or bad luck when we do not achieve what we set out to achieve. But, in fact, change comes about by changing the way we think and perceive things. According to this presupposition, you have all the inner resources you need. You just have to identify and use them to fulfil your outcomes. What goes on in your mind falls uniquely within your ownership and control. Even in the most difficult of external circumstances you can create your own thoughts, making any meaning or responding in any way you wish. No one can *make* you unhappy any more than they can make you happy if you decide and act otherwise.

We tend to underestimate how these internal resources can bring about change in ourselves and others. What you believe about yourself and your abilities largely determines, of course, what you achieve. But we know that these beliefs form part of the neurology we have *ourselves* created by our interpretation of past experience, and the way we have 'filtered' experience. We also know that some of these have passed their 'sell by date', and no longer empower us in our present life. And what we can install we can also *uninstall*.

As well as beliefs, you have already learnt how to change how you feel and thus harness a crucial resource for motivation and success. But what about our physical resources? We often complain about our bodies. But we do not have to look far to find examples of extraordinary achievements by people with far inferior physical endowments – another example of 'If anyone can, I can'. By accepting this presupposition (from Day 16) you can identify and use your more or less unlimited neurophysiological resources to the full.

TODAY'S TO DOs

- Decide on an empowering state you will need in some specific situation in the future and set up an anchor to empower you.

- Extend your repertoire of Milton and Meta Model language patterns by further listening and observation. You may need to refer back to the patterns in Days 9 and 10. Start to use Meta Model question responses in low-sensitivity situations, where it doesn't matter if you blow it. But check back on the rules all the same. You will find it easy and enjoyable as you explore people's mental maps and start to communicate more effectively.

- Use your pacing and leading skills some time today whenever you get a chance, either in one-to-one conversation or in a group. Again, start with low-key situations until you have the confidence to use the skills intuitively.

DAY 21

All Change

This chapter covers:
- **Change techniques**
- **Change personal history**
- **Phobia cure**
- **Detailed personal history questionnaire**

NLP involves change: change in what you do, in how you think, in your attitudes and beliefs. In many cases you can bring about change in other people, as we saw on Day 4, for instance, creating rapport in order to improve better communication. But changing others usually starts with making changes yourself. In the case of creating better rapport it might mean understanding that the other person sees things differently from you, has different beliefs and values, and has goals and aspirations as genuine and sincere as your own. Or you may need to change habits that annoy the other person and break rapport.

CHANGE TECHNIQUES

Today we will cover three popular NLP change techniques which will help consolidate much of what you have learnt throughout the 21-day course. You will need to draw on your sensory acuity and rapport skills, for instance, as well as the anchoring skills you have just learnt. At the same time these three techniques illustrate NLP's power in bringing about change.

1. **The Change Personal History technique**: This works well on minor negative feelings that have become familiar, established, but unwanted habits.

2. **The Phobia Cure**: This technique has particular associations with NLP and its co-founder Richard Bandler. Traditional psychotherapeutic methods usually take months to dislodge a phobia. But this technique does not require sophisticated methods or long psychiatric training, and takes only about 10 minutes. We have chosen one of several versions.

3. **Detailed Personal History Questionnaire**: This offers a series of questions that you can use with a person to reach a much deeper level than the stated or 'presenting' problem. We have based it on a questionnaire designed by Tad James, co-author of *Time Line Therapy* (Meta Publications Inc.).

CHANGE PERSONAL HISTORY

You can use this technique to remove negative emotions, unwanted habits, and beliefs that cause low self-esteem. It readily adapts to all sorts of personal problems.

1. Identify the negative state, elicit it, calibrate to it (meaning, watch for non-verbal evidence, as well as the words you hear, matching also for rapport), and anchor it (see Days 19 and 20).

2. Hold the negative anchor and ask the person to go back and think of a time when he or she had similar

feelings. Continue until you reach the earliest experience the person can identify. Release the anchor, 'break state' and bring the person fully back to the present.

3. Ask the person, in the light of what they now know, to think what resource they would have needed in that early situation to make it a satisfying or at least OK experience rather than a problematic one. The resource may take the form of a word or phrase like 'security' or 'being loved'. This resource must come from within the person themselves rather than from other people in the group, if you find yourself working in a group situation.

4. Elicit and anchor a specific and full experience of the needed resource state, and test this positive anchor (see Days 19 and 20).

5. Holding the positive resource anchor, take the person back to the earliest experience. Invite him or her to watch from outside themselves with this new resource and notice how it changes the experience. Then invite the person to step inside the situation with the resource (keep holding the resource anchor) and run the experience through as if happening again. Ask them to notice what happens: other people's responses and their own feelings and conclusions. If dissatisfied at any stage, go back to step 4 and add more resources that will enable resolution. (Resolution means that the person can experience it without the familiar bad feeling and learn from the experience.)

6. Still holding the resource anchor, take the person forward through the other similar experiences they visited on their way back and check that these no longer elicit the familiar bad feeling. Add further resources if needed. Remove the anchor and break state.

7. Finally, test the change by asking the person to remember any of the experiences that previously elicited the bad feeling and notice how those memories have changed. Calibrate to the person's physiology (see Day 5) to collect your own evidence. Then future pace by asking the person to imagine a situation in the future which, in the past, would have created the negative feeling. Notice the resources working to change the person's experience.

A couple of extra tips may help:

●   Set a positive resource anchor before you start, in case the person gets sucked into negative feelings (see 'How to create an empowering anchor' in Day 19 and 'Using anchors' in Day 20).

●   If you can identify no resource that will sufficiently change the experience, get the person to step inside *others* they think have the resource – 'Imagine acting confidently like Bill', or 'What would go through Sally's mind . . .?' Identify the positive intent behind the behaviour, and offer them the resources they need.

PHOBIA CURE

Phobias illustrate the power of negative anchors. But although they can seem extreme, they follow a straight-forward trigger–response process that most of us experi-ence to a lesser extent all the time. Phobias simply have more extreme or unpleasant effects. You will note that this change technique avoids direct association with what may cause stress to the person. Also notice the use of percep-tual position (see Day 12) and dissociation devices (see Day 7).

1. First establish a safety (positive resource) anchor kinaesthetically and test it. A safety anchor will immediately produce a positive, empowering state of mind, such as calmness.

The following steps take the form of actual verbal instructions to the person with the phobia. You can adapt them to the circumstances and the individual, using your rapport skills.

2. I will ask you to do a few things that you can do in your mind really quickly, so that your phobia won't bother you at all, ever again. I'll give you the directions one part at a time, and then you go inside and do it. Nod when you've finished.

3. First I want you to imagine yourself sitting in the middle of a cinema. Up on the screen you can see a black and white snapshot in which you see yourself in a situation just before you had the phobic response.

4. Then I want you to float out of your body up to the projection room, where you can watch yourself, *watching yourself*. From that position you can also see yourself in the still picture up on the screen.

5. Now turn that snapshot up on the screen into a black and white film, and watch it from the beginning to just beyond the end of that unpleasant experience. When you get to the end, stop it by freeze-framing. Then jump inside the picture and *run the film backwards*. All the people will walk backwards and everything else will happen in reverse, just like rewinding a film, except that it now features you.

6. Now think about what you used to fear. See what you would see if actually there.

7. Now, what seemed to you to cause the problem?

Adapted from *Using Your Brain for a Change* by Richard Bandler (see Further Reading).

DETAILED PERSONAL HISTORY QUESTIONNAIRE

You have learnt a lot of techniques for change so you have tools available for your own use or to apply to others. Sometimes, however, in say a counselling or therapy situation, you may not know which technique to use. While the right technique will often take no more than 15 minutes to work, you may need to spend a lot more time beforehand, determining the nature and extent of the problem. This will involve detailed questioning – detective work, if you like – to find the root of the problem. Treating the symptoms (rather than the cause) will only provide a short-term solution. So, by identifying the root problem, you will save a lot of time in the long run. The Detailed Personal History Questionnaire helps in this process.

This questioning technique presupposes that the presenting problem simply *exemplifies* a greater problem, as a symptom rather than the cause. Typically, dealing with the root problem not only affects the stated problem. As a bonus, it usually affects many other aspects of the person's life. This may involve 'ecology' which you met on Day 3. Not everyone really wants to change, at least at the level of the underlying problem revealed. So always check this out first.

As well as the questions below, you can use the Cartesian questions we covered on Day 3. If the underlying problem remains unidentified, the presenting problem (or another version of the root problem) will almost certainly reappear. However, the questionnaire process, on its own, can bring about personal transformation, just by changing thinking. Experiment with it and find out more about yourself and others.

We have only partly E-Primed these questions, as some

involve Milton language (see Day 8) and reflect everyday speech. However generally expressed, the questions all relate to a 'presented problem':

1. What do you want? What else? . . . What else?
   This will establish their true goals or outcomes and also congruence. Does their non-verbal behaviour match their 'presented' outcomes? Remember what you have learnt about sensory acuity.

2. How does that pose a problem to you?
   This will establish complex equivalence (see Days 9 and 10) – how *this* means *that*.

3. How do you know it is a problem?
   This should establish a 'reality strategy' – it calls on real, sensory evidence.

4. (a) When did the problem start?
   (b) When didn't you have it?
   (c) When don't you have it now?
   (d) What have you done about it up to now?
   These questions will define the boundaries of the problem.

5. (a) Can you recall the very first time you experienced this problem – how did you feel then?
   (b) What examples of the problem have occurred since? How do you feel about these?
   These questions will give the history of the problem.

6. Looking at and listening to these events, how do they relate to your current situation?
   This and the next two questions may reveal a pattern.

7. Tell me about your family situation – parents, etc. How do they relate to your current situation?

8. Does anything in your early life bear some relationship or relevance to this problem?

9. If this problem had a purpose or intention for you, what would it be?
   This will identify the positive intention behind behaviour.

10. (a) When did you choose, at some level, to create this situation?
    (b) For what purpose?
    These questions involve the person themselves as the cause or source of the problem.

11. Do you need to learn or understand anything that would allow a solution to the problem now?
    This establishes the availability of learning.

12. Do you agree, at both a conscious and unconscious level, to clear the problem today and to know that you have a solution when we have completed the work?
    This seeks a 'contract' for change.

Your skill in sensory acuity will increase the value of the questionnaire. Watch out for incongruence. Agreement at the unconscious level may not come from the words spoken, but from the total physiology and voice characteristics. So use your rapport skills.

You can adapt this technique to use on yourself, of course. As you will not have the benefit of observing body language, you can use it in conjunction with other approaches, such as outcome clarification, reframing, perceptual positions and neurological levels. All these methods help you understand yourself more deeply and define the problem more accurately.

PRESUPPOSITION FOR TODAY

> **A person cannot not respond.**

On Day 12 you met a similar presupposition that applied to learning: 'we cannot not learn'. Today's presupposition has even wider application and means, for instance, that we will always respond in some way to a behaviour, an event, or any sensory input. The fact that a person responds in a different way to what you would expect just reflects their different map of the world. To get a response, you may well have to change your own behaviour. But this presupposition means that you will always get *some* response. You should therefore try different approaches until you achieve your outcome.

TODAY'S TO DOs

- Think of a personal situation you want to change. In a relaxed, undisturbed state, go through the change questionnaire, allowing your creative, unconscious mind to help you answer the questions. Note how you feel after doing this, and any ideas that come to you about what you want to change.

- Experiment more with perceptual positions (see Day 12). Why not take on a particular third position role, such as that of a lawyer, prime minister, or five-year-old child? Apply it to any behaviour during the day, things people say, events that happen and circum-stances that arise. Note how your perceptions change, sometimes dramatically, and how your emotions differ from normal.

- Start to control your response to any behaviour or event. Use your anchoring skills to get into the state you want, and experiment more with reframing (see Day 15). Start to elicit specific response outcomes in others using your pacing and leading (see Day 5) and language skills (see Days 8, 9, 10 and 11).

Today's three techniques illustrate NLP in personal change. However, everything you have learnt from Day 1 onwards will bring change. Even accepting a single presupposition can change your attitude enough for close friends and relatives to notice the difference. As you carry out deliberate matching (see Day 4) and build rapport, you will gain more benefits.

The main effect of NLP, however, comes from the *accumulation* of principles or presuppositions, and the range of skills. An approach like this avoids the trap of relying on one or two all-purpose techniques. Whilst NLP uses techniques, you usually have a choice. The wisdom of the approach means that if something doesn't work you can try something else.

We hope you have enjoyed the practical 'To Do' exercises. By experiencing what you learn as you go along, you multiply your learning. And you also enjoy the immediate benefits of what you learn in your life.

Remember:

Whatever you think you are, you are always more than that.

Enjoy discovering your own limitless potential. Take up the challenge of personal change. Start programming yourself for continuous, enjoyable improvement. Make NLP work for you – starting *now.*

Appendix

CERTIFICATION STANDARDS – PRACTITIONER LEVEL

Demonstration of ability to identify the following basic skills, techniques, patterns and concepts of NLP, and to utilise them competently with self and with others.

1. Behavioural integration of the basic presuppositions of NLP:
    - outcome orientation with respect for other's model of the world and the ecology of the system
    - distinction between map and territory
    - there is only feedback (cybernetic) – no failure
    - meaning of your communication is the response you get
    - adaptive intent of all behaviour
    - everyone has the necessary resources
    - resistance is a signal of insufficient pacing
    - law of requisite variety

2. Rapport, establishment and maintenance of

3. Pacing and Leading (verbally and non-verbally)

4. Calibration (sensory experience)

5. Representational systems (predicates and accessing cues)

6. Meta Model

7. Milton Model

8. Elicitation of well-formed, ecological outcomes and structures of Present State

9. Overlap and translation

10. Metaphor creation

11. Frames: Contrast, Relevancy, As If, Backtrack

12. Anchoring (V, A, K)

13. Anchoring techniques (contextualised to the field of application)

14. Ability to shift consciousness to external or internal as required by the moment's task

15. Dissociation and Association

16. Chunking

17. Submodalities

18. Verbal and non-verbal elicitation of responses

19. Accessing and building of resources

20. Reframing

21. Strategies: Detection, elicitation, utilisation and installation

22. Demonstration

Duration of Training

Minimum of 130 hours training in the basic NLP patterns led by a Certified Trainer, or a Certified Master Practitioner under the supervision of a Trainer.

Glossary Of NLP Terms

Accessing cues   The ways we tune our bodies by breathing, posture, gesture and eye movements to think in certain ways.

Anchoring   The process by which any stimulus or representation (external or internal) gets connected to and triggers a response. Anchors can occur naturally or be set up intentionally.

As-if frame   Pretending that some event has happened, so thinking 'as if' it had occurred; encourages positive, creative problem-solving by mentally going beyond apparent obstacles to desired solutions.

Associated   'Inside' an experience, seeing through your own eyes, fully in your senses. Used in the sense of subjective as compared with objective perspective.

Auditory   To do with the sense of hearing.

Backtrack   To review or summarise, using another's key words and tonalities; to re-present a communication to ensure the meaning is understood.

Chunking (*see also* **Stepping**) Moving along a spectrum of general or ambiguous to specific or 'big picture' to detail or vice versa. Changing your perception by going up or down a 'logical level'.

Complex equivalence   Two statements that are considered to mean the same thing, e.g. 'He is not looking at me, so he is not listening to what I say.'

Congruence   State of being completely sincere, with all aspects of a person working together toward an outcome. Agreement, or unity between the 'parts' of a person.

Content reframing   Taking a statement or situation and giving it another meaning, asking, 'What else could this mean?'. Focusing on whatever you choose to gain another perspective.

Context reframing   Changing the context of a statement or behaviour to give it another meaning, by asking, 'Where (in what context) would this be an appropriate behaviour, way of thinking, or response?'

Conversational postulate   Hypnotic form of language in which a question is interpreted as a command.

Crossover matching (*see also* **Mirroring**)   Matching a person's body language with a different type of movement, e.g. tapping your foot in time to a person's speech rhythm.

Deep structure (*see also* **Surface structure**)   The complete linguistic form or meaning of a statement from which the 'surface structure' of everyday communication is derived after generalisation, deletion and distortion.

Deletion   In speech or thought, missing out a portion of an experience.

Dissociated (*see also* **Associated**)   Seeing or hearing from 'outside' an experience, rather than from 'inside'. Used in the sense of objective or 'removed', or when accessing a memory from the perspective of another person.

Distortion   Representing an internal experience or the 'deep structure' of an experience in a limiting, or changed or incomplete way, along with generalisation and deletion or omission.

Downtime   A light trance state in which your attention is towards your own thoughts and feelings rather than the immediate world around you, e.g. as in daydreaming.

Ecology In NLP, the overall relationship between a person and their thoughts, strategies, behaviours, capabilities, values and beliefs. Concern for congruence, and awareness of the wider effects of outcomes. The study of consequences.

Elicitation Acquiring information, whether by direct observation or (Meta Model) questioning, about a person's behaviour or thought processes (strategy), e.g. when modelling a person's behaviour or identifying their values and outcomes.

Eye accessing cues Movements of the eyes in certain directions which indicate visual, auditory or kinaesthetic thought processing.

First position (*see also* **Second position**; **Third position**; **Associated**) Perceiving the world from your own point of view only. Being in touch with your own inner reality.

Frame A context, viewpoint or way of perceiving something, as in outcome frame, rapport frame, backtrack frame.

Future pace Mentally rehearsing or 'testing' an outcome to ensure that the desired behaviour or state will occur.

Generalisation The process by which one specific experience comes to represent a whole class of experiences; typical of the 'surface structure' of common communications.

Gustatory To do with the sense of taste.

Identity A person's self-image or self-concept; who you take yourself to be; the totality of your being.

Incongruence Internal conflict, as when not totally committed to a statement or an outcome. May be apparent from the disparity between a person's words and (even the subtlest) actions or disposition.

Intention   The purpose or desired outcome of an action. A positive although 'unconscious intention' may lie behind apparently negative or purposeless behaviour.

Internal representations   Patterns of information we create and store in our minds in combinations of images, sounds, feelings, smells and tastes. Sensory thought-processes or 'modalities'.

Kinaesthetic   The 'feeling' sense, tactile sensations and internal feelings such as remembered sensations, emotions, and the sense of movement and balance.

Leading   Changing your own behaviours with enough rapport for the other person to follow or 'match'.

Lead system   The representational system (visual, auditory, kinaesthetic) that accesses information to input into consciousness.

Map of reality   Sometimes referred to as 'model of the world'. Each person's unique representation of the world built from their individual perceptions and experiences.

Matching   Adopting parts of another person's behaviour in order to establish or enhance rapport.

Meta Model   A model that identifies language patterns that obscure meaning in a communication through the processes of distortion, deletion and generalisation. It includes specific questions to clarify and challenge imprecise language to connect it back to sensory experience and the 'deep structure'.

Metaphor   Indirect communication by a story or figure of speech implying a comparison. In NLP metaphor may cover similes, parables and allegories.

Milton Model   The inverse of the Meta Model, using artfully vague language patterns to pace another person's experience and access unconscious resources.

Mirroring   Matching portions of another person's behaviour as in a mirror image.

Mismatching   Adopting different patterns of behaviour to another person's, breaking rapport for the purpose of redirecting, interrupting or terminating a meeting or conversation.

Modal operator of necessity   A linguistic term for rules (should, ought, etc).

Modal operator of possibility   A linguistic term for words that denote what is considered possible (can, cannot, etc).

Model   A practical description of how something works, whose purpose is to be useful. A generalised, deleted or distorted copy.

Modelling   The process of discerning the sequence of ideas and behaviour that enable someone to accomplish a task. The basis of accelerated learning.

Model of the world   Each person's unique representation of the world built from his or her individual perceptions and experiences. The sum of an individual's personal operating principles.

Neuro-Linguistic Programming   The study of excellence and a model of how individuals structure their experience.

Neurological levels   Also known as the different logical levels of experience: environment, behaviour, capability, belief, identity and spiritual.

Nominalisation   Linguistic term for the process of turning a verb into an abstract noun, and the word for the noun so formed.

Olfactory   To do with the sense of smell.

Outcome   A specific, sensory-based, desired result that meets the well-formedness criteria.

Pacing   Gaining and maintaining rapport with another person over a period of time by joining them in their model of the world. You can pace beliefs and ideas as well as behaviour.

Perceptual filters   The unique ideas, experiences, beliefs and language that shape our model of the world.

Perceptual position   The viewpoint we are aware of at any moment can be our own (First Position), someone else's (Second Position), or an objective and benevolent observer's (Third Position).

Phonological ambiguity   Two words that sound the same, but there/their difference is plain/plane to see/sea.

Predicates   Sensory-based words that indicate the use of one representational system.

Preferred system   The representational system that an individual typically uses most to think consciously and organise his or her experience.

Presuppositions   Ideas or statements that have to be taken for granted for a communication to make sense.

Punctuation ambiguity   Ambiguity created by merging two separate sentences into one.

Rapport   Mutual trust and understanding between two or more people, facilitating communication.

Reframing   Changing the frame of reference round a statement, behaviour or situation to give it another meaning. Getting another perspective, e.g. an insight on a problem.

Representation   An idea: a coding or storage of sensory-based information in the mind.

Representational system How we code information in our minds in one or more of the five sensory systems: Visual, Auditory, Kinaesthetic, Olfactory (smell) and Gustatory (taste).

Resourceful state The total neurological and physical experience when a person feels resourceful. The state of mind conducive to achieving an outcome.

Resources Any means that can be brought to bear to achieve an outcome, including physiology, states, thoughts, strategies, experiences, people, events or possessions.

Second position (*see also* **First position; Third position**) Perceiving the world from another person's point of view, such as when communicating ('putting yourself in the other person's shoes').

Sensory acuity The ability to make finer and more useful distinctions about the sense information we get from the world. The skill of 'reading' non-verbal behaviour.

State How you feel, your mood, or state of mind. The sum of all neurological and physical processes within an individual at any moment.

Stepping Used to mean 'chunking', as in 'step up' or 'step down'.

Strategy A sequence of representations leading to a particular outcome.

Submodality Distinctions, qualities or characteristics within each representational system which give them unique, subjective meaning and may reflect a state of mind. The smallest building blocks of our thoughts.

Surface structure Linguistic term for the spoken or written communication that has been derived from the deep structure by deletion, distortion and generalisation.

Synaesthesia   Automatic link from one sense to another. Illustrated in apparently illogical 'sensory predicates' in expressions such as 'I'll see how I feel about it'.

Third position (*see also* **First position; Second position**) Perceiving the world from the viewpoint of a detached and benevolent observer. One of three different Perceptual positions, the others being First and Second position.

Timeline   The way we store pictures, sounds and feelings of our past, present and future.

Trance   An altered state with an inward focus of attention on a few stimuli.

Triple description   The process of perceiving experience through First, Second and Third Positions – a wider perspective that can give insight, and a choice of meaning.

Universal quantifiers   Linguistic term for words such as 'every', 'never' and 'all', implying absolutes that admit no exceptions; one of the Meta Model categories.

Unspecified nouns   Nouns that do not specify to whom or to what they refer.

Unspecified verbs   Verbs that have the adverb deleted, so they do not say how the action was carried out. The process is not specified.

Uptime (*see also* **Downtime**)   State where the attention and senses are committed outwards.

Visual   To do with the sense of sight.

Visualisation   The process of seeing images in your mind. Sometimes refers to imagining in any or all representational systems, or mental rehearsal.

Well-formedness criteria A way of thinking about and expressing an outcome which makes it achievable, verifiable and motivating, and congruent with other personal outcomes. The basis for consistent achievement and win–win outcomes.

Further Reading

Frogs into Princes, Richard Bandler and John Grinder, Real People Press (1979).

Heart of the Mind, Connirae Andreas and Steve Andreas, Real People Press (1989).

Introducing Neuro-Linguistic Programming, Joseph O'Connor and John Seymour, HarperCollins (1990).

NLP for Managers, Harry Alder, Piatkus (1996).

NLP for Trainers, Harry Alder, McGraw Hill (1996).

NLP: The New Art and Science of Getting What You Want, Harry Alder, Piatkus (1994).

NLP: The New Technology of Achievement, Steve Andreas and Charles Faulkner (eds), NLP Comprehensive (1994).

Reframing, Richard Bandler and John Grinder, Real People Press (1982).

Timeline Theory, Tad James and Wyatt Woodsmall, Meta Publications (1988).

To Be or Not To Be, David Bourland, Jr and Paul D. Johnston (eds), International Society for General Semantics (1991).

Train Your Brain, Harry Alder, Piatkus (1997).

Training with NLP, Joseph O'Connor and John Seymour, Thorsons (1994).

Turtles All the Way Down, John Grinder and Judith De Lozier, Metamorphous Press (1995).

Using Your Brain for a Change, Richard Bandler, Real People Press (1985).

Index